D1259287

Architectural Judgement

Architectural Judgement

PETER COLLINS

Professor of Architecture
McGill University, Montreal

McGILL–QUEEN'S UNIVERSITY PRESS

Montreal

1971

Printed in Great Britain by
W & J Mackay & Co Ltd, Chatham
All rights reserved

ISBN 0 7735 0114 2

Library of Congress Catalog Card No. 75-148116

To
FRIEDRICH KESSLER, M.A., J.U.D.
Sterling Professor of Law, Yale University

as a token of gratitude,
affection and esteem

CONTENTS

CONTENTS

ILLUSTRATIONS

between pages 112 and 113

PREFACE

The idea of relating the theory of architecture to that of law suggested itself quite fortuitously two or three years ago, when comparing the curricula of schools of architecture with those of other professional disciplines. Prompted by the suspicion that architectural schools had never really freed themselves from the old Art School mentality (however emancipated they might seem in a University setting), my sole purpose in making this comparative study was to see whether legal and medical education possessed any distinctive qualities which (a) were lacking in architectural training, and (b) could be identified as generically 'professional'. However, when examining the curriculum of the Faculty of Law, I was so struck by the pedagogical congruities which seemed implicitly shared by the philosophy of law and the philosophy of architecture that I purchased a number of text-books on Jurisprudence, and started studying these in the hope of bringing new light to bear on my own particular discipline.

The inadequacy of the result, though now embarrassingly obvious, did not become apparent to me until I enrolled as a research fellow at the Yale Law School in 1968–69 (for which McGill University generously granted me a year's leave of absence). But once there, it was made excitingly evident that the affinities between legal judgement and architectural judgement were not only far more numerous than I had suspected, but were most clearly discernible in the standard introductory courses on Contracts, Torts and Civil Procedure, as taught in that School.

I have no illusions as to the limited knowledge of the law which even the most conscientious freshman can obtain after only a few months' application; but I should nevertheless like to thank those professors whose lectures I attended (and who would, I am sure, prefer to remain anonymous) for tolerating a middle-aged enthusiast among the ranks of their First Year students. I should also like to

express my gratitude to many colleagues and other friends—
especially Max Ferro—for their comments on the first draft of this
text (which led to the prompt removal of its more blatant defects).
The final draft contains several modifications suggested by the ten
architectural students who participated in an optional seminar on the
topic given at McGill University in 1969–1970. The proofs were
corrected by the same person who performed the drudgery for
Concrete : the Vision of a New Architecture and for *Changing Ideals in
Modern Architecture*; and it is no small tribute to her patience and
equanimity that she is still my wife.

PART ONE

The Analysis
of Professional Judgement

In the middle ages our forefathers followed the identical course with regard to their fine arts which we follow with regard to our laws. They took the same time, used the same processes of division of labour and aggregation of experiences, and employed the same class of intellect to design, employing the mason as we do the lawyer, only to execute; and thus in consequence, raised to themselves a monument, of a lower class perhaps, but in itself as perfect as ours. This mode we have entirely abandoned in the department of the fine arts to follow the French constitutional one . . . Success by such means is impossible, and our systems of art are as hollow and ephemeral as the one of their constitutions.

James Fergusson. *Principles of Beauty in Art* (1849) p. 167

Nothing is so ill-made in our island as the laws . . . Our houses are filled with conveniences which the kings of former times might have envied. Our bridges, our canals, our roads, our modes of communication, fill every stranger with wonder. Nowhere are manufactures carried to such perfection. Nowhere is so vast a mass of mechanical power collected . . . Is, then, the machinery by which justice is administered framed with the same exquisite skill which is found in other kinds of machinery? Can there be a stronger contrast than that which exists between the beauty, the completeness, the speed, the precision with which every process is performed in our factories, and the awkwardness, the rudeness, the slowness, the uncertainty of the apparatus by which offences are punished and rights vindicated? Look at that series of penal statutes, the most bloody and the most inefficient in the world, at the puerile fictions which make every declaration and every plea unintelligible both to plaintiff and defendant, at the mummery of fines and recoveries, at the chaos of precedents, at the bottomless pit of Chancery. Surely we see the barbarism of the thirteenth century and the highest civilisation of the nineteenth century side by side; and we see that the barbarism belongs to the government, and the civilisation to the people.

T. B. Macaulay, Speech on the Reform
Bill, delivered in the House of Commons
on 5 July 1831 (*Collected Works*, 1891 ed.,
Speeches, pp. 496–7.)

CHAPTER ONE

Judgement as an evolutionary process

The first, and most surprising thing the freshman law-student learns about law is that 'the history of law' is, by definition, apparently regarded as something which can have no practical utility. A law school lecturer on Contracts may begin a discussion with *Paradine v. Jane* (1647),[1] which held that the occupation of one's leasehold-property by Prince Rupert and his troops is not sufficient grounds for refusing to pay the rent. A lecturer on Torts may start with the accidental discharge of a musket in 1616.[2] But no teacher of either Contracts or Torts would regard this as 'history', and he would be aghast if any of his students were so misguided as to imagine that it was. It cannot be history, the student would probably be told, because it is *relevant*; hence in university law schools, whenever there does exist a 'legal historian', his interests are expected to be confined to the analysis of mediaeval plea rolls, or to the relationship between Justinian's Pandects and the social life of the Roman Empire.

The reason for this attitude becomes obvious if we reflect on the way litigation actually works. When a lawyer argues for his client in court on the basis of *Coggs v. Bernard*[3] (a case concerned with a cask of brandy damaged in the reign of Queen Anne) he would no more

[1] Cf. *Halsbury's Laws of England* (Simonds edition), vol. viii, p. 179, para. 311 and footnote.

[2] Ibid., vol. xxviii, p. 80, para. 84 (*Weaver v. Ward*). 'Torts' concern the legal remedies for wrongful acts or injuries which infringe rights created otherwise than by contract, and constitute a clearly-defined branch of Anglo-American law.

[3] 2 Ld. Raymond 909. The case is cited thirty times in *Halsbury's Laws of England*.

be accused of historicism or antiquarian irrelevancy than Chief Justice Holt himself, who had settled *Coggs v. Bernard* to everyone's satisfaction in 1703 on the basis of the notions of *depositum, commodatum, locatio* etc., as expounded in Bracton's *De Legibus*, and borrowed by him from Justinian's Civil Code.[1]

In other words, lawyers make a clear distinction between historical records which are *precedents*, and historical records which are not precedents; and it is impossible to over-emphasize the importance of the distinction in a consideration of professional judgement. Insofar as any recorded legal decision (whether decided one year ago or five hundred years ago) is a rationally justifiable argument for taking a similar legal decision today, it is a precedent. Insofar as any legal decision (whether decided a year ago or five hundred years ago) is irrelevant to a legal decision today, it is, as far as practising lawyers are concerned, 'mere history'.

Let us consider, for example, a case where a plaintiff has purchased a painting under the delusion that it is a genuine Le Corbusier, and five years later is assured by a highly reputable auctioneer that it is not. Can he rescind the contract if the dealer who sold the painting honestly believed, and still believes, that the picture was painted by Le Corbusier? Or is he stuck with a painting for which he was induced to pay a relatively high price, but which, on the open market, has been assessed by experts to be worth considerably less money?

The answer to this problem in English law is to some extent conditioned by whether or not a 'reasonable time' has elapsed before making the claim; but judged solely from the point of view of contractual obligations, it would be to the effect that if payment has been made, and delivery received, before 22 April 1967, the contract could not be rescinded, and it would be uncertain as to whether or not the plaintiff could obtain damages; but if these events had occurred after that date, the dealer would be statutorily obliged to pay damages, and could probably be obliged to take back the painting and refund the purchase price. And the reason for this difference would be that whereas the validity of such a contract had been upheld in 1950[2] (when the decision of the Court of Appeal was sup-

[1] Cf. the article by S. D. Elliott in *California Law Review*, vol. vi, pp. 91 ff.
[2] 2 K.B. 86. *Leaf v. International Galleries.*

ported by two cases decided in 1843[1] and 1905[2] respectively) the
Misrepresentation Act of 1967 changed the law,[3] whereby these
decisions could no longer be cited as precedents for such a situation,
even though they might well be valid precedents for other situations.

Such applications of 'precedent' are not simple, mechanical,
judicial processes. Let us suppose another hypothetical case,
identical in all circumstances to the previous example, except that
whereas, in the previous example, the plaintiff purchased a painting
from a merchant, and then asked an auctioneer to offer it for sale as
a genuine Le Corbusier, in this new hypothetical case the plaintiff
buys the painting at an auction and then offers it for sale five years
later to a dealer who doubts its authenticity. In view of the dis-
claimers of warranty which, since 1967, usually precede the 'Conditions of Sale' printed at the beginning of auctioneers' catalogues
in England, it seems unlikely that the plaintiff could obtain the
equitable remedy of rescission granted by the Misrepresentation
Act, or even succeed in a claim for damages. On the contrary, the
auctioneer could probably still rely successfully on *Mesnard v.
Aldridge*,[4] settled in 1801, as an adequate defence. *Mesnard v.
Aldridge* had nothing to do with the authenticity of oil paintings. It
involved a dispute as to whether a horse, purchased at an auction
sale, could rightfully be returned if it was subsequently found to be
physically defective, and whether the auctioneer was thereby bound
to refund the purchase price. But it was held by the Court that the
sale of goods by auction is subject to the published Conditions of
Sale, and that, provided these have been adequately communicated
to the bidders, and are not unreasonable, the purchaser has no

---

[1] *Wilde v. Gibson* (1 H.L.C. 605).

[2] *Seddon v. North Eastern Salt Co.* (1905, 1 Ch. 326).

[3] Cf. *Halsbury*, cumulative supplement for 1968, referring to vol. xxvi, para.
1629. Note, in *Leaf v. International Galleries*, the concluding remarks by the
Master of the Rolls: '. . . There has been opportunity for Parliament to alter
the law if it was thought to be inadequate'. The first section of the Misrepresentation Act (1967 c. 7) states that 'Where a person has entered into a contract
after a misrepresentation has been made to him and (a) the misrepresentation
has become a term of the contract; or (b) the contract has been performed; or
both; then, if otherwise he would be entitled to rescind the contract without
alleging fraud, he shall be so entitled, subject to the provisions of this Act . . .'

[4] 3 Espinasse 271.

remedy against the auctioneer for a bad bargain if the Conditions of Sale were complied with.

Now it may be argued that the lawyer's attitude towards history, as described here, is no different from that of a number of distinguished and influential art-historians, such as the authors of *Pioneers of the Modern Movement* or of *Space, Time and Architecture*, who were also concerned with 'precedents', and with what seemed 'relevant', in the sense that their histories are chronologically arranged antecedents of contemporary architecture. But the similarity between the art-historian's approach to history, and the lawyer's approach to history ends here. No specialist in contract law would see any point in studying its evolution by reference to its 'pioneers'. No specialist in the law of Torts, however interested in its emergence from the feudal law of trespass, would think it worth his while to make a detailed study of wrongful pre-historic injuries, and then call it *The Eternal Present*. Nor would a specialist in international law, after having published the standard and most authoritative text-book on *Leading Cases of the Nineteenth and Twentieth Centuries*, feel urged to write a monograph on *Rococo Ecclesiastical Law in Lower Franconia*.

The foregoing remarks are not intended to deride famous architectural histories written by distinguished scholars. Their purpose is to emphasize, as vigorously as possible, a fundamental difference of attitude between the lawyer's concept of history and the architect's concept of history during the last two hundred years. There may be schools of architecture which have now come to regard historical relevance from the same point of view as schools of law. If so, well and good. But the most recent curricula seem to indicate a trend in the opposite direction. Far from replacing the nineteenth-century archaeological approach (as exemplified by Banister Fletcher's *History of Architecture*) with histories which emphasize the evolution of currently relevant principles, there is a tendency to replace the history of architecture with even broader courses on the general history of art—i.e., survey courses of painting, sculpture and architecture as exemplified by selected masterpieces of the last five thousand years.

The legal profession, then, takes two distinct attitudes towards its own past, whereby certain elements are seen as an integral part of the web of the current law, whilst other elements are seen as only remotely related to current practice, and are thus rarely considered of interest to busy practitioners or ambitious neophytes. At first sight, the distinction might seem comparable to the late nineteenth-century distinction between architectural theory, as conceived by Julien Guadet, and architectural history, as conceived by Auguste Choisy, so that the first legal attitude might seem to correspond to the theory of architecture, and hence be entitled to the name 'theory of law', or Jurisprudence.[1] Unfortunately, however, legal theory is not only a well-established discipline but (and this is the fascinating thing about Anglo-American Jurisprudence) it is usually studied in a complete historical vacuum. There are indeed scholars, such as H. M. Hart and Albert Sacks,[2] who have concluded that, even philosophically, the legal process can only be evaluated and discussed in a historical context. But the normal procedure is to treat the concepts of Jurisprudence as if, by their nature, they enjoyed philosophical immortality. Vigorous discussions about the concept of sovereignty, as expounded by John Austin in his *Province of Jurisprudence Determined*, are developed in learned essays as if the notion of sovereignty must be something absolute and eternal: as easy to identify in the reign of William IV as during the American Civil War. Hypotheses as to the extent to which laws passed by 'Rex I' would still be valid on the accession of his son 'Rex II'[3] are discussed as if modifications to the Plantagenet coronation oath had never existed, or as if there had been no controversy or practical dilemma which prompted the mediaeval nobility to bring such modifications into effect. The 'philosophy of law', like 'aesthetics', is thus generally thought of as something which, though it can occasionally be illustrated by real laws or real works of art, would be vitiated by too much emphasis on actual legal systems or actual artistic practices.

These distinctions are important because whereas the legal

---

[1] Unless otherwise stated, the word is always used in this essay in its Anglo-American sense. Its significance with respect to Codified legal systems is indicated in chapter ten.

[2] Their book, entitled *The Legal Process*, does not seem to have been printed, but the multilithed text has been widely circulated since 1958.

[3] Cf. H. L. A. Hart, *The Concept of Law* (1961), p. 52.

attitude towards 'history', and the legal attitude towards 'theory', are often paralleled in schools of architecture, the legal attitude towards what Professor Lovejoy called 'the history of ideas', emphasizing the evolution of contemporary practice and thought, is only just beginning to find its way into architectural education. Yet architecture, like law, or any other profession, can only be taught effectively to future generations of practitioners as a process of 'becoming'; as something which, theoretically, has no absolute forms, but is in constant transition from 'was' to 'is'. However much architectural theorists may disagree with the legal concept that the past is in many respects part of the fabric of the present, it is surely indisputable today that students of both law and architecture can only learn to deal effectively with what *will* be if they understand the process by which 'what was' became transmuted into 'what is'.

It thus seems evident that the traditional division, in architectural schools, between 'history' and 'theory', might profitably be abandoned in favour of something corresponding to the legal concept of *precedent*; and although legal precedents are only faintly analogous to architectural precedents, a brief analysis of this legal concept may perform a useful heuristic function for architects by helping them to determine the weight they should accord to precedent in judging any phase of architectural design.

A judicial precedent has been defined by a former Lord Chancellor as 'a judgement or decision of a court of law cited as an authority for deciding a similar state of facts in the same manner, or on the same principle by analogy'.[1] As such, it is a peculiarity of the Anglo-American Common Law tradition. The extent to which this definition requires qualification need not concern us here. In the present context, all we need note is, firstly, that according to the definition, precedents are *cited*, and secondly, that they are cited not only to obtain or justify decisions concerning *similar states of facts*, but also decisions on the *same principles*, or by *analogy*.

Theoretically, if A sues B, and if it can be shown that the circumstances are identical to a previous case where C obtained judgement against D, then the doctrine of precedent would imply (assuming no statute has been passed in the meantime to change the law) that judge-

[1] Lord Jowitt: *Dictionary of English Law* (1959), p. 1385.

ment should be awarded to A. But in fact, circumstances rarely *are* identical; and if B appeals against the judgement, it is usually because he contends that the precedent did *not* apply.

As an illustration, let us consider the famous leading case of *Rylands v. Fletcher*,[1] which concerned liability for subterranean damage to a distant coal-mine caused by a badly constructed reservoir. During the final appeal to the House of Lords, Counsel for the Plaintiff in Error (i.e. Rylands) asked the court to give judgement in his favour on the grounds that in *Acton v. Blundel, Chasemore v. Richards, Smith v. Kennick*, and about eight other cases, the decisions exonerated their client from legal liability. Counsel for the Defendant in Error (i.e. Fletcher) contended, on the contrary, that the circumstances of the case bore so close a similarity to the facts in *Hodgkinson v. Ennor* that the decision in this latter case should apply. Now it should be noted that the court not only decided that *Hodgkinson v. Ennor* was indeed the precedent which governed the cause at issue; it also specifically 'differentiated' *Smith v. Kennick*, in such a way as to demonstrate that, far from supporting the contentions of the Plaintiff, it could be seen, if correctly interpreted, to support the contentions of the Defendant.

Imagine this procedure applied to an architectural dispute. Let us assume, for example, that one of the participants in the Toronto City Hall Competition [Pl. I] were to sue the municipal authorities for breach of contract, on the grounds that the design by Viljo Rewell was inferior to the plaintiff's own entry. Counsel for the plaintiff might bring forward expert witnesses to assert that the requirements of this new city hall, as described in the programme forming part of the conditions of entry, were almost identical with those of the London County Hall begun in 1912; and that since the plaintiff's design bore a close resemblance to that of the London County Hall, it merited the first prize. Counsel for the defendants would doubtless bring forward expert witnesses to declare that the requirements of the Toronto City Hall could only be fitted appropriately into the forms used by Oscar Niemeyer for the Congress Building of the Brazilian parliament (which *was* in fact the precedent followed by Rewell). Meanwhile, an *amicus curiae* submits a brief to the effect that since the essence of any city hall is its historical

[1] (1868) L.R. 3 H.L. 330.

continuity with the evolving life of the city, the municipal authorities should have followed the precedent of the Paris City Council by enlarging the original City Hall with unobtrusive additions, designed to harmonize with the original structure. The court would undoubtedly have reserved judgement, so as to take time to consider the matter; but whether it would ever reach a conclusion on the facts as stated here is highly doubtful.

Stated thus, it is clear that whatever relationship the legal concept of precedent may or should bear to the architectural concept of precedent, it differs radically from the architectural concept of precedent as we generally understand it today. Whatever lip-service architectural theorists may pay to the doctrine that form follows function, there is no corresponding belief that a form which still fulfils a specific function should be taken as a precedent for any new form intended to fulfil the same function. On the contrary, any concept of precedent, insofar as it exists, is based on the art-historical doctrine that form follows form, whereby John Jacobus, in *Twentieth Century Architecture, 1940–1965*, rightly considers it art-historically meaningful to juxtapose photographs of the Guggenheim Museum with Boullée's Cenotaph to Newton, and the Chandigarh Assembly building with the eighteenth-century astrological observatory in New Delhi. That the Pont du Gard at Nîmes really was the precedent for Frank Lloyd Wright's Marin County Centre [Pls. IV & V] is extremely likely; whether it *should* have been the precedent is precisely the point here raised.

The selection of precedents

'Some cases, of course, there are where one route and only one is possible. They are the cases where the law is fixed and settled. They make up in bulk what they lack in interest. Other cases present a genuine opportunity for choice—not a choice between two decisions, one of which may be said to be almost certainly right and the other almost certainly wrong, but a choice so nicely balanced that when once it is announced, a new right and a new wrong will emerge in the announcement'.[1] These genuine opportunities for *choice* are usually cases in which everything depends on the choice of *precedent*.

[1] B. N. Cardozo, *The Growth of the Law* (paperback edition), p. 58.

In architecture the emphasis given to 'originality' has tended to obscure the liberty which the choice of precedent bestows. But even in the two centuries before 1750, when the 'rules' of antiquity were perhaps unduly venerated, the *selection* of precedents and their *adaptation* created far more originality than we now perceive, in that, for example, the proportions of columns and entablatures varied considerably in accordance with the different requirements and locality of each specific building.

Today, the selection and adaptation of precedents not only should fill, but clearly does fill, a far greater rôle than it ever filled in the architecture of the past. It fills a greater rôle in architecture than it does in law. The genuine opportunities for choice, which as Mr. Justice Cardozo observed, constitute a comparatively small percentage of litigated disputes, are seldom absent from an architectural problem. But just as there can be such a thing as 'mechanical jurisprudence' in law, so there can be and is 'mechanical eclecticism' in architecture. Despite the fact that every good architect, like every good judge, must not only select from precedents, but must select creatively, the inhibition created by the extravagances of nineteenth-century eclecticism are such that few architects will admit to the practice, and fewer still would ever assent categorically to the thesis (recently put forward by the Archigram Group) that such selection is the essence of their creativity. Instead, the emphasis is almost invariably on 'originality', as if originality and precedent were mutually exclusive. Yet even the most superficial study of the judicial process demonstrates that the only genuine and fruitful originality derives precisely from the accurate, vigorous and imaginative manner in which precedents are analyzed and compared. Fortunately, the architectural profession has, during the last decade, paid far more attention to precedent than in the first half of this century; but its spokesmen still tend to resist giving full recognition to this aspect of the design process in their public pronouncements; and although a conscientious architect, faced with a commission to design a new city hall, would invariably make a thorough (though possibly surreptitious) study of other city halls, his public assertions might well induce the belief that these studies were only of value because they showed where and how all his precursors had ignominiously failed.

Precedent and continuity

The manner in which precedents were regarded three centuries ago as an aid to architectural continuity is well exemplified by the enlargement of the courtyard of the Louvre, where a succession of architects quadrupled its size between 1625 and 1750 without noticeably deviating from the precedent established in 1546 by Pierre Lescot. Such an attitude no longer appeals to us; and rightly so, because we, unlike Lemercier, Le Vau and A. J. Gabriel, no longer use the same structural materials and structural systems as were used by our ancestors. But one unfortunate effect of this reaction has been to lead us at times to exaggerated extremes, and to follow subconsciously the archaeological theory (which was, paradoxically, an off-shoot of Gothic Revivalist research) that extensions to any building must make manifest the decade in which they were built.

One recent example of this phenomenon is the method of completing the Royal Festival Hall in London [Pls. VI & VII]. Whatever may have been the shortcomings of the original auditorium constructed for the Festival of Britain (built when materials were in short supply as a result of World War II), it certainly cannot be dismissed as an architectural mediocrity. It was designed under the supervision of Sir Leslie Martin, one of the most vigorous pre-war leaders of the Modern Movement in Britain who, when he eventually left the architectural department of the London County Council (of which he was ultimately the director) was appointed professor of architecture at Cambridge University. The Festival Hall is described in at least one authoritative guide-book, published in 1958, as both artistically and acoustically one of the finest concert halls in Europe.[1] It occupies one of the most prominent sites on the Thames embankment. At the time it was built, its only indisputable defect was that, since it was incomplete, its unfinished eastern flank had to be given a temporary covering. Yet when, twenty years after its inauguration, the contemplated addition was built next to it, the group-leader of the project apparently decided that because of the architectural difficulties of placing one concert hall next to another after a span of nearly twenty years, it was advisable to seek 'contrast

[1] F. R. Banks, *The Penguin Guide to London* (1958), p. 66.

rather than similarity': a contrast achieved by designing a 'cluster of sculpted elements' in rough concrete. The characteristics of the resultant juxtaposition are explained by Peter Moro as follows: 'The Royal Festival Hall is a formal building in the classical sense. The new building, in spite of its apparent informality, is nevertheless also a formal building in the sense that the deliberate pursuit of ir-regularity in itself becomes a formalistic mannerism . . . When seen across the river, the old and new concert halls form an attractive composition, only marred by the banality of the building in the background'.[1] This building in the background was designed in the 1950s by Sir Howard Robertson, former Principal of the Archi-tectural Association School, past president of the Royal Institute of British Architects, Royal Gold Medalist, and author of *The Prin-ciples of Architectural Composition*. Whether or not it is a formal building in the classical sense, or a formal building in the sense that its deliberate pursuit of irregularity becomes a formalistic mannerism, Mr. Moro does not say. All we know for certain is that the spaces between the buildings are not so much 'plazas' as 'generation-gaps'.

Whatever the merits or demerits of the addition to the Royal Festival Hall, it exemplifies an attitude which is clearly yet another legacy of nineteenth-century historicism; of the conviction that every fragment of a building must be capable of accurate chronological identification by future archaeologists on the basis of their visible and tangible shape. The present age, which has seen so much pro-gress in the detection of art-historical forgeries by the analysis of technological rather than formal qualities, may find it easier to renounce this heritage, especially now that the Metropolitan Museum in New York has decided to continue displaying its beautiful 'antique' horse (originally dated 470 B.C.) though it was proved in 1967 to be a modern forgery. This is not to condone the irrational imitation of ancient tectonic forms in new structural materials. It is simply to assert that a greater conformity with the legal attitude towards precedent may make architects pay more than lip-service to the ideal of constructing extensions to buildings in harmony with the existing environment.

The logic and economy of designing reinforced concrete frames

[1] *R.I.B.A. Journal*, June 1968, p. 252.

in harmony with eighteenth-century masonry has been amply demonstrated; yet the art-architect's urge towards self-expression and originality frequently over-rides his sense of duty towards his environment and towards the past. When, in 1961, an international competition was held for an addition to the early eighteenth-century library of Trinity College, Dublin [Pl. VIII], four of the judges (i.e. the Vice-Chancellor, a Professor of Library Science from Harvard, and two architects: Raymond McGrath and Sir Hugh Casson) congratulated the prize-winner on 'the architectural relationship with the older buildings', adding that 'the façade exhibits a sensitive progress of windows which is carefully proportioned, and is both less affected and more logical than might appear at first sight'. But the fifth judge (a Professor of Architecture from the University of Venice) dissented, and expressed the opinion that the architecture 'does not seem to me to harmonize with the surroundings in which the new building is to be situated'.[1]

Whether or not the premiated design was more in harmony with the environment than the other two hundred and seventeen entries; whether or not it *would* have harmonized more with its environment if it had been built according to the original plans, will never be known, since few of the designs submitted were published, and the building, as finally executed, bore little resemblance to the prize-winning project. But the architect was consistent to this extent: whatever changes he made, he clearly paid great attention to the official request for 'a design in a contemporary idiom which will express the middle of the twentieth century as faithfully as the building of 1712 expresses the age of reason'.[2]

In an assessment of the finished building published in 1967, Alan Colquhoun argued that the new building really did harmonize with its setting because it was essentially a 'foil' to the old library.[3] But a 'foil' means the very opposite of what 'precedent' means in law. A 'foil' is a contrast; and to contrast two cases is to *distinguish* or differentiate them, i.e., to demonstrate that one is *not* a precedent for the other. In fact, as Mr. Colquhoun correctly asserts, the precedents of this new building are to be found in Le Corbusier's

[1] *Architectural Review*, August 1961, p. 77.
[2] *Architectural Review*, March 1960, p. 154.
[3] *Architectural Review*, October 1967, pp. 265–7.

Musée à Croissance Illimitée and in that same architect's monastery at Evreux.

Precedent as a means of effecting change

H. L. A. Hart, in *The Concept of Law*, illustrates what he calls 'the persistence of law' by recounting how in 1944 a woman was convicted of telling fortunes in violation of the Witchcraft Act of 1735. 'This', he says, 'is only a picturesque example of a very familiar legal phenomenon: a statute enacted centuries ago may still be law today'.[1] Picturesque it may well be, but it is singularly inept as an illustration of the point he wishes to make. The Act in question, though later referred to as 'The Witchcraft Act',[2] was in fact an act to *repeal* the Witchcraft Acts of Elizabeth and James I (as is clearly stated in its preamble);[3] and all it asserts, essentially, is that after 24 June 1736, no person shall be prosecuted for witchcraft in any court in Great Britain. The clause relevant to *R. v. Duncan*[4] (the case to which Professor Hart refers) simply provided that, for the more effective prevention and punishment of persons claiming occult arts or powers ('whereby ignorant persons are frequently deluded and defrauded'), anyone convicted of undertaking to tell fortunes, etc., should be put in jail.

But this example illustrates one way, and certainly the most clear-cut way, of effecting lasting changes in Anglo-American law; namely, by statute. It is, moreover, the *only* 'officially' recognized way of effecting such changes in countries such as France, where the law is codified. But it is clearly a very clumsy way; so clumsy, in fact, that even in countries where Civil Codes are established, precedents set by courts of appeal can, under certain circumstances, change laws without awaiting legislative intervention. In the Anglo-American Common Law, the doctrine of precedent has proved to be an extraordinarily effective way of *modifying* the law, since by virtue of their judicial power to 'distinguish' cases, judges can create new precedents as new circumstances may require.

Nevertheless (and this is why the subject is introduced in the present context) it can be seen that new precedents cannot be

[1] *Op. cit.*, p. 60.   [2] 59 & 60 Vict., c. 14.   [3] 9 Geo. II, c. 5.
[4] 1944, 1 K.B., 713.

effective if they are created whimsically or eccentrically, but only if the judiciary's ideals of justice indicate that the old precedents are untenable. There are many cases where injustice must be tolerated by the courts (and also by the unfortunate litigant) simply because the exceptional character of the litigation does not warrant changes in the law. It is not unusual for a judge to say—as Lord Justice Phillimore once said: 'With reluctance—I might almost say with sorrow—I concur in the view that this appeal must be dismissed. I trust that the case will proceed to the House of Lords'.[1] In fact, this particular case did proceed to the House of Lords, where the appeal was allowed. But sometimes fairness does not eventually triumph. In *L'Estrange v. Graucob*,[2] Lord Justice Maugham prefaced his opinion (to the effect that the plaintiff was estopped from asserting that she had not read a document she had signed) by saying: 'I regret the decision to which I have come, but I am bound by legal rules and cannot decide the case on other considerations'. However, changes are in fact continually being made to the law by virtue of the compelling influence of new circumstances, and these legal attempts to achieve a balance between preservation and innovation might profitably be applied to judgements concerning changes in our architectural environment.

Consider, for example, a wider aspect of the problem posed by the Trinity College Library Competition, that is to say the problem of adding any building to any university campus. At Dublin, the existing environment was such that it could reasonably be regarded as a dominant factor in the design of a new structure. But there are many campuses where the existing buildings are neither sufficiently extensive nor of such high quality that it would be reasonable to regard them as setting a precedent for later work. The designer of a new building might here justifiably say: 'The buildings which at present enclose my site will inevitably be demolished within the next few years to make way for other and more appropriate buildings. In my own design, therefore, I shall consider the kind of environment which will form its eventual frame, rather than its existing frame, and shall design it in such a way as to facilitate the

[1] *Olympia Oil & Cake Co. Ltd. v. Produce Brokers Ltd.* (1915), 112 L.T. 744. See R. Cross, *Precedent in English Law* (1968), pp. 33-4.

[2] 1934 2 K.B. 394.

task of my successors'. Whether or not his successors would pay any attention whatsoever to his endeavours seems in the present mood of architecture highly doubtful; but it need hardly be said that any such decision by the architect in question must be made in good faith both as regards the past and the future. Good intentions towards the future are common enough; but the frequency of decisions to ignore an existing environment suggests that good faith towards the past is uncommonly rare.

Precedent and cases of first impression

A case of first impression (*primae impressionis*) is defined as 'a case of a new kind, to which no established principle of law directly applies, and which must be decided entirely by *reason*, as distinguished from authority'.[1] But from what has already been said about the infrequency of identical cases, and the obligation to apply precedents by *analogy* whenever a similarity of facts or an identity of principles is lacking, it will be clear that the border-line between 'a new kind of case' and 'a case with very few analogous precedents' is virtually impossible to define. The usual example given of a case of first impression is *Mirehouse v. Rennell* (1832);[2] an extraordinarily dull case concerning whether or not the executor of a deceased prebendary has the right of presenting an ecclesiastical benefice attached to the defunct prelate's endowment. But even here, Mr. Justice Parks asserted that the case was only 'in some sense new'; and whilst he affirmed every judge's right and duty to decide for himself, according to his own judgement, what was just and expedient in such circumstances, he specifically denied that any judge was at liberty to reject analogies with existing rules simply because he thought that the rules were not as convenient and reasonable as he himself could have devised.

The difficulty of identifying a case of first impression is emphasized here because in recent years it has been fashionable to consider every architectural design as '*primae impressionis*'. Louis Kahn is not

---

[1] Lord Jowitt, *Dictionary of English Law*, p. 1402. However it should be noted that neither the words 'first impression' nor '*primae impressionis*' occur in the reference cited (viz. *Mirehouse v. Rennell*).

[2] 8 Bing. at 515.

the only famous architect to assert that 'it is good for the mind to go back to the beginning because the beginning of any established activity of man is its most wonderful moment'. At that time, he was designing a building in Africa where he saw many huts the natives had made. 'There were no architects there. I came back with multiple impressions of how clever was the man who solved the problem of sun, rain and wind. I came to the realization that every window should have a free wall to face.'[1]

Kahn's patriarchal remarks could be benevolently construed solely as a poetic rephrasing of the nineteenth-century demand that more attention be paid to 'vernacular' architecture; but their danger lies in the implicit mixture of two romantic fallacies: firstly, the idea that the most primitive solutions are always the best solutions, and secondly, the idea that we must abandon accumulations of judgements (i.e. precedents) so as to be free to design every building as if it were the first of its kind. Now there have indeed existed, during the last two hundred years, certain buildings which can undoubtedly be classified as *primae impressionis*. The Crystal Palace is an example. However analogous it may have been to pre-existing conservatories, it is still indisputably the first successful example of a temporary international exhibition hall, just as, somewhere, there was at some time built the first bank, the first hotel, the first office building. But it would be as foolish for an architect, commissioned to design an office building today, to regard his own problem as *primae impressionis*, as it would be for a judge, faced with a claim for damages against the operators of a new mode of transportation, to declare that all previous decisions concerning Common Carrier Liability were irrelevant, since the case involved a new mechanical invention. Even Walter Gropius, who was less sympathetic than most pioneering architects of his generation towards historical precedents, observed in *The New Architecture and The Bauhaus* that 'since theory represents the impersonal cumulative experience of successive generations, it offers a solid foundation on which a resolute band of fellow-workers can rear a higher embodiment of creative unity than the individual architect'.[2]

---

[1] Reprinted in V. Scully, *Louis I. Kahn* (1962), pp. 114–21, from *The Voice of America Forum Lectures* (1960).

[2] *Op. cit.* (1935 ed.), p. 53.

Mr. Justice Cardozo once pointed out that 'in law, as in every other branch of knowledge, the truths given by induction tend to form the premises for new deductions'.[1] This philosophy is common enough among architects involved in building performance research; but except when applied to mass building-types such as schools and offices, it tends to be limited by scientists to the investigation of standards of lighting, velocity gradients in wind tunnels, and similar problems.[2] The suggestion here is that the philosophy should extend throughout the whole field of architectural judgement, and hence throughout every phase and activity of architectural education. The educational system of any profession has, as its main duty, to inculcate and synthesize the criteria by which all judgements are made; and society is cheated if architectural design is treated like painting and sculpture, whereby the artist is ultimately to be regarded as the sole judge as to whether or not his creation is right.

Precedent and creativity

The creativity inherent in the judicial process has been insisted upon by many legal scholars, but perhaps never so persuasively as by Benjamin Cardozo, who was himself a famous judge. In the series of lectures he gave at the Yale Law School on 'The Growth of the Law', the concept of creativity is the climax of his whole theme. 'In the development of law', he remarks when discussing Symmetry and Justice, 'as in other fields of thought, we can never rid ourselves of our dependence upon intuition or flashes of insight transcending and transforming the contributions of mere experience'; and a few pages further on, he quotes approvingly from Windelband's *Introduction to Philosophy*: 'The artistic activity exhibits a mutual play of conscious and unconscious processes which can never be rationally explained . . . *The creation is accompanied by conscious criticism*, but the positive element of achievement is not a matter of

[1] *Op. cit.* (paperback ed.), p. 47.
[2] These titles are taken from the current list of research projects published by the Department of Architecture and Building Science at the University of Strathclyde.

cunning and calculation; it comes as a fortunate chance from the unconscious depths of life.'[1]

Cardozo's conception of the creativity of the judicial process has one implication which may seem to contradict an assertion previously made in this essay. 'Let us admit', it may be argued, 'that legal judgement in its noblest and ablest sense is creative. But then it must also be admitted that few judges attain this ideal, and once having attained it, they are esteemed by their contemporaries and revered by posterity. They are, in fact, the "Pioneers" or "Form-Givers" of the law. And if this is so, then surely, by analogy, it is proper that we should also venerate the "Form-Givers" of architecture.'

The law does indeed have its 'Form-Givers'; but it is of the essence of the legal concept of 'precedent' that forensic fame does not automatically, in itself, confer authority on any judicial decision. Lord Mansfield undoubtedly deserved to have a large monument erected to him in Westminster Abbey by his contemporaries; but his personal authority did not prevent his important dictum about the validity of contracts which lacked a 'consideration' from being declared contrary to the laws of England by the House of Lords.[2] Similarly, the saying (with respect to the New York Court of Appeals in the 1920s) that 'when Cardozo and Pound are both on the same side, the judgement is sound' may be a useful guide to law students; but in that decade itself it never had any force of law. The evaluation of a novel judicial decision is not based on the reputation of the judge, however creative he may be known to be, but on the clearly enunciated reasons for the decision, on the known context of the decision, on the welfare which society can expect from the decision, and on the oratorical felicity with which the decision is expressed.

A famous architect is expected to produce great buildings; but his fame cannot, and certainly should not, automatically confer

[1] B. N. Cardozo, *The Growth of the Law* (paperback ed.), pp. 89–92.

[2] I.e., when his dictum in *Pillans v. Van Meirop* (1765) was over-ruled by *Rann v. Hughes* (1778). The particular problem is discussed later in this essay. As Sir William Holdsworth pointed out in his review of Cecil Fifoot's biography of Lord Mansfield (L.Q.R., vol. liii, p. 231), the real error was that Lord Mansfield, being a Scotsman, had unfortunately decided *Pillans v. Van Meirop* in accordance with Scottish law.

greatness upon them. Hence architectural judgements will only be truly professional when we learn not only to distinguish Form-Givers from lesser mortals, but to distinguish clearly, among every Form-Giver's *oeuvre complète*, those designs which are below the standards which the Form-Giver himself has given the public the right to expect.

CHAPTER TWO

Judgement as a rational process

Any opinion expressed about a building or group of buildings can, in its widest sense, be called a rational judgement. In this sense, Ruskin's rapturous assessment of the merits of St. Mark's, Venice, is just as much a reasoned judgement as a surveyor's report on the condition of a mediaeval barn. In the narrower and stricter sense of the term, however, it may be assumed that professional judgements in architecture are neither the dithyrambic transmutations of poetic experiences induced by the contemplation of a building, nor the bare catalogue of a building's physical merits and defects. They are, we may presume, sober and sensitive critical assessments of the total quality of a building envisaged as a synthesis of every aspect of its design. Such assessments are rarely put into writing (even by judges of architectural competitions); nor are they elaborated into lengthy detailed expositions customary in Courts of Appeal. But elaborations of such judgements, and even attempts to reconcile or distinguish conflicting opinions, by means of reasoning, seem to be an indispensable part of the architect's *creative* process. The only controversial aspect of the activity concerns the difficulty in reaching general agreement as to what exactly this 'rational' element implies.

The nineteenth-century theory of Rationalism, as expounded most eloquently by Viollet-le-Duc, has been criticized from two diametrically opposed points of view. First there are those who contend that an architect, being an artist, designs intuitively, and hence judges intuitively, so that the merits of his work are incapable of assessment by Aristotelian, Cartesian or any other 'rational' methods. Secondly, there are those who contend that nineteenth-century Rationalism was just a clumsy and obsolete substitute for judgements now capable of solution with absolute precision by computers. The only common ground of these two dissenting points of view is the shared implication that *debate* about architectural judgement is impossible. Hence those who hold either view would presumably deny that legal judgements could possibly provide any useful analogy to architectural judgements, since the former, being based in Anglo-American law on an 'adversary system', assumes that there must be two points of view, even if one point of view is virtually untenable.

Scepticism as to the reality of 'Rationalism' as a dialectical process cannot be ignored, because such scepticism was expressed even by those who were most influential in popularizing the doctrine in the nineteenth century. César Daly, in an editorial in the 1866 issue of the *Revue Générale*, stated that although the Rationalist School (with which he sympathized) was assuming considerable importance in France, its virtue in assuring technological progress was offset by its inevitable tendency to retard aesthetic progress.[1] John Summerson (whose essay on Viollet-le-Duc and his theory is a masterpiece of its kind) considered that Rationalism was vitiated by the fact that it was possible to envisage two kinds: the first depending wholly on the extent to which function can be mathematically stated, and the second depending on the architect's personal interpretation of function. 'The first sort is ruthless in its application of means to ends; the second sort adapts both means and ends to a game of its own. The first sort of architecture is, as a matter of fact, almost impossible of conception . . . the second sort of architecture is a perfectly feasible one, the only proviso being that the function of the building be considered as of sufficient emotional interest to make this dialectical mode of expression significant.'[2]

The credibility of nineteenth-century Rationalism has been affected in the present century by the introduction of parallel concepts, such as the idea of 'organic architecture' developed by Frank Lloyd Wright, and the cult of 'functionalism'. Moreover, there are doctrinal ambiguities inherent in such architectural labels as

[1] Op. cit., vol. xxiv, col. 3.
[2] J. Summerson, *Heavenly Mansions* (paperback ed.), p. 149.

'rationalism' and 'functionalism' which are well exemplified by the title of Alberto Sartoris's 'panoramic synthesis of modern architecture', published in Milan in 1935, where the title on the front cover reads: *Gli Elementi dell' Architettura Funzionale*, whilst the title on the spine reads *Architettura Razionale*. In this instance, the confusion was to some extent due to misgivings expressed by Le Corbusier in a letter written in 1931; a letter which Sartoris published in the preface. In this letter, Le Corbusier contends that the term *architettura razionale* is too limited, and adds: 'our rationalist cenacles negate, though only theoretically, the fundamental human function of beauty, namely the beneficial and invigorating action which harmony has upon us'.

Walter Gropius also rejected the term 'rationalism' in *The New Architecture and the Bauhaus*, though this was mainly due to the disrepute into which *Die neue Sachlichkeit* had fallen in the 1930s.[1] 'Rationalism,' he wrote, 'which many people imagine to be the cardinal principle (of the New Architecture), is really only its purifying agency. The liberation of architecture from a welter of ornament, the emphasis on its structural functions, and the concentration on concise and economical solutions, represent the purely material side of that formalizing process on which the *practical* value of the New Architecture depends. The other, the aesthetic satisfaction of the human soul, is just as important as the material'.[2]

These emphatic repudiations of Rationalism by both Le Corbusier and Gropius, and their reasons for repudiating it, are important, because the nineteenth-century ideal of Rationalism, as expounded by Viollet-le-Duc and exemplified by Henri Labrouste, had never implied that 'Rationalism' must necessarily exclude emotion. Following Boileau (whose *Art Poétique* was written in 1674), these French theorists regarded reason only as an arbiter of architectural criticism, and never as the sole mechanism of architectural creativity. Hence any discussion as to whether architecture should be either rational or emotional would, as far as these theorists were concerned, be intrinsically futile.

[1] See B. M. Lane, *Architecture and Politics in Germany, 1918–1945* (1968), p. 130.

[2] Op. cit. (1935 ed.), pp. 19–20.

Judgement as a rational process

The validity of Rationalism as a basis for architectural criticism must surely depend on whether or not the essential qualities of good architecture can be assessed by *debatable* judgement. Before the Freudian era, this concept of a 'reasoned' judgement, though difficult to define with philosophical precision, was at least relatively free from ambiguities in this respect. But since the middle of the last century, when the verb 'to rationalize' was gradually introduced into our vocabulary, the difference between 'reasoning' and 'rationalizing' has obscured and complicated the essential nature of the problem. Nevertheless, it is some consolation to reflect that the complexities which this ambiguity has introduced into architectural theory are minuscule compared with its devastating effect on legal theory; and although American jurisprudence has now more or less recovered from Jerome Frank's shattering assault on the traditional theory of legal judgement, the nature of this assault, and the peculiar vulnerability which theories of legal judgement display to such attacks, makes legal theory an ideal 'model' (as the sociologists would say) for elucidating the fundamental problems of professional judgement in architecture.

Professor Frank's argument in *Law and the Modern Mind* may be summarized as follows: 'It has long been a tradition among lawyers to assert that judicial decisions are reached by a process of reasoning. But in fact this overt display of reasoning is sheer bunkum. When a judge hears a case, he gradually makes up his mind (since the law insists that he *must* make up his mind); but he does so in response to a variety of factors which have nothing to do with "reason", and range from the bias of his social prejudices to the rawness of his ulcers. The so-called "reasons" which he finally sets forth in his official opinion are nothing more than rationalizations of pre-determined hunches. If he has decided to give judgement in accordance with precedents cited on behalf of the plaintiff, his trained intelligence and mastery of legal jargon will easily allow him to demonstrate their relevance. If, on the contrary, he favours the defendant, he can just as easily demonstrate the opposite. Judicial opinions are simply the expression of a subconsciously persisting childhood image of a "father-figure"; and anyone who studies such opinions in the hopes of understanding the nature of law will be wasting his time.'

39

Much of the force was taken out of Jerome Frank's argument by the simple expedient of promoting him to the Bench, when, as Judge Frank, he discovered that the judicial process was rather more objective than he had hitherto supposed. But even if we accept that Jerome Frank's original theory has now been shown to be incorrect, we are not thereby dispensed from analysing the rationalist theory of architectural judgement with the same scepticism that he displayed. Viollet-le-Duc, the father of modern architectural rationalism, approached the same problem from the other end when he wrote: 'Observe in how many cases Reason confirms the judgement pronounced by Taste. Often—perhaps always—what we call taste is but an involuntary process of reasoning whose steps elude our observation.'[1]

Similarly, the careful analysis made by Mrs. Johnson Abercrombie with respect to the psychology of perception and reasoning[2] must not be allowed to obscure the fact that the legal profession long ago accepted, as one of the facts of life, that eye-witnesses frequently give contradictory evidence without the slightest taint of perjury. Indeed, it is one of the commonplace duties of a court of law to fashion justice from such contradictions and inconsistencies, asserted in perfectly good faith. Hence, although it is certainly useful for an architect to understand the psychology of perception, professional judgements in architecture, like professional judgements in law, become little more than academic exercises if we subscribe to a theory that all humanity can be so schooled in perceptiveness as to describe uniformly both the shape and significance of objects seen, and to draw identical conclusions from occurrences observed.

Every architect knows perfectly well that, when designing a building, his initial reasoning process is a sequence of 'rationalizations', in the sense that it is a series of 'inspirations rigorously

[1] E. E. Viollet-le-Duc, *Entretiens* (1863), vol i, p. 29, here given in Bucknell's translation, p. 29. ['Très-souvent (peut-être toujours) le sentiment du goût n'est qu'un raisonnement involontaire dont les termes nous échappent'.]

[2] In *The Anatomy of Judgement* (1960), ch. 2 and 3. The author of this book is now Reader in Architectural Education at London University; but when it was written she was in the Department of Anatomy, studying 'Perception in cerebral palsied children'. The book is not therefore specifically concerned with architecture.

analyzed by reason'.[1] He visualizes some relationship of forms intuitively, and then tries to justify it in relationship to the programme. Often it is only with the greatest reluctance that he can bring himself to abandon his brain-child and search his mind for another. In practice, therefore, the question is not so much 'why does the architect *choose* certain relationships of spaces?' but rather 'why does he *reject* certain relationships of spaces?' The quality of an architect's creative talent may well be measured by the variety of spaces he is capable of conceiving; but the quality of his judgement depends upon his criteria of rejection, and the scruples with which they are applied.

Here, perhaps, lies the only real difference between the judicial functions of law and architecture. However creative the cerebration of a High Court judge may be, it must necessarily be of a somewhat different order from that of an architect. Admittedly, it is quite possible, in theory, for a High Court judge, like an architect or an advocate, to envisage the solution of each particular problem as a process of selection and permutation from among every precedent he has ever encountered throughout his career. But in practice, judges rarely need to range beyond those precedents which are actually cited to them by the lawyers in charge of the case. Famous disputes have indeed been decided on the basis of one of the judge's own discoveries. Chief Justice Best's decision in *Jones v. Bright* (1829) was largely influenced by a precedent not cited at the bar.[2] *Norway Plains Co. v. Boston & Maine R.R.* (1854)[3] was decided on the basis of *In re Webb*, which Chief Justice Shaw seems to have come across accidentally when looking up another case in the same unreliable volume of Taunton's Law Reports.[4] But such occurrences must be rare. In fact, architectural judgement seems to be an amalgam of the functions of all the participants of a legal trial, in

---

[1] Viollet-le-Due, *op. cit.*, vol. i, p. 179: '. . . l'inspiration revêtue d'une distinction particulière à toute oeuvre produite par un sentiment vrai analysé rigoureusement par la raison, avant d'être exprimé'.

[2] 5 Bing. 533 at p. 543: 'However, I do not narrow my judgement to that, but think on the authority of a case not cited at the bar, *Kain v. Old* . . . &c., &c.'

[3] Supreme Court of Massachusetts, 1 Gray 263.

[4] Unfortunately, the eighth volume, to which Chief Justice Shaw referred, was notoriously unreliable. Cf. remarks (quoted in a footnote to chapter six) by Baron Parke in *Hadley v. Baxendale*.

that an architect must not only weigh the merits of arguments, both for and against each potential solution, with judicial impartiality, but he must simulate the 'adversary system' of a Common Law trial by some kind of private intellectual debate within his own mind.

If this analysis of the creative process of architecture is correct; if architectural judgement is in fact more concerned with rejection than selection; then perhaps the most apt legal definition of 'reason' is that given by Blackstone two centuries ago, when defining customary law. 'Customs', he wrote, 'must be reasonable, or rather, taken negatively, they must not be unreasonable.'[1] This, essentially, is all that the traditional Rationalist has ever demanded of an architectural design. He does not ask that it should demonstrably fulfil its function to perfection, that its structural system should demonstrably be the most elegant and economical that any civil engineer could devise, and that its environmental amenities must be proved to be unsurpassably exquisite. He simply asks that no architect should continue working on a project once he has become aware that it is unsuitable in its composition, illogical in its structure and incapable of harmonizing with its environment or with its component parts. This moderation partially explains why Rationalism is so unfashionable today. Rationalism has always been essentially a tolerant doctrine; hence it is as uncongenial to those for whom architectural creativity is analogous to Action Painting as it is to technocrats who dream of creating an everlasting urban utopia within five years.

Another reason why Rationalism is unpopular is that it conceives of reason in much the same way that the law conceives of 'a reasonable man'. Whenever litigation involves alleged negligence, the traditional Common Law test is usually: 'what would a reasonable man have done in the circumstances?' Judicial definitions of 'a reasonable man' have been numerous, varied and picturesque; but the frequency with which a jury of twelve reasonable men can stubbornly refuse to give a reasonable verdict has so persistently exasperated the judiciary, that jury trials in civil cases are becoming increasingly rare. 'Reasonable men' also exasperate famous architects; for whatever definition we may choose for 'a reasonable man',

[1] Sir William Blackstone, *Commentaries on the Laws of England*, p. 77 (Intro., sec. 3).

it is unlikely that any architectural 'Form-Giver' would recognize him as his ideal client. The basis of Le Corbusier's housing units (as they evolved from the mock-up exhibited in Paris in 1925 to their culmination in the various *Unités d'Habitation*) has been the Parisian artist's ideal dwelling since the mid-nineteenth century, i.e. a large glazed studio at the front, with an indoor balcony at the back covering the kitchen area and containing a bed. How suitable this is for 'a reasonable man', in the sense of an ordinary citizen of moderate means, is difficult to assess, though the transformation of Pessac,[1] and the alacrity with which *béton brut* interior walls are covered with wallpaper suggest that the proletariat is more conservative than *avant-garde* architects care to admit. The sociological surveys of three housing units (including the *Unité d'Habitation* at Nantes) conducted by Paul Chombart de Lauwe estimated that thirty-two per cent of the housewives at Nantes considered their kitchens to be too small, whilst forty-five per cent considered them so small as to be totally inadequate.[2] 'Whilst granting to architects the rôle of educator of the occupants, and wise promoter of a new way of life in new dwellings and new cities, we nevertheless think that more attention should be paid to the needs and desires of families', the author writes. 'For example, the solution which consists in providing a wide opening from a bedroom onto a living room is unacceptable.'[3]

Rationalism has recently come under attack from another quarter. With the sudden advent to popularity of architectural theorists who advocate complete permissiveness, and affectionately regard Las Vegas as the twentieth-century equivalent of Versailles, it is no longer enough for Rationalists simply to demand greater tolerance in judging what is reasonable; they must reaffirm their belief that their kind of tolerance does not exclude criteria, and that such criteria can be enunciated in the form of rational principles.

The classical concept of 'architectural principles' was unfortunately undermined by well-meaning but inept treatises published in the first half of this century, when 'principles' were discussed rather aridly in terms of platitudinous generalizations such as 'unity',

[1] See: Philippe Boudon, *Pessac de Le Corbusier* (1969).
[2] P. Chombart de Lauwe, *Famille et Habitation* (1960), p. 80.
[3] *Ibid.*, p. 107.

'contrast', 'balance', 'punctuation', 'inflection', and so on. In the present context, it will be profitable to forget such classifications for the moment, and examine whether any help can be obtained by analogy with the notion of 'principles' as understood by practitioners of the law.

The popular idea of a legal principle is of an orotund Latin epigram. This idea was probably first popularized by Lord Bacon, who announced in his *Elements of the Common Laws of England* that 'the rules themselves I have put in Latin, which language I chose as the briefest to contrive the rules compendiously, the aptest for memory, and of the greatest authority and majesty to be avouched and alleged in argument'.[1] However, the idea proved so infectious that when, in 1863, Chief Baron Pollock absent-mindedly made the comment: *res ipsa loquitur*[2] instead of simply saying 'the thing speaks for itself', the phrase was adopted with such enthusiasm and alacrity by the Bar, that it was eventually used to designate a principle enunciated by Chief Justice Erle (in *Scott v. London & St. Katherine Docks*)[3] to the effect that 'where an accident is such as in the ordinary cause of things does not happen if those who have the management use proper care, it affords reasonable evidence, in the absence of explanation by the defendants, that the accident arose from want of care'. By 1896, we find the principle being specifically referred to as 'the rule of *res ipsa loquitur*' in an American court of law;[4] and it has been so termed ever since.

If, however, we seek the essential character of legal principles, as expounded or implied by judges when deciding cases, it seems clear that they stem from an entirely different concept, first enunciated (also in Latin) about a century ago: the concept of a *ratio decidendi*. The full implications of *rationes decidendi* are a favourite topic of professors of jurisprudence, since they allow full play for the intellectual sport of demonstrating the inherent contradictions of previous scholars' definitions. For our purposes, however, it can be

[1] *Op. cit.*, Preface.

[2] A phrase he doubtless recollected from Cicero's *Oratio pro Milone* (though Cicero wrote '*res loquitur ipsa*'); or from *Roberts and Tremayne's Case* reported in Cro. 16 Jac. I, p. 508.

[3] 1865, 3 H. & C. at 601.

[4] In *O'Neal v. O'Connell* (167 Mass. 390), per Lathrop J. The term appears in the 1897 edition of Bouvier's Law Dictionary, but in no earlier edition.

defined quite adequately as the doctrine that there must always be some fundamental 'reason for deciding' a case one way rather than another, and that this reason is the 'principle', or fundamental criterion, on which the case has been adjudged (whatever other remarks may have been made by the Court in its published opinion).

To demonstrate the relevance of this concept to the problems of architectural judgement, let us take, as an example, a critique published by Professor Peter Prangnell on the Amsterdam City Hall Competition.[1] After describing the Toronto City Hall, the Boston City Hall, and Wilhelm Holzbauer's winning project for the Amsterdam City Hall as 'three monuments to the idiocy of our times', he justifies this rebuke by explaining that, traditionally, city halls have housed the secular organization by which city services are provided and regulated, and thus a city hall should demonstrate those qualities that citizens really value. Such qualities, he says, vary with the occupations and interests of each citizen; hence a city hall should be, in microcosm, the image of streets and places of cities; freely accessible and 'interiorized'.

After describing the prize-winning Amsterdam scheme as 'simple-mindedly boorish', Professor Prangnell amiably continues: 'the whole package does not make one civil gesture towards that extraordinary example of the city—Amsterdam. This must be the crucial issue . . .'. Then, after elaborating upon the nature of this crucial issue, he expresses the view that two projects, one by Heijdenrijk and the other by Hertzberger, *did* take it into account.

If Professor Prangnell had been one of the official judges of the competition,[2] he would obviously not have asserted that the qualities praised in these schemes were *alone* sufficient to justify giving their authors the prize. He would, for example, have had to make sure that both Heijdenrijk and Hertzberger had complied with all the published conditions of the programme. But if we assume, for the sake of argument, that the judges were wrong in specifically asserting that Heijdenrijk did not comply with the conditions,[3] then the *ratio decidendi* of Professor Prangnell's judgement could be stated as the principle (which he enunciates) to the effect that 'a project for any

[1] *The Canadian Architect*, March 1969, pp. 60 ff.
[2] Which included Professor Sir Robert Matthew and Professor J. Schader.
[3] *Jury Report*, p. 23.

public building must have, at its root, a concern with a city-like fabric of support and fill, and must be concerned primarily with supporting all those elements and actions of life that make for agreeable citizenship'.[1]

Whether or not this *ratio decidendi* is valid, or whether it means anything at all, is, in the present context, immaterial. It need simply be noted that Professor Prangnell very logically based his judgement of this whole complex issue on one single principle which he considered of over-riding importance, and that he supported it by reference to two *precedents* which he considered authoritative, namely Shadrach Woods' Free University of Berlin and Le Corbusier's Venice Hospital.[2]

The second important aspect of Professor Prangnell's principle of judgement, which is also relevant to the judicial theory of a *ratio decidendi*, is its implicit assumption of a context. This will be discussed in more detail in the next chapter; but it is appropriate here to note that there has long been a lively controversy among jurists as to whether a *ratio decidendi* is totally dependent on its context, or whether it constitutes a principle with a life of its own. Cardozo seems to have taken the latter viewpoint, since in *The Nature of the Judicial Process* he criticized[3] Lord Halsbury's pronouncement that 'a case is only an authority for what it actually decides. I entirely deny that it can be quoted for a proposition that may seem to follow logically from it. Such a mode of reasoning assumes that the law is necessarily a logical code, whereas every lawyer must acknowledge that the law is not always logical at all'.[4] Yet if we examine the context of Lord Halsbury's statement, there seems much to be said for his point of view, which was by no means novel, and had been made by numerous judges, as for example by Chief Justice Best in *Richardson v. Mellish* (1824).[5]

The particular case referred to by Cardozo (*Quinn v. Leatham*, 1901) revolved round the general issue as to whether a dispute between members of a trade union and an employer of non-union workmen was a trade dispute within the meaning of the *Conspiracy and Protection of Property Act* of 1875. The crucial problem which

---

[1] *The Canadian Architect*, March 1969, p. 62.   [2] *Ibid.*
[3] *Op. cit.* (paperback ed.), p. 32.
[4] *Quinn v. Leatham* (1901) A.C. 495 at 506.   [5] 2 Bing. at 248.

eventually confronted the House of Lords was whether or not a decision in an earlier case (*Allen v. Flood*, 1898) constituted a binding precedent. Lord Halsbury contended that it did not, since in *Allen v. Flood*, it had been decided[1] that the defendant had uttered no threat, the trade union had passed no resolution, and the defendant had done nothing except express his personal views in favour of his fellow members. In *Quinn v. Leatham*, however, the evidence had shown that there had indeed been a conspiracy to induce the plaintiff's workmen to go on strike; hence whatever might have been the *ratio decidendi* of *Allen v. Flood*, it could never, according to Lord Halsbury, be applicable to a lawsuit based on the Statute in question.

This doctrine had been stated even more forcibly by Lord Halsbury in an earlier case (*Monson v. Tussaud*, 1894):[2] 'I have some difficulty', he said, 'in following the argument that a decision of the Court on one set of facts is an authority upon another and a totally different set of facts. Of course, if the two sets of facts are governed by some principle of law, the principle of law affirmed by the Court is equally authoritative to whatever facts the principle may be applied; but where the strength and cogency of the facts themselves, or the inference derived therefrom, is in debate, I cannot, as a matter of *reasoning*, compare one set of facts with another and bring them within any governing principle.'

These judicial opinions have been quoted in detail since they illustrate a principle of legal judgement which seems highly relevant to architectural judgement, even though it seems to have been generally overlooked by those who have written about architectural 'rules'. There is undoubtedly a whole *corpus* of architectural principles, enshrined in precedents, which can be adduced by the aid of reason, and applied to new or even hypothetical situations. But the congruity of the context is essential to the proper application of such principles, otherwise they produce only mechanical, alien and moribund *pastiches* of a type which brought 'the rules of architec-

[1] It is important, in the present context, to note that when *Allen v. Flood* was decided in the House of Lords, Lord Halsbury dissented from the majority opinion. In other words, he differed as to the interpretation of the facts constituting the subject of the *ratio decidendi*.

[2] 1894 1 Q.B. at 689.

47

ture' into justifiable disrepute. According to Howard Robertson's *Principles of Architectural Composition*, 'the examination of the practical factors which influence the design of buildings in a direct and concrete sense forms a study quasi-independent of the consideration of design in the abstract'.[1] But even the most superficial study of legal judgements will convincingly demonstrate that there is no such thing as 'the consideration of adjudication in the abstract', and that even the broadest legal generalizations depend for their application, in the last resort, on the context in which they are applied. Consider, for example, the maxim which can be translated as: 'no one will be heard to assert his own shameful conduct'.[2] At first sight, this proposition that no one may come into Court simply to ask for punishment might seem so obviously in accordance with the administration of temporal justice as to be applicable automatically, as indeed it *was* so applied by Lord Mansfield when he refused to allow a juror to testify to his own impropriety.[3] But it eventually became clear that if a jury *does* reach its decision by improper means (such as by casting lots), there is literally no other way of detecting such impropriety other than by a sworn confession from one of its members.[4]

I claim, then, that if we regard the principles of architecture in the same light that judges regard the principles of law, those principles are equally meaningful and genuine, since they form part of a creative 'cybernetic' process involving *reasoning within an appropriate context*. For although the primary context of legal reasoning is ostensibly the specific issue in dispute, just as the primary context of architectural reasoning is ostensibly the specific requirement of a client, in law and architecture any valid decision must depend on wider contexts: the context of history (which provides precedents), the context of society (which provides safeguards

[1] *Op. cit.*, p. 3.

[2] '*Nemo turpitudinem suam allegans audietur*'. Professor Wigmore, in his famous treatise on *Evidence*, describes this as an eighteenth-century maxim; but in fact it occurs in Coke's *Institutes* (Bk. IV, ch. 64) in the form: '*allegans suam turpitudinem non est audiendus*'.

[3] *Vaise v. Delaval* (1785) 1 Term. Rep 11.

[4] Cf. the Pennsylvania case of *Commonwealth v. Weizman* (1936) (25 Pa. Dist. & County 469), where the members of the jury were fined $10.00 for Contempt of Court.

for the public with regard to the possible effects of any decision on those not immediately involved) and the context of the physical environment (which provides both a sense of place and the judicial guidelines of customary law). All these factors must be involved in the process of reasoning, just as the process of reasoning must be involved in the process of evaluation; and when an architect can enunciate his reasoning with the same clarity and precision as a High Court judge, he may feel assured that his judgement is professional in the noblest and most apt sense of the term.

CHAPTER THREE

The environmental context of judgement

In the practice and criticism of architecture, 'context' affects, or should affect, judgement in at least four different ways. First, there is the physical and economic environment which every building constitutes in itself, and in which it is situated: a context which not only involves the programme of the new building and the nature of the terrain, but will also involve many other physical and economic factors, such as the character of the surroundings, the prevalent climatic conditions, the state of the money-market, and the ability of the building contractors to deliver specific materials or equipment at specific times to the building site. Secondly, there is the political context, ranging from statutory zoning restrictions to all the various political pressures which can be exerted on an architect to force him to design in one way rather than another. Thirdly, there is what may be called the procedural context of the design itself, i.e., the sequential influences of ideas by which the final scheme evolves from the architect's initial sketches, and the reasons which cause him to favour one form of evolution rather than another. Fourthly, there is the historical context of the project, i.e., the relationship between the building and other buildings of the same type, or the relationship between this particular design and earlier work by the same architect. There may well be other contextual factors which should be taken into account; but it is probable that they can all be placed within one of these four categories so far mentioned.

The environmental context of judgement

The full importance of the physical context of a building has only begun to be appreciated in recent years. Indeed, the success of writers like Lewis Mumford in arousing wide public recognition of this factor is probably the twentieth century's most important contribution to the theory of architecture. But like all truths which have suddenly illuminated man's creative mind, there has been a tendency for idealism to push the logic of their basic tenets to unrealistic extremes. The mid-twentieth-century reaction against the eighteenth-century concept of urban spaces, exemplified at Nancy (with its emphasis on the orderly disposition of enclosing façades, regardless of what happened behind them) was certainly timely; but it has sometimes induced critics to vie with one another as to which of them can envisage integration at the most grandiose scale. For example, everyone would concur with the premise that a building to be constructed on Beacon Hill, in Boston, should relate in some way to its immediate neighbourhood. The premise that the neighbourhood in which this new building is to be situated should be integrated with the rest of Boston is less easy to demonstrate, but one can well envisage plausible arguments in its favour. The premise that Boston should be integrated within the whole galaxy of its suburban setting can certainly be defended as an ideal. But the premise that no architect can design a building for Beacon Hill without redesigning the whole of Massachusetts can lead only to arid academicism and frustration; yet it is a thesis which by no means lacks advocates in our architectural schools.

Of more immediate relevance than such visionary criteria would be the maxim (here submitted for consideration) that it is impossible to design or criticize a building adequately unless the designer or critic is familiar with the site. I contend that it is inconceivable that a journalist can write an adequate criticism of a major building during a single brief visit, especially if he has never visited the environment before. I would similarly contend that it is incredible that the best project for the Toronto City Hall Competition could have been that of a competitor who had never visited Canada. But whether credible or not, such things do happen, and architects must therefore interrogate their professional consciences scrupulously when trying to adumbrate general maxims concerning the relationship of a building to its environment.

The minority report of the judges of the Toronto City Hall Competition (written by Professor Sir William [now Lord] Holford and Professor Gordon Stephenson) based its dissenting opinion specifically on the unsuitability of that monumental design to the site prepared for it. But the *ratio decidendi* of the majority report was stated specifically to be 'the need for a distinctive building, different in form and materials from standard commercial buildings —impressive when seen from the Square and its immediate neighbourhood, and also a distinctive feature of the silhouette of Toronto as seen from the distance'.[1] The majority decision may well have been right; but its *ratio decidendi* has clearly little to do with the environment of downtown Toronto. On the contrary, its justification was related solely to the avowed purpose of the competition, which, according to the published Conditions of Entry, was that 'One of the reasons for this competition is to find a building that will proudly express its function as the centre of civic government. How to achieve an atmosphere about a building that suggests government, continuity of certain democratic traditions and service to the community are problems for the designer of the modern city hall. These were qualities that the architects of other ages endeavoured to embody in the town halls of their times.'[2]

Which 'architects of other ages' were in the minds of those who drafted the competition conditions is not clear. Presumably they were alluding to mediaeval city halls in northern Europe. But they were obviously not thinking of the architects of the mid-eighteenth-century extension to the old city of Nancy, where the façade and silhouette of the city hall was composed of standardized bays common to every other building in the plaza, and derived from standardized bays built in adjoining plazas of the newly-expanded city. Nor were they thinking of the City Hall at Metz (designed in 1764 by the Professor of Architecture at the French Academy School) which had not only to harmonize with the mediaeval cathedral opposite, but had also to conform to the configurations of an irregular sloping site. Sigfried Giedion justly remarked with reference to the buildings at Nancy that 'an immense fund of archi-

[1] *A Synopsis of the City Hall and Square Competition for Toronto, Canada* (1958), Appendix A, p. 3.
[2] *Ibid.*, p. 2.

52

tectural knowledge is revealed in each of these squares. It appears equally in the way the heights and proportions of the buildings are regulated and in the handling of the materials used . . . each element is co-ordinated with all the others; isolated phenomena are synthesized to form the most effective whole'.[1]

When Sir William Holford and Professor Stephenson presented their dissenting opinions on the Toronto award, they nevertheless prefaced their remarks by asserting that the judges were *unanimous* in regarding the winning design as 'the most original in conception of any of those submitted'.[2] But it is by no means clear that the originality of this one scheme, as compared with the other 519 schemes, had anything to do with the specific urban context in which the building was to be situated. On the contrary, the resemblance of the scheme to the new parliament buildings in Brasilia suggests that the urban, climatic, economic and historic context of downtown Toronto was given relatively little attention. Perhaps it was proper that these factors should have been regarded so lightly; but if so, many currently popular dogmas about environmental design need to be radically revised.

In contrast to the procedure adopted by those who organized and judged the Toronto City Hall Competition, it may be instructive to study the evolution of the competition held a hundred years ago for the Royal Courts of Justice in London. Throughout the whole development of this project, from the establishment of the programme to the choice of site, the views of practising lawyers were given predominance; and the fact that these lawyers naturally approached the problem with minds conditioned by the techniques of legal procedure may help us to evaluate the legal attitude towards 'context' by comparison with that of the architectural profession.

There is no need to describe in detail the history of the Law Courts Competition, since this has been admirably summarized by Michael Port in an essay published in *Architectural History*.[3] All that is necessary here is to indicate the manner in which (a) the

[1] S. Giedeon, *Space, Time and Architecture* (1967 ed.), pp. 146–7.
[2] *Synopsis*, Appendix A, p. 7.
[3] M. H. Port, 'The new Law Courts competition (1866–67)', in *Architectural History* (Journal of the Society of Architectural Historians of Great Britain), vol. xi (1968), pp. 75–93.

programme was established, (b) the site was selected, (c) the competitors were briefed, (d) the entries were judged and (e) the winning design was modified—all with reference to the environmental problems as understood in the 1860s. For this purpose, earlier proposals for Courts of Justice, such as Sir Charles Barry's project of 1842 for a building in the middle of Lincoln's Inn Fields, may be disregarded. All that need be observed with reference to such projects is that, when the acquisition of the site for the new Courts of Justice was authorized by Act of Parliament in 1865, the problem had already been under close parliamentary scrutiny for a quarter of a century.

First, then, let us consider the establishment of the programme, the selection of the site and the briefing of the competitors. This was an age before persons in authority employed 'consultants' to study the space needs in detail,[1] so the Royal Commission on the Concentration of the Courts of Law and Equity relied initially on an architectural surveyor, H. R. Abraham, who was in fact the brother-in-law of the Attorney-General (Sir Richard Bethell). This choice of H. R. Abraham as surveyor for the government proved unexpectedly fortunate for the leaders of the architectural profession, since it was probably the subsequent accusations of nepotism[2] that induced the government to establish a limited competition. Abraham seems to have fulfilled his allotted task efficiently enough, and gave creditable replies to the two hundred questions asked of him by the Select Committee of the House of Commons which took evidence with respect to the Courts of Justice Building Act.[3] Nevertheless, he admitted that he had not thought it necessary to trouble the judges personally, and he apparently obtained most of his factual inform-

[1] The programme for the Toronto City Hall Competition was based on a 60-page report by a firm of Management Consultants (Woods & Gordon). The Consultants who prepared a report in 1956 for the proposed Los Angeles Auditorium (i.e. Arthur D. Little, Inc.) themselves 'acknowledged the valuable contribution by five consultants', one of which was a firm of architects in Boston!

[2] *The Builder*, vol. xix, p. 432 (22 June 1861). Since Bethell (who became the first Lord Westbury) was forced to retire from public office in 1865 'for having unworthily used his position to advance his relatives' (*D.N.B.*), the accusation may well have been justified.

[3] See the published *Minutes of Evidence* of 11 July 1861.

ation either from their clerks, or from various lawyers whom he preferred not to name.[1]

To appreciate the complexity of the problem, it should be understood that at this time, the British judicial system, as evolved throughout the centuries, had come to consist of a congerie of disparate jurisdictions, which, though basically classifiable within the two main branches known as 'law' and 'equity',[2] were in fact subdivided into many different types of courts, often situated in widely different localities. Thus the architectural concentration of all these courts into a single building was an important preliminary stage in achieving their amalgamation into a single judicial system, and may well have been a proximate cause of this much-needed reform. At all events, the Judicature Act by which the reforms were achieved was not passed until five years after the competition was held.

When it was finally decided to select a design by means of a limited competition, another Royal Commission, this time under the chairmanship of the Lord Chancellor, was appointed to supervise the whole thing. Members were nominated by the senior judges of the various courts, by the Benchers of all the Inns of Court, by the Law Society and by the Commissioner of Works (i.e. the minister responsible for public buildings). One member of the Commission, Sir Roundell Palmer, Q.C. (who was now Attorney-General), was also a member of the 'Committee of Judges of Designs' which was to select the competitors and eventually make the award.

The drafting of the Book of Instructions was the responsibility of a 'Works Committee', which began its work by forming four sub-committees: two to study the requirements of the Bar and Solicitors respectively, and two to study the access for lawyers and for the public. The means of access for the lawyers was considered by them to be particularly important because (as George Denman, Q.C., M.P., insisted when giving evidence before the Select Committee of 1869)[3] the impossibility of giving a barrister ample warning of the time when a case was to be called in court, together with the

---

[1] *Ibid.*, questions 179, 180.   [2] See Chapter 10.

[3] *Minutes of Evidence taken before the Select Committee on the New Law Courts*, 20 July 1869, question 2528.

desirability of allowing him to spend most of his time in his own chambers, made it essential that no barrister's chambers should be more than two hundred and fifty yards from the Courts. The means of access for the public was clearly more difficult to predict, since whereas a map had been made showing the location of every law office in London, it was impossible to know from which direction litigants, jurors and witnesses might be expected to arrive. Nevertheless, much time was spent studying, and making proposals for, the widening of existing thoroughfares and the creation of new streets. Similarly, attention was paid to the rehousing of those who would be displaced by the clearing of the proposed site.[1]

As regards the designs of the courtrooms, the Commission obtained all the information it could about courtrooms existing in England, and, through diplomatic channels, about new courtrooms constructed abroad. The latter proved of little help, since although several countries, notably France and Prussia, provided plans of provincial palaces of justice, the countries which sent drawings seldom followed the British legal system, whilst those countries which did have the Anglo-American Common Law, such as the United States of America, seldom had suitable prototypes, since their courthouses were generally too small. However the Commission could report that it had 'received plans of some excellent Courts in Toronto'[2] [Pl. XXIB]. It was eventually decided that the English Assize Courts were generally too large, and that the ideal size would be that of the Court of Exchequer at Westminster[3] [Pl. XXIA]. This had been constructed against the west flank of Westminster Hall, where its width was determined by the spacing between the Hall's mediaeval buttresses. According to Sir John Soane's drawing prepared for the Select Committee of 1824, the Exchequer Court measured 42′ 8″ × 31′ 11″, and was the largest of the courts at Westminster.[4]

---

[1] *Minutes of Evidence taken before the Select Committee on the Courts of Justice Building Act (Money) Bill*, 11 July 1861, question 134.

[2] *Report of Royal Commission of 1865* (submitted 1870), p. xxii, para. 59. See also House of Lords Standing Order (bound with miscellaneous papers relevant to the Royal Courts of Justice in the R.I.B.A. Library: SR 725.151: 42.1) at p. 116.

[3] *Report of Royal Commission of 1865* (submitted 1870), p. xvii, para. 18.

[4] Plans in Sir John Soane's Museum.

The most important feature of the instructions was not the written schedules, but the arrangement whereby the competitors were to 'visit and revisit all the existing Courts and Offices to familiarize themselves with the extent, order and method of performing the business of each'.[1] It was this requirement, more than any other, which prompted the government to resist Mr. Bentinck's resolution, moved in the House of Commons on 22 March 1866, that the competition be made open to all. In replying for the government, the minister responsible (Mr. Cowper) pointed out that it was necessary for the competitors to 'study for at least seven months the minute details of the required building',[2] and that 'arrangements had accordingly been made that the selected architects should have access to the present Courts and Offices when they pleased, in order that they might be enabled to see how the business was transacted, and thus by their own eyes and their own judgement ascertain what kind of building would be best adapted for the business carried on'.[3] He insisted that 'the object was to get the very best Palace of Justice in the world', and that it was totally at variance with the government's instructions that 'they should endeavour to develop rising talent among architects', or 'secure such an exhibition of architectural drawings as might be interesting to the public'.[4]

As regards the method of judging the entries, it was decided to give full responsibility to the clients, that is to say to the legal profession (represented by the Lord Chief Justice of England and the Attorney-General), to the Treasury (represented by the Chancellor of the Exchequer and Sir William Stirling-Maxwell, M.P.) and to the first Commissioner of Works, W. F. Cowper. Only two of them were thus lawyers, and none had any architectural expertise. Cowper and his wife were friends of John Ruskin,[5] so this may account for the general assumption that the building would be neo-Gothic; but there is no reason to believe that Cowper himself (who had had a varied military and political career) had any marked

---

[1] *Report of Royal Commission of 1865* (submitted 1870), p. xxiv, para. 74.
[2] *Hansard*, 22 March 1866, col. 786.   [3] *Ibid*.   [4] *Ibid*., col. 784.
[5] In Peter Quennell's biography of Ruskin, Mrs. Cowper is referred to as Mrs. Cowper Temple. Mr. Cowper was a son of the 5th Earl Cowper, but his mother married again to Lord Palmerston (i.e. Viscount Palmerston and Baron Temple); and when he inherited his step-father's estate in 1869, he changed his name to Cowper-Temple.

architectural prejudices. Sir William Stirling-Maxwell was distinguished as a historian and a connoisseur of art; but his cultural interest was in all things Spanish. There was thus good reason to assume that the criteria of assessment would be those stated by the Commission, namely that 'the chief points to be kept constantly in view, and to be treated as superseding, so far as they may conflict, all considerations of architectural effect, are the accommodations to be provided and the arrangements to be adopted so as in the greatest degree to facilitate the dispatch and the accurate transaction of the law business of the country'.[1] Two architects, John Shaw and George Pownall, had been appointed to assist the judges in interpreting the drawings, and they were eventually added to the jury at the request of the competing architects.[2] Expert opinions were also obtained to advise on the heating, ventilation, police supervision, fireproofing, and cost-analysis, whilst in addition, the Commission's sub-committees of the Bar and the Solicitors examined the plans and checked the report drawn up by their representatives on the Commission itself.[3]

It came therefore as a shock to the architectural profession when the 'Judges of Designs', after studying the projects for six months, reported on 30 July 1867 that since Barry had submitted the best plan, and Street had submitted the best elevation, they should be appointed jointly [Pls. XII & XVII]. It came as an even greater shock when, as a result of Barry's protest that he alone was entitled to the commission, the award was made to Street. Presumably Street was given the commission because he was considered more skilful at Gothic detailing; but Barry's claim should not be given too much weight, since it was mainly based on Shaw and Pownall's tabulated assessment. This assessment merely listed eighty-eight items, such as 'offices and staircases to offices', 'water closets and urinals', 'separation of traffic', etc., and awarded one point for the best solution, forty-one points being awarded to Barry, as compared with three to Street. But this hardly justifies Barry's implied assertion that his own plan was fourteen times better than Street's, and

[1] *Report of Royal Commission of 1865* (submitted 1870), p. xxiv, para. 78.
[2] *Ibid.*, p. xxiii, para. 69. (This request had the unanimous support of the R.I.B.A. [Resolution of 23 March 1867].)
[3] *Ibid.*, p. xxvii, para. 103.

there is every reason to suspect that Barry's insistence on a monumental Gothic dome (to be used for storing documents) would have
been disastrous. The only really incredible feature of the whole
competition is that, as compared with the many voluminous transcripts of the various Select Committees, the Judges' Final Report
apparently occupied only five lines of notepaper![1]

Nevertheless, the legal profession had a final opportunity to
display the merits of its own brand of judicial procedure when (as a
result of the decision to construct a Thames Embankment) a suggestion was made in 1869 that the site of the Courts of Justice should
be moved three hundred yards further south so that its main façade
would overlook the river. Another Select Committee was therefore
formed, and Street was called to give evidence. In the course of six
hundred and forty-eight questions, involving the exchange of fifty
thousand words, and lasting two days, Street cautiously emphasized
the magnificent 'opportunity of architectural effect'[2] given by the
new site, and referred approvingly to Fergusson's comments on
Somerset House[3] (which the new alternative site would have ad-
joined). He even went so far as to suggest that 'from Waterloo
Bridge it would be a singularly good view, for this reason: that
Waterloo Bridge is thirty-seven feet above the ground level of the
Embankment, so that you get naturally what, when I made my
competition design for this building, I was obliged to get artificially.
In order to show the whole scheme, including the great central hall
rising above the other buildings, I was obliged to take a bird's eye
view [Pl. XIII], which is entirely an imaginary thing; but from
Waterloo Bridge you do get, to a great extent, the effect of a bird's
eye view . . . I think it is a magnificent site for a public building'.[4]
But in reply to leading questions from Beresford Hope, a Member
of Parliament and former President of the R.I.B.A., who tried to
get Street to admit that 'the main reason for the proposed change of
the building from Carey Street to Howard Street is of an artistic
nature', Street insisted that he personally had 'made no objections

[1] *The Builder*, vol. xxv, p. 607 (17 August 1867).
[2] *Minutes of Evidence taken before the Select Committee on the New Law Courts*
(9 July 1869), p. 37, question 633.
[3] *Ibid.*, p. 40, question 660.
[4] *Ibid.*, p. 40, question 663; p. 57 (13 July), question 972.

to the Carey Street site artistically' and added: 'If you ask me which site affords the greatest opportunity for architectural display, I should say the Embankment site; but granted that you are going to make the land round my building decent, I have no objection to the Carey Street site'.[1] It would certainly be difficult to accuse Street of trying to build what Professor Prangnell would have termed 'a monument to the idiocy of his times'. Indeed, the advantage of the Embankment site which seems to have most strongly attracted Street was the comparative ease with which building materials could be brought to it by barge along the Thames, with a corresponding saving of an estimated five per cent in construction costs.[2]

In any event, the matter was finally settled by the lawyers, who persuaded the Select Committee that the proposed variation of three hundred yards would, when considered within the environmental context of the Inns of Court, place intolerable shackles on the administration of justice (despite the fact that half the courts were then situated nearly two miles away, at Westminster). They also successfully convinced the Select Committee that the mediaeval Inns of Court (i.e. the traditional abode of the profession) would never be abandoned merely for the sake of finding chambers closer to wherever the Courts of Justice might be built. As a result, the Strand (or 'Carey Street') site was, after lengthy argument, retained.

One conclusion which could be drawn from this vast mass of published records is simply that lawyers' ideas of architectural context are based solely on mundane practicalities, to the exclusion of the total environment, and that their views are so limited by tawdry aspects of utility that they are impervious to nobler ideals of urban design. But something more useful may possibly be learned by studying the *procedures* which were followed when selecting the site, and comparing these to the procedures followed when selecting the designs. The system of interrogation used in the former, whereby questions were put by members of a tribunal, and the replies of those called to give evidence were carefully recorded, seems equally applicable to both problems; and it seems a pity that the two eminent jurists who were included among the 'Judges of Designs' were not able, or did not choose, to impose such a procedure on their colleagues. Such a procedure might not have resulted in the selec-

[1] *Ibid.* (13 July), p. 64, question 1134.   [2] *Ibid.* (9 July), p. 41, question 673.

tion of a better architect, or in the construction of a better building; but by recording the judges' deliberations (including the interrogation of each competitor on the merits of his design) posterity would have been presented with a means of correlating the questions asked with the results achieved. This scientific method was then, as it is now, adopted when the problem was seen solely as one involving finance. Perhaps it could profitably be extended to solve architectural problems whose value cannot be assessed in terms of monetary cost.

It may of course be objected that any such procedure in architectural competitions would necessarily involve sacrificing the anonymity of competitors, and that this anonymity is essential if judgements are to be fair, and manifestly seen to be fair. But in the legal profession, the attitude towards procedural fairness is precisely the opposite. Whereas in an architectural competition, all the competitors are told well in advance who the judges will be, but no judge is supposed to have any idea who will compete, in law, the parties to a dispute rarely know who the judge will be, but once the trial has started, only the most exceptional circumstances (such as those involving alleged blackmail) allow cases to be conducted with any degree of secrecy. Indeed, it is of the very essence of Common Law ideals of fairness that judges, juries, witnesses, advocates and parties to a dispute must all confront one another, with a full knowledge of the identity of each.[1]

Anyone who, as regards the Sydney Opera House Competition, might be inclined to wonder if Eero Saarinen would have awarded the commission to Jørn Utzon had he been aware of his identity should wonder instead whether Utzon might have conceived his project rather differently had Eero Saarinen been replaced by Philip Johnson. If we assume, out of respect for Utzon's integrity, that his project was in no way influenced by his knowledge of who was to be the judge, we must pay the same respect to the memory

[1] Cf. Viollet-le-Duc, *Entretiens* (1872), ii, p. 413: 'Il faudrait donc, pour que la valeur des concurrents fût appréciée avec autant d'équité que possible, une discussion devant leurs oeuvres, entre gens de métier, notoirement capables, habiles à faire valoir les motifs de leurs préférences ou leurs critiques, et que cette discussion fût entendue par un jury . . . Imagine-t-on quel serait le sort des accusés traduits en Cours d'assises, s'ils devaient être jugés par les conseillers, l'avocat général et les avocats plaidants ?'

of Saarinen by assuming that his decision would in no way have been affected by any previous knowledge of the identity of the designer. The doctrine of anonymity, established for academic reasons two centuries ago at what became the Ecole des Beaux-Arts (to the effect that projects for the Grand Prix and Concours d'Emulation must be marked with a pseudonym) was abandoned with alacrity in schools of architecture whenever and wherever the 'Beaux-Arts' system itself was abandoned. Its retention in architectural competitions is thus almost as anachronistic as the procedure of Star Chamber.

These reflections have led rather far from their starting point, which was the judicial attitude towards environmental requirements when assessing competitive designs. But if, in conclusion, we enquire by what evolutionary process environment has assumed such importance in the concept of architecture, it can readily be demonstrated that this relatively recent architectural doctrine derived mainly from the legal doctrines of Montesquieu, which were enunciated a century before any scientist had put forward the biological doctrine we usually associate with the environmental implications of 'organic architecture'. From the Renaissance to the mid-eighteenth century, architectural form had been conceived as universal—the same in Greece as in Scandinavia, the same in Russia as in the United States. The change in attitude came with Montesquieu's *Esprit des Lois*. Book XIV discusses law as relative to the nature of climate; Book XVIII discusses law as relative to the nature of the land (*terrain*); Book XXIII discusses law as relative to the density of populations.

Many years were to pass before anyone would formally assert the same relationship in architecture. The initial credit for this must be given to Gothic Revivalists, such as Pugin, who asserted in his *True Principles* that he would 'maintain and prove that climate has always had a large share in the formation of domestic architecture'[1] and that in ecclesiastical architecture, 'our northern climate requires an acute pitch of roof'.[2] But the idea only assumed special

[1] A. W. Pugin, *The True Principles of Pointed or Christian Architecture* (1841), p. 55. Cf. also Georg Moller's *Essay on Gothic Architecture* (c. 1819), chapter one (1st English translation published in 1824).

[2] *Ibid.*, p. 48.

importance with the introduction of the cult of 'vernacular architecture' at the end of the nineteenth century, and it is perhaps for
this reason that Sir Banister Fletcher's father seems to have been
the first professor of architecture to preface methodically each
historical survey with descriptions of the geographical, geological
and climatic milieu. Since then, the concept of environment has
been given even wider connotations, until we have now come to see
architectural contexts in all their confusing ecological complexity, as
admirably exemplified in the standard text-book by John Burchard
and Albert Bush-Brown. Nevertheless, as these authors demonstrate,
it is easier to describe complexity than to understand its architectural
significance, even historically. Wistfully, their awe-inspiring statistical accounts of the technological changes which occurred in transportation, communication and industrialization during the last
fifty years are interspersed by art-historical lamentations that 'it
becomes clear in an instant that the work in American music was
far more experimental than in architecture',[1] and that 'the other
arts, as they were being practised in America, seemed to have little
to say to the art of architecture'.[2] But it is precisely because music
and painting have no specific environment that such free experi-
mentation (with every artist acting as his own judge) is still possible.
The restrictions which our new technological environment increasingly impose on architectural design may well be off-set by
liberating factors; but as more and more experts become involved,
it seems logical to suppose that methods of judgement will need to
become far more objective and sophisticated, whereby those based
on legal procedure—which may be regarded as the judicial process
par excellence—may prove to be of increasing relevance in future
decades.

[1] J. Burchard & A. Bush-Brown, *The Architecture of America, a social and
cultural history* (1961), p. 332.
[2] *Ibid.*, p. 412.

CHAPTER FOUR

The political context of judgement

Few aspects of architectural design have a more obvious relationship with law than that which concerns the political control of urban and rural environments. Lawyers who specialize in Land Development Law may be deluded into thinking that they can dispense with the assistance of architects and planners; but few specialists in urban design have any doubt that legislative sanctions of some kind are essential if their work is to be effective. The main dilemma facing urban planners is in fact that of legal draftsmanship: the difficulty of so phrasing legislation that it will be specific enough to be enforceable, yet flexible enough to allow modifications whenever unpredictable needs make changes desirable.

However, apart from litigious problems arising from this type of legislation (such as disputed decisions concerning the 'aesthetic' control of buildings), it will be clear that any study concerned with architectural judgement must consider the term 'politics' in its widest sense, as meaning the governmental controls which influence, or should influence, such judgements. Here we are at once confronted with a number of ambiguities of which the most important is that between two overlapping concepts: the concept of State control and the concept of government control. In England, and other countries of the Commonwealth, there still survives a constitutional distinction between 'the State' and 'the government', whereby although the legislature, judicature and and executive are inextricably intermingled, none of these either separately or conjointly is identified with the State. Parliament, which combines legislative, executive, and to some extent judicial functions, is composed of

'Her Majesty's loyal opposition' as well as 'Her Majesty's government'. Hence however much the theoretical distinction between serving the State and serving a political party may have been attenuated by the televised influence of the American 'presidential' system (where the Head of State has more arbitrary powers than George III could have envisaged even in his wildest dreams), the concept of 'serving the State' still retains fewer political implications in British territories than in the United States.

The distinction is inevitably of great significance in the legal profession, where the concept of 'Royal Justices', independent of political parties and the electorate, gives the British judiciary an aura of impartiality which is not entirely illusory, especially when compared with the status of judiciaries elected by universal suffrage, or appointed by the elected leader of the ruling political party. This distinction is less relevant to the status of State-employed architects; but the distinction may have something to do with explaining why, in England, a larger proportion of practising architects choose to be salaried State employees.

Even in England, however, the ambiguity between 'State employment' and 'government employment' is, as far as architects are concerned, almost as confusing as in the United States. Adrian Cave, in his study of 'Architects in the Civil Service', uses the terms 'Civil Service departments' and 'government departments' interchangeably, and this ambiguity probably explains his *cri de coeur* about 'the frustration of being involved in the policy-making machine with little opportunity of influencing it'.[1] According to Thomas Balogh, the same frustration is shared by the whole of the Civil Service. 'How purposive positive policy can be formed under these conditions is a mystery', he writes, 'or rather it would be a mystery if purposive policy were formed'.[2]

The difficulty of fulfilling architectural ideals by political influence thus seems as great among State-employed architects as amongst those in private practice; and even architects who acquire direct political influence by gaining election to the legislature are not necessarily those who, in the opinion of the younger members of the profession, are most likely to make the best use of it. Without

[1] Published in the *R.I.B.A. Journal*, October 1968, p. 447.
[2] *Ibid.*, quoting Thomas Balogh, *Crisis in the Civil Service* (1968).

any disrespect to those architects who have been elected to legislatures, either in Europe or America, it can be asserted without fear of contradiction that professional eminence has seldom been their basic qualification. The same assertion would not, however, be entirely true of lawyers. Admittedly, one does not have to be an eminent lawyer to be elected to parliament. But it is unlikely that a member of parliament would be appointed Attorney-General unless he had proved his forensic ability, whereas a Minister of Works or of Town and Country Planning is not expected to have any professional qualifications peculiar to these special responsibilities.

The inter-relationship of political power and architectural evolution has only recently received from historians the attention it deserves. Allusions have of course frequently been made to the political jobbery current in the organization of the British Office of Works during the eighteenth century, and to the political pressures which shaped French architecture in the same period. But Barbara Miller Lane's *Architecture and Politics in Germany 1918–1945*, published in 1968, seems to be the first monograph of its type, although it was preceded by a number of essays by other authors, such as Anthony Jackson's 'The Politics of Architecture: English Architecture 1929–1951'.[1]

Professor Jackson interpreted the effects of Hitler's seizure of power in Germany by the assertion: 'architecture became political'. But the most fascinating aspect of Professor Lane's book is that, according to her, the influence of this particular dictatorship on architecture was negligible. From the evidence she has produced, she not only demonstrates that Nazi politicians were incapable of deflecting the course of German architecture (as it had evolved by the methods described in histories of 'The Modern Movement'), but also makes clear that so-called 'Fascist' architecture was confined almost exclusively to buildings used specifically for political propaganda, such as the Nuremburg arena and consular offices abroad.

Whether or not 'Fascist' architecture really was totally retrogressive is open to discussion. Since this kind of architecture bore a marked resemblance to the monumental buildings designed before World War I by Peter Behrens and other Pioneers of the Modern

---

[1] Published in the *Journal of the Society of Architectural Historians*, vol. xxiv, p. 97 (March 1965); esp. p. 101.

Movement, it could certainly be regarded as stylistically *ana-chronistic* from the point of view of art-historical taxonomy. But at the same time it can hardly be denied that the derisive attitude towards authority and precedent which has characterized *avant-garde* painting and sculpture during the last fifty years was carried over to architecture in the era between the two World Wars, to such an extent that it left those in authority who desired monumentality few alternatives. Whether or not contemporary society has substituted anything equivalent to the concept of 'monumentality', or whether, indeed, it has substituted anything at all, is debatable.[1] Whether the High Court at Chandigarh is more monumental or less monumental than the Royal Courts of Justice in London is a point of great nicety, as lawyers used to say.[2] But since few important government buildings were ever built by *avant-garde* architects between 1919 and 1939, it seems reasonable to suggest that those then responsible for government buildings—whether German, Italian or Russian—had little alternative but to adopt some form of 'classicism' (whether it be what H. R. Hitchcock calls 'scraped classicism', 'dilute classicism', 'pseudo-classicism', or 'neo-neo-classicism')[3] if they wanted to express their political concept of power.

Just what kind of political power the new German architecture associated with the Bauhaus really did express is still obscure, and there have been few more fascinating episodes in the history of architecture than the enthusiasm with which the *avant-garde* architects of Germany identified their cause with the political ideals of Communism from the end of World War I until the advent of Hitler's régime. Mies van der Rohe designed the memorial to Rosa

[1] Cf. Walter Gropius, *The New Architecture and the Bauhaus* (1935 ed.), p. 44: 'Our ultimate goal, therefore, was the composite but inseparable work of art, the great building, in which the old dividing-line between monumental and decorative elements would have disappeared for ever.'

[2] Le Corbusier's phrase: 'l'architecture est chose de plastique' (*Vers une Architecture*, p. xxv), is a curious echo of Beresford Hope's reference to 'the plasticity of Gothic architecture', when questioning G. E. Street during the Select Committee hearings of 13 July 1869 (*Minutes of Evidence*, p. 64, question 1133).

[3] H. R. Hitchock, *Architecture, Nineteenth and Twentieth Centuries* (1958), pp. 341, 315, 316, 381.

Luxemburg in Berlin. Gropius designed a similar memorial at Jena. Moreover, his Total Theatre was designed for Erwin Piscator, the most fervent protagonist of the theory that dramatic art is essentially a medium for Marxist propaganda. But when, in 1932, the Russian government suddenly denounced as 'bourgeois' the architecture which the Nazis were then calling 'bolschevik', it became clear that the *avant-garde*'s enthusiasm for Soviet Russian politics had merely been prompted by the belief that communist governments could be relied upon to further their particular architectural ambitions. As soon as the Russians repudiated *avant-garde* architecture, the *avant-garde* architects repudiated Soviet politics. As late as 1934 Gropius was still hoping for aid from Dr. Goebbels, and addressing private appeals to the Reichskulturkammer.[1] Mies van der Rohe did not abandon hope until 1937; and though the conclusion which Sibyl Moholy-Nagy draws from his activities during the previous five years (to the effect that he actively co-operated with Fascist politicians)[2] is probably unjust, Mies van der Rohe's unswerving devotion to his architectural ideals certainly bore little apparent relationship to the fluctuating political milieu in which he was obliged to practise.

The relevance of this phenomenon to the relationship between legal judgement and architectural judgement bears on the fact that whereas it is axiomatic among British legal theorists that the administration of justice is incompatible with political affiliations, and that the only way to safeguard justice is to ensure that elected government has no power to influence or remove a judge, architectural theorists seem to take the opposite view. It was the *avant-garde* theorists who were the most fervent protagonists of the political control of architecture fifty years ago; and in so far as radical architectural theorists may now object to any such political controls as exist, it is seldom because of the existence of such controls *per se*, but rather because the party in power does not subscribe to their own architectural beliefs.

The same divergence of view occurs with respect to the virtues

---

[1] B. M. Lane, *Architecture and politics in Germany, 1918–1945* (1968), p. 181.
[2] 'The Diaspora' in *Journal of the Society of Architectural Historians* (March 1965), vol. xxiv, pp. 24–25; and the vigorous exchange of correspondence published as 'letters to the editor' in the October 1965 issue (vol. xxiv, pp. 254–6).

of allowing architects and lawyers to be salaried employees of the State. When Roscoe Pound lectured to the Massachusetts Medical Society in 1949, the steady rise of the idea of the Service State seemed to him at that time to be the major threat to the legal profession, and to the ideals of professional service in general. 'The tendency of our economic development', he asserted, 'is to bring about something very like a class of employees of corporations called law clerks who may yet be seen forming a law clerk's union affiliated with the CIO, and exerting themselves not to advance the administration of justice but to advance the compensation of law clerks. An incidental bad effect of this course of development of the metropolitan lawyer is that the Bar often comes to be divided into two classes, habitual plaintiff's lawyers and habitual defendant's lawyers, each with its staff of lawyers, law clerks, experts and, one suspects, witnesses'.[1]

This distinction between plaintiff's lawyers and defendant's lawyers does not correspond to any aspect of architectural practice, so Dean Pound's reasons for distrusting the nationalization of lawyers have little apparent relevance to any discussion concerning the advantages or disadvantages of nationalizing architects. Nevertheless, despite the basic differences in the premises on which theories of professional involvement in politics are based, both professions are being increasingly influenced by the growth of political science as an academic discipline, and particularly by the emphasis placed by many political scientists on the view that their field of study is simply one aspect—though for them the most vital aspect—of a general sociological and psychological study of power. Hence, paradoxically, architectural students and law students are now less concerned with political control over their professions than with professional control over politics. The control of politics by lawyers has of course been a commonplace since the time of de Tocqueville. But whereas the study of legislative processes forms an increasingly important part of academic legal training, the architectural student finds no natural affinity between his professional studies and those of political science. He is therefore finding more difficulty in transmuting his ideals from professional into political terms.

The general concept of 'professional ideals' will be discussed

[1] *New England Journal of Medicine* (8 September 1949), vol. 241, p. 354.

separately in the final chapter; but it will be appropriate here to comment on one curious development in legal ideals which has particular relevance to the political context of architecture, namely the shift in emphasis from the ideal of 'justice' to the ideal of 'public policy'. If one compares the law reports of the last century with those published today, one is struck by the increasing infrequency of the word 'justice' and the tendency to replace it by the term 'public policy'. This is certainly not due to any ignorance on the part of nineteenth-century judges as to the legal implications of 'public policy'. On the contrary, it is precisely because they were so keenly aware of its implications that they were able to keep the two notions distinct. By 'justice', they meant giving a person what was legally due to him. By 'public policy' they meant restricting an individual's legal rights for the general benefit of mankind. Since the time of Henry VIII it had been held, in *Maleverer v. Spinke*,[1] that a man might justifiably commit a tort if it was for the public good, as, for example, by pulling down a burning house for the safety of neighbouring houses. Lord Mansfield, in *Walton v. Shelley* (1786), considered that the rule which stated that 'no party who has signed a paper or deed shall be permitted to give testimony to invalidate that instrument' was 'a rule of law founded on public policy'—a rule which governed the decision in *L'Estrange v. Graucob* (1934) already mentioned.[2] Similarly the doctrine that a contract to commit a crime is void, is also based on the notion of public policy.[3] The decision in *Coggs v. Bernard* (1703) (as reported by Lord Raymond),[4] to the effect that common carriers are absolutely responsible for all mishaps to goods entrusted to them, except those occasioned by the King's enemies or by the Almighty, was regarded as 'a politick establishment, contrived by the policy of law'. Finally, the classic statement of the relationship between law and public policy was given by Lord Truro in *Egerton v. Brownlow* (1853)[5] when he said: 'Public policy, in relation to this question, is

---

[1] Dyer's Reports, p. 36 b. verso (1793 ed.), para. 40.   [2] See Chapter 1.

[3] Jessel, M. R., in *Printing & Numerical Registering Co. v. Sampson* (1875), L.R. 19 Equity Cases at 465.

[4] 2 Ld. Raym, at 918. The report in 3 Salkeld 11 uses the phrase 'a politic establishment, for the safety of all persons concerned'.

[5] 4 H.L. Cas. 1 at 196.

that principle of the law which holds that no subject can lawfully do that which has a tendency to be injurious to the public good, or against the public good'. Nevertheless, most judges of the time would have supported Chief Justice Best and Mr. Justice Burrough, in *Richardson v. Mellish* (1824),[1] when the former asserted: 'I am not much disposed to yield to arguments of public policy'; the latter adding: 'I, for one, protest, as my Lord has done, against arguing too strongly upon public policy. It may lead you from sound law. It is never argued at all but when other points fail.'

With the modern predilection for deciding cases ostensibly on the basis of 'public policy' (if one may so interpret judicial reluctance to enunciate the word 'justice') there has been a tendency to do less than justice towards nineteenth-century concepts of legal judgement in this respect. For example, a standard text-book on Contracts asserts that in the opinion of Sir George Jessel (the Master of the Rolls) in *Printing & Numerical Registering Co. v. Sampson* (1875):[2] 'if there is one thing which more than another public policy requires, it is that men of full age and competent understanding shall have the utmost liberty of contracting, and that their contracts entered into freely and voluntarily shall be held sacred and shall be enforced by courts of justice.' But Sir George Jessel never asserted anything of the kind. He was simply paraphrasing the argument of the defendant before giving judgement for the plaintiff. He admitted that the public policy of not lightly interfering with freedom to contract was of paramount importance; but since he vigorously denied that the case at issue (where an inventor had formally agreed to sell whatever he might eventually invent) did in fact involve a contract contrary to public policy, the statement was simply an *obiter dictum*. 'Does one imagine that it is against public policy for an artist to sell the picture which he has never painted or designed, or for the author to sell the copyright of the book, the title of which is even, as yet unknown?', he asked rhetorically. On the contrary, he asserted, the dictates of public policy have presumably precisely the opposite effect, since such contracts 'encourage the poor, needy, and struggling author or artist. They enable him to pursue his avocations, because people rely upon his honour and good faith'.[3]

[1] 2 Bing. at 242, 252.   [2] L.R. 19 Equity Cases at 465.   [3] *Ibid.*, at 466.

These views have been cited at length because it is important to note that they were Common Law maxims, based on what, for want of a better term, we may call 'principles of natural justice'. But modern theories of political science have not only caused the ideal of 'public policy' to encroach upon other ideals, including those referred to by Sir George Jessel as 'honour and good faith'; they have caused them to be regarded as a purely legislative device, evolving from the many complex reasons which cause modern legislators to see themselves as instruments of compulsory egalitarianism, destined to fulfil the rôle of Robin Hood. These new statutes are not concerned with limiting a person's legal rights by virtue only of the equitable rights of society. They are penal laws which control legal rights as effectively and as arbitrarily as any sumptuary laws passed by the Tudor Monarchy. Doubtless there are many occasions when persons *should* be deprived of their rights; but without getting involved in such controversial matters, and without even expressing any view as to whether such a concept of legislation is either necessary or desirable, it is important to emphasize that the modern judicial concept of public policy is essentially different from the concept of 'public policy' held in earlier centuries.

Few examples exemplify the distinction better than *Leeds Industrial Co-operative Society v. Slack*,[1] which was decided in the House of Lords in 1924 by a majority of 3:2 in favour of the appellants. The respondent had applied for an injunction to prevent the appellants from constructing a building so high as to interfere with his right of light. The appellants contended that under Lord Cairns's Act of 1858 the courts could, and in this case should, award damages in lieu of an injunction. In other words, they implied that it was in the public interest to allow them to infringe another property-owner's rights if they themselves were willing to pay such compensation as might be considered equitable by the courts, whereas the respondent argued that, on the contrary, it was manifestly against the public interest to allow someone to buy permission to do something which would otherwise be illegal.

The problem was unfortunately complicated by an obscure but important point of law, in that whereas most of the clauses of Lord Cairns's Act (passed when Equity and Law were still distinct) had

[1] 1924 A.C. 851.

been repealed by the Statute Law Revision & Civil Procedure Act of 1883, the jurisdiction to grant damages instead of an injunction had been confirmed by the Judicature Act of 1873, and apparently re-confirmed by the Statute Law Revision Act of 1898. But the real problem, as seen by the two dissenting judges, was the interpretation of the phrase 'apprehended injury' in terms of an easement. None of the judges denied that the ordinary remedy for the threatened violation of a legal right is to obtain an injunction; but it was by no means clear to Lord Sumner and Lord Carson that the High Court had jurisdiction both to refuse an injunction and to award damages in lieu when such an award was tantamount to licensing the continuance of a tort on payment of money compensation. Indeed, it was their view that such an interpretation would have meant that any individual could be compelled by law to sell his rights to any other individual if the latter was wealthy enough to buy them. As Lord Sumner put it: 'I doubt whether it is complete justice to allow the big man, with his big building and his enhanced rateable value and his improvement of the neighbourhood, to have his way, and to solace the little man for his darkened and stuffy little house by giving him a cheque that he does not ask for'.[1]

Lord Sumner was prepared to admit that the jurisprudence on which the appellants relied might be 'wise policy', though he cited *Krehl v. Burrell* (1878–9)—a case dealing specifically with easements—to illustrate his assertion that 'it was a thing which judges have repeatedly described in terms of not exaggerated disfavour'. But it should be noted that when discussing the moral issues involved, he had spoken of 'complete justice' and not of 'public policy', arguing that if it were in fact in the public interest to oblige persons to sell easements to other private individuals for the benefit of urban improvements, it was up to the legislature to make statutory provisions accordingly.

The delusion of monarchs and other legislators that their statutes are necessarily in the public interest has of course deep historical roots, and appears as early as 1423, when Henry VI started the tradition of prefacing his statutes with the announcement that they were 'made and established to the honour of GOD, and for the

[1] *Ibid.*, at p. 872.

wealth of the King and of his realm'.[1] Moreover, since these statutes were published in both English and French, we know that the English word 'wealth' corresponded to the French word '*bien*'. Hence 'Common Wealth', 'Common Weal', 'Publique Weal', 'Public Good' and 'Public Policy' all meant much the same thing, when used in statutes, though 'Public Good' does not seem to appear before 1662, and 'Public Policy' apparently makes its first appearance in the Act of 1706 which united England and Scotland. Its most common application to the law of Obligations was, in that century, with respect to contracts in restraint of trade.[2]

The political dilemma which thus confronts both lawyers and architects is this: Even if we firmly believe that an increase in the compulsory statutory controls over social obligations is both desirable and inevitable, we must recognize that these controls must, of their nature, now be legislative, and not judicial. And if we consider it desirable that legislatures should have absolute and un-limited power to determine, as matters of 'public policy', the obligations of every citizen toward every other citizen, it seems to follow that it would be inconceivable for any legislature to delegate part of such power to the judiciary. Yet the very complexity of such regulations is leading to more and more delegated authority, whereby judgements are not delegated to members of the judiciary, but to other officials—often quite junior officials—employed by the State.

In the United States of America, legislative powers to regulate architecture in accordance with 'public policy' are limited by the Supreme Court's interpretation of the Federal Constitution, written two centuries ago, and preserved inviolate, despite the alacrity with which the constitutions of each individual State are so frequently re-written. Thus it was asserted in *Ayer v. Commissioners on Heights of Buildings in Boston* (1921)[3] that aesthetic considerations alone cannot justly form the basis for the exercise of 'police power' (i.e. legislative control) to limit the use of private property. Similarly, in *City of New Orleans v. Levy* (1953),[4] the Court decided that the

[1] That is to say, the various 'chapters' of statutes for the year are prefaced in this manner from 1423 onward.

[2] Cf. Lord Mansfield's dicta in *R. v. Norris* (1758) 2 Keny. 300.

[3] 242 Mass. 30.   [4] 223 La. 14.

preservation of the famous 'Vieux Carré' was 'not only for sentimental value, but also for its commercial value, and hence such
legislation constitutes valid exercise of public power'. The Supreme
Court's decision in *Berman v. Parker* (1954),[1] upholding the consti-
tutionality of expropriating a privately-owned department store as
part of a statutory slum-clearance and rehousing project in the
District of Columbia, is sometimes described as having revolution-
ized the accepted interpretation of the Fifth Amendment in this
respect; but in fact it only asserted that it was constitutional to
legislate for visual environmental amenities when the State was
exercising the power of 'eminent domain' (i.e., the compulsory
purchase of property by the State).

In England, where no such constitutional limitations exist, the
power to exert judicial control over the appearance of buildings was
delegated to local planning authorities by the Town and Country
Planning General Development Order in 1950. Such authorities
have power to order the alteration of any design or external appearance which would injure the amenity of the neighbourhood; a
power limited only by the proviso that the design must be (a)
reasonably capable of modifications so as to conform with such
amenity, or (b) of such a character that it ought to be, and could
reasonably be, constructed elsewhere on the same plot of land. Yet
only the most ardent anglophile would contend that these wide
powers to determine and enforce 'public policy' have uniformly
produced environments which are vastly superior to those in America;
and the reason for this is probably that no two architects—and
certainly no two civil servants—are in full agreement as to exactly
what the ideal 'public policy' (in the sense of an environmental
'common weal') really is.

If such a conclusion may appear excessively gloomy, this is only
because architectural theorists seldom admit that controversies
about the specific fulfilment of generally accepted ideals are the
very essence of all learned professions, and perhaps even the cause
of their existence. Idealistic lawyers may feel depressed at the
thought of so much injustice in the world, just as idealistic architects feel depressed at the thought of so much squalor and ugliness.
But few practising lawyers would be so naïve as to believe that an

[1] 348 U.S. 26.

International Committee for Solving Contemporary Problems of Law[1] could produce a universally valid solution, or offer anything more than a partial hint as to their permanent solution. Magna Carta, like the Athens Charter, gave the self-appointed leaders of the society of its time a sense of direction; but even though laws are more easily changed than physical environments, it seems doubtful if any charter will ever bring either perfect and prompt justice, or permanent environmental harmony, to all the nations of the earth.

The distinction between justice and public policy is thus the political aspect of a dilemma which will be discussed in more detail later, namely the problem of finding a just mean between 'minimum' and 'optimum'. 'Justice' is the optimum; but perfect justice is only attainable in law (just as perfect harmony is only attainable in architecture) when an individual's right to pursue happiness is un-limited by any other individual's right to pursue his own particular kind of happiness. This limitation is what brought the professions into being, and still dictates their essential task. The academic lawyer is right to dream of an ultimate *Restatement of Contracts* which will replace all other *Restatements of Contracts*, and codify, once and for all, the quintessential perfection of all contractual relationships. The academic architect is right to dream of ideal cities for ideal people, and may be forgiven for prefacing a treatise on ideal architecture with the phrase '*ed io anche son pittore*'.[2] But lawyers are not legislators, nor are architects painters. The legal neophytes of a generation ago thought the first *Restatement of Contracts* really was the eternal law of Reciprocal Obligations, just as those who studied architecture in the 1930s thought that *Vers une Architecture* said all that need be said about the eternal laws of architecture. Both must now marvel nostalgically at their youthful over-simplification of what professional obligations and professional progress really imply.

[1] Cf. Le Corbusier, *Oeuvre Complète*, vol. i, p. 175, and his establishment of C.I.R.P.A.C. (*Comité International pour la Réalisation des Problèmes Architecturaux Contemporains*).

[2] 'And I also am a painter': the preface to E. L. Boullée's Treatise.

CHAPTER FIVE

The procedural context of judgement

'Procedure' is such an essential concomitant of law that, in practice, the two are virtually inseparable. Indeed, in the United States, the hallowed constitutional phrase: 'due process' has become so popular that assertions of its non-observance by the authorities is now relied upon by every radical reformer as a conventional device for flouting the law with impunity. The term itself is of course far older than most Americans imagine, for although not as old as Magna Carta (as has been asserted by some English commentators) it occurs in English statutes as early as 42 Edw. III c. 3 (i.e. 1368); a statute which is still in force, and which asserts that 'no man be put to answer without presentment before justices, or matter of record, or by *due process* and writ original, according to the old laws of the land'. In fact, it means nothing more than 'a fair trial' (despite all that has been written about its Constitutional implications in America), though how one decides what is 'fair' is of course another problem.

The procedural context of architectural judgement seldom receives the attention from architectural critics which it deserves, because the traditions of art-criticism, despite much scholarly research into the procedural evolution of great works of painting and sculpture, place all the emphasis on the final product. In architecture, the conclusive importance of final results would be indisputable if their procedural context had only a negative influence. It is true that a building owner who finishes up with an unsatisfactory building derives no more consolation from explanations of the procedural impediments which prevented success than a litigant who loses his case because his lawyer entered a claim for the wrong remedy. But the issue here is not the extent to which mastery of procedural techniques helps or hinders satisfactory solutions; it is whether procedures form, or do not form, an integral part of the creative process; because if they do, they must necessarily be included among the criteria by which any professional art is judged.

Architectural design, whatever else it may be, is undoubtedly a *process*. Some arts comprise more than one creative process, each relatively discrete, however closely related. Such relationships are best exemplified by comparing 'The Performing Arts' with the basic creative arts on which they depend for their existence. Music and drama are good examples, but so, of course, is the art of building, especially today, when design and construction are generally conceived of as distinct operations.

When a famous pianist gives a public performance, he must necessarily be influenced by the total environment in which he performs. He may be so stimulated by an awareness of the enthusiasm of his audience, and the elegance of the architectural setting, as to surpass himself. He may be so hyper-sensitive to environmental distractions that he eventually abandons 'live' performances in favour of recordings. But in either event, whatever he plays relates directly to the musical score, and constitutes, and is intended to constitute, a faithful rendering of the composers' intentions; a fact which places his artistic talent in a special category. A music critic who asserts that some soloist's performance of a particular sonata is the best he has ever heard does not imply that the pianist has created something which the composer would never have been capable of inventing. He is asserting, on the contrary, that the soloist has expressed, with unusual felicity, the essence of what the composer was only able to indicate diagramatically on his score.

Do the same criteria apply to the art of building? Nowadays, building contractors are usually given such detailed working drawings, and other instructions, that they have little scope for initiative. Even during and before the eighteenth century, when more latitude was granted them, and when working drawings were far more diagrammatic, it was nevertheless customary for the supervising architect to draw all the details at full-size on a temporary plastered wall near the site; details which the masons could than trace onto their templates. The art of the builder was seldom recognized as contributing anything fundamentally additional to the architect's design; and since the distinction between the arts of space and the arts of time inevitably implies far less differentiation between design and performance in the former, the names of building contractors are seldom considered of any historical interest.

Yet it is surely not a coincidence that two of the greatest pioneers in the evolution of reinforced concrete architecture, namely Auguste Perret and P. L. Nervi, were primarily building contractors, whose contribution to the art of building was due as much to their concern for the *process* of building, and their mastery of constructional techniques, as their intuitive sense of form. Moreover a distinguished Canadian architect recently suggested, when giving the R.I.B.A.'s 1968 Annual Discourse, that the processes of building and of financing buildings are so intimately connected to the process of architectural design that large building-complexes can only be built if experts in all three aspects of building join together, from the very beginning, as professional members of the design-team. Indeed, it is significant, as regards the present context, that his lecture was entitled 'The City as Process'.[1]

But whatever the validity, or even the general practicality, of such collaboration, one implication of the relationship which exists between a finished building and its working drawings is that the sanctity of modern 'historical monuments' would seem to be yet another survival of nineteenth-century historicism. The archaeological justification for James Fergusson's derisive comments about reproductions of the Parthenon in foreign surroundings have little relevance to the present age. Hence although the restoration of Le Corbusier's Villa Savoie—now officially declared a historical monument—may well have been prompted by valid sentimental reasons, anyone who saw it when it was in ruins, with its original environment obscured by new low-cost apartment buildings, might cogently argue that it would be more intelligent, and artistically just as valid, to build a new Villa Savoie from the original working drawings on a more appropriate site.

[1] *R.I.B.A. Journal*, June 1968, pp. 258–261.

Nevertheless, if we disregard, for the moment, the relationship between working drawings and finished buildings, and consider simply the nature of the design-process itself, it will be apparent that whatever technique is used, the *process* of architectural design is inseparable from the final product. This is particularly obvious now that scientists have popularized the idea that 'feed-back' is a component part of decision-making in architecture; but even before this cybernetic terminology was used, the process existed, however unsystematically.

The same can be said of other professions, particularly of law. It is even true of that aspect of law which seems to the layman to play so insignificant a rôle in the judicial process as to render analogies between architecture and law defective—namely what may be called the 'aesthetic' content. Mr. Justice Cardozo pointed out that the creative processes whereby 'the sordid controversies of litigants are the stuff out of which great and shining truths will ultimately be shaped'[1] have a marked affinity with the processes of literary creativity. 'We find a kindred phenomenon in literature, alike in poetry and in prose. The search is for the just word, the happy phrase, that will give expression to the thought, but somehow the thought itself is transfigured by the phrase when found. There is emancipation in our very bonds. The restraints of rhyme or metre, the exigencies of period or balance, liberate at times the thought which they confine, and in imprisoning release.'[2]

There is indeed one major difference between the art of architecture and the art of law, in that whereas an architect, finding himself pursuing the wrong track, can always throw his sketches in the waste-basket and start again, the lawyer, once embarked upon the development of a case in court, cannot change his plans. Yet this dilemma is probably no more severe than that confronting architects once the building process has begun. Indeed, the ingenuity demanded of an advocate when confronted with unexpected evidence is probably no less than that which an architect has to display when the building contractor confronts him with an unforeseen structural problem. These differences spring not so much from a difference between the nature of the two professions as from the fact that in

[1] B. N. Cardozo, *The Nature of the Judicial Process* (paperback ed.), p. 35.
[2] B. N. Cardozo, *The Growth of the Law* (paperback ed.), p. 89.

architectural design, architects *simulate* the rôle of all the participants of a trial. All the time design-decisions are being made, the architect must be the advocate supporting a particular solution, the advocate opposing this particular solution, the witnesses testifying both for and against its adoption and the judge who makes the final decision. 'Surprise witnesses', in this intellectual context, are not unknown to the architectural designer. On the contrary, it is often the clues provided by unexpected evidence, as tentative solutions evolve, which constitute new guide-lines along which he charts his exploratory course.

The accomplishment of any professional task must inevitably start with general ideas as to the type of solution envisaged, and in the days when Julien Guadet lectured on architectural theory, it was accepted that, in architectural design, there was a traditional sequence of three processes, which he referred to as 'disposition' (or what was generally called composition), 'proportion' (i.e. study) and 'construction' (i.e. the scientific control of studies, followed by the execution of the design).[1] In recent years the complexity of the building industry has made this sequence appear to be an over-simplification. Even by the end of the nineteenth century, new developments in building technology and more complex programmatic requirements had made any firm distinction between the three processes unrealistic. Indeed, Guadet himself specifically denied that the triad implied anything more than a logical sequence relying for its efficacy on the interdependence of all three.[2] But today, this interdependence is so complex that the traditional idea of a 'composition' as something which can be elaborated in detail prior to any collaboration with engineers and building contractors is impractical in any large project, as was explained by Raymond Affleck in the R.I.B.A. lecture just mentioned.[3]

Such developments in architectural procedure would seem to raise again the whole question of the validity of international competitions. The relationships of architectural judgement to competitive projects must inevitably postulate the assumption that a design can be selected on the basis of cardboard models and small-scale drawings [Pl. I]; and even though most competitions allow

[1] J. Guadet, *Eléments et théorie de l'architecture* (1904), vol. i, p. 100.
[2] *Ibid.*, p. 194. [3] *R.I.B.A. Journal*, June 1968, pp. 258–261.

competitors to submit written reports (in which they can justify the forms employed by reference to technical analyses) such reports are inevitably subordinated to judgements concerning what Guadet would have called 'the composition', and is still in fact a 'composition', whatever modern euphemism may be used to make us think otherwise.

Yet this traditional approach to the process of architectural design raises problems of judgement which are well exemplified by comparing the structural system of the Toronto City Hall, as envisaged in a prize-winning project [Pl. II], with the structural system as actually executed. The feature of Viljo Rewell's design which most clearly commended itself to rationalist observers was the concept of constructing the office towers as vertical shell vaults. This concept can be simply explained by reference to the principle of shell vaulting whereby its strength relates to its curvature, and hence some device must always be incorporated to maintain undistorted the curvature of these thin membranes. The usual technique is to place a series of stiffening membranes at right angles to the vault surface. The towers of Rewell's City Hall were in fact envisaged as what might be described as vertical shells, in which the stiffening membranes constituted the floors.

The only apparent defect of the system, as presented to the judges in the final project, was that the required floor areas obliged these stiffening membranes to form cantilevers of extravagant projection. The judges therefore suggested that 'structurally, the greatest economy which, it appears, could readily be pursued would be in devising ways of reducing the size of the cantilever at present shown'.[1] But this advice was adopted with such alacrity that not only were columns introduced at mid-span so as to halve the projection of the cantilevers; they were also introduced at the ends of the cantilevers behind the curved concrete wall, whereby the latter ceased to perform any structural function whatsoever, and, as finally built, became simply a series of pre-cast slabs hanging from a reinforced concrete frame. Thus the structural concept which had been one—if not the major—ostensible justification for the compositional shape (the other justification being the symbolic

[1] *Synopsis of the City Hall & Square Competition for Toronto, Canada* (1958), Appendix A, p. 6.

enclosure of the centrally isolated circular council chamber) was nullified.[1]

It can be argued that this structural concept was never regarded by right-minded architects as of any consequence, and that the judges had indeed specifically stated that the merit of the two office towers was simply that they were 'superb aesthetically, their carefully shaped and related curves achieving a balance and total effect of strength and dignity'.[2] It could also be argued that any adverse criticism of the structural changes just indicated are obsolete survivals of nineteenth-century theories based on the 'frank expression' of masonry construction, whereby, according to Viollet-le-Duc, mediaeval building forms were the direct result of the structural system. Once the aesthetic superbness of Rewell's carefully shaped and related curves had been widely recognized, it could be argued that the architect was at liberty—indeed was morally obliged—to construct these office towers as cheaply as possible, even if this entailed, for example, substituting load-bearing brickwork for the reinforced concrete walls. It could, in other words, be argued (as it has been cogently argued by Reyner Banham and many other distinguished art-historians) that the real Pioneers of Modern Architecture were those who first perceived that architecture is simply large-scale packaging, whereby the distinction between modern architecture and earlier architectures has nothing to do with new structural systems, but is simply an inevitable extension of the new art of Industrial Design. The real Pioneers of the Modern Movement, it would be claimed, were men like Walter Gropius, who designed chairs, buildings and whole cities with the same ease

[1] In this instance, structural virtuosity was sacrificed to the budget; but the opposite happened at Sydney, where the winner of the Opera House Competition, determined to build what he had sketched, found that instead of costing $9m, the building would cost $49m. As a result, it seems doubtful whether the half-finished structure will ever be completed. According to Sigfried Giedion (in the fifth edition of *Space, Time and Architecture*), the fiasco was due to the fact that 'another political party came into power and decided . . . to cheapen it and simplify all details' (p. 686). But it seems more likely that the real trouble was that 'Utzon has said that this solution was inspired partly by the organic-dynamic movements of a bird's wing and partly by the many connections of an automatic telephone . . .' (*Ibid.*, p. 678).

[2] *Synopsis of the City Hall & Square Competition for Toronto, Canada* (1958), Appendix A, p. 5.

that they designed diesel engines and automobiles. Their real disciples were men like Walter Dorwin Teague,[1] who, without any academic training as an engineer, or practical experience as a builder, designed not only photographic equipment, vacuum cleaners and cash registers, but buildings and urban renewal projects. The trouble with nineteenth-century Rationalism, such critics would doubtless argue, is that its theories were developed before the era of machine production and modern engineering analysis, and hence it never took these new developments into account.

Whether or not this controversy is capable of solution by reasoned argument, it is impossible to say. But there are at least three aspects of the anti-Rationalist thesis which deserve consideration in the present context. The first is that however valid such a philosophy may be for the machine age, it certainly does not *derive* from it, since it was traditional in Italy from the days of the Roman Empire to the final decline of its Renaissance. The second argument is that, however much this philosophy may have encouraged collaboration between 'designers' and 'performers' in industrial design, it is inimical to close technological collaboration in architectural design. The 'architecture as packaging' theory is surely the strongest support for the idea of selecting projects for major buildings on the basis of cardboard models; miniature ornamental artefacts which are chosen on the basis of appearance, and which can then be evaluated by independent consultants as to the cheapest method of constructing them to full-size. Indeed, it is the traditional philosophy on which the whole concept of international architectural competitions is based. As the Mayor of Toronto announced in March 1955: 'I am going to suggest we hold a competition . . . somewhere there may be a Wren, a Michelangelo, or a Leonardo';[2] and anyone who saw the 520 models laid out in juxtaposition will understand just what he had in mind.

The third aspect of a possible rebuttal of the Bauhaus philosophy does not, strictly speaking, involve an argument, since it simply adduces certain ideas by analogy with the legal profession. But it

[1] See also *infra*, p. 126.

[2] I should like to express my appreciation to Dr. Eric Arthur, the Professional Advisor, for directing my attention to the documents relating to this competition, deposited by him in the Canadiana section of the Toronto Public Library.

may have some heuristic value and carry some persuasive weight. Is it possible, in fact, to envisage a lawyer planning and designing the strategy of a case without full cognizance of the total technique of his art? Is it conceivable that any Queen's Counsel, briefed for a plaintiff, would be capable of sketching out for his junior, or for his client, or for a student working in his chambers, the general procedure to be adopted, if he himself were ignorant of the full implications of the implementation of that strategy, and of the type of precedents on which he would have to rely?

Let us imagine Sir Roundell Palmer (the future Attorney-General who was to fulfil such an important rôle in the Royal Courts of Justice Competition) discussing the best strategy for making the final appeal in the famous case of *Rylands v. Fletcher*[1] (in which he was leading counsel for the Plaintiff in Error). This litigation (already mentioned briefly in the first chapter) concerned the flooding of Fletcher's coal-mines as a result of the structural failure of a reservoir built for Rylands on nearby property. As developed in the lower courts, the litigation had become an issue on the crucial question of 'absolute liability', i.e., whether or not the mere existence of ancient concealed mine-shafts under the foundations of the reservoir, though unknown to any of the parties involved, made Rylands automatically responsible for any subterranean injury caused to nearby property as a result of this storage of water.

Sir Roundell Palmer might well have said to his client: 'It is not procedurally possible for Fletcher to maintain an action against you, because you had no knowledge of the state of the subsoil, you had no malicious intentions, and you were in no way negligent in that you employed experienced engineers to do something which was in itself perfectly *lawful*. All we need argue, then, is that since it is a rule of law that knowledge or wilfulness are necessary for *your* liability in tort, only the engineers can be held liable if there was in fact evidence of negligence. If we can only argue this point strongly enough, the case against you must inevitably be decided in your favour'. Sir Roundell Palmer did in fact half-heartedly argue this point of view, but it was obvious to him, from what is here termed the 'procedural context' (i.e. the way the case had actually evolved

[1] This is reported as *Fletcher v. Rylands* (3 H. & C. 774) and afterwards as *Rylands v. Fletcher* (English & Irish Appeals, L.R. vol. iii, p. 330).

to date), that his client's cause depended entirely on the highly technical issue of liability for trespass. During the previous appeal to the Court of Exchequer, it had already been more or less decided that negligence on the part of the engineers was so minor an aspect of this important question of principle as to be virtually irrelevant. Thus, despite one of the judges' eloquently-expressed doubts, the other two members of the Exchequer court had held that even if the engineers *had* been negligent, they could be regarded as agents of Rylands, and hence the responsibility would still be his. Thus any strategy evolved by Rylands' lawyers could only succeed if it argued persuasively enough against imposing absolute liability in the particular circumstances.

The legal alternatives in this case have been summarized in some detail, because they demonstrate that although, in law, 'procedural context' may not provide much creative impetus or direction during the planning of a single trial, it plays a big part in the design of litigation when this goes through several courts of appeal. The point insisted upon is essentially the same as that which will be argued in chapter eight, namely that there can be no true profession where the 'art' can be distinguished from the 'technique'. It is of no relevance to the concept of a profession (however relevant it may be to the theory of Fine Art) that a musician can compose what he cannot perform, or that a preliminary sketch can be regarded by connoisseurs as more praiseworthy than the finished painting which resulted from it. Nor is it relevant that sculptors today can 'design' objects which they have not the technical skill to create. Girardon was incapable of casting in bronze the equestrian statue of Louis XIV for the Place Vendôme; but the finished product was identical with the full-sized effigy he modelled. Whether we like it or not, the procedural context of a professional art is the context of a finished product which is logically indivisible. For an architect, the finished product is a complete set of contract-drawings and specifications. He may of course specialize in some particular type of building. Lawyers and surgeons often specialize in some branch of the legal or medical arts. But any lawyer who initiates specialized litigation on behalf of a client, any surgeon who initiates specialized therapy on behalf of a patient, must be potentially capable, however young he may be, of envisaging and solving *all* the detailed incidental problems involved in its fulfilment, even if assistants, technicians and consultants are required to do some of the tasks under his supervision. In law and medicine, there is no such thing as a 'designer' who specializes in devising processes which he cannot supervise.

The architectural relevance of these contentions is that they pose three fundamental critical and pedagogical questions. Firstly, is it realistic to judge any design without considering the process or procedure by which it came into being? Secondly, is it realistic to expect a high standard of architecture if prosperous firms employ 'design teams' composed mainly of fledgling graduates with plenty of young ideas, but virtually no experience of detailing or supervising the construction of buildings? Thirdly, is architecture, when defined as the art of building, still a true profession even though architects are no longer capable, like Philibert de l'Orme, of constructing the buildings with their own hands?

Let us consider the first question, namely whether one can judge a finished building without studying the process by which it was designed. There must undoubtedly be architectural geniuses who, one suspects, had the same intellectual ability to conceive immediately, *in toto*, the right solution as that ability which allowed Mozart to write the entire overture to *Don Giovanni* the night before the first performance. But most architects, however gifted they may be, are usually compelled to spend many hours, days, weeks, and even months, trying out various solutions. Some of their rejected solutions are of course completely sterile; but there are many in which the false step potentially contains within itself suggestions as to the appropriate path to be followed.

The possibility of taking such preparatory studies into account when judging a finished building is at present remote, since limitations of storage space (in addition to many other considerations) usually prompt an architect to jettison all his preparatory studies once the final project has been decided upon. But since the pedagogical value of assessing final projects in conjunction with preparatory studies is now widely recognized, it seems a pity that more active steps cannot be taken to assess really important buildings by similar techniques. At present, journalists and historians, faced with the task of architectural assessments, are inevitably frustrated by the need to deal with this problem in a purely negative manner. If extensive preparatory studies still exist, they can provide the material for a useful doctoral thesis; but few editors are prepared to make space available for publishing them. If they do not exist, the contextual study of a building can only deal with this problem by discussion with the architect (if he is still alive), and even then, questions seldom elicit responses more substantial than: 'We tried that in one of our earlier solutions, but it proved completely impractical'. Interrogation of this kind is obviously a clumsy and ineffectual way of studying systematically the procedural causes by which a sequence of studies produced the formative stimuli for the final design. Yet the impossibility of the systematic analysis of procedural creativity increases the limitations already inherent in the pedagogical methods based on such analyses; methods which are already badly hampered by the fact that academic projects are rarely constructed.

The second problem concerns the validity of the practice, common in many large architectural firms, of employing a 'design team' of bright young Form-Givers fresh from graduate school. The efficacy of the system in a profession dominated by the concept of architecture as 'prestige packaging', or as 'sculpture big enough to walk about inside',[1] is uncontestable; but it is precisely this concept which is here in dispute. It may be that architects, like certain types of scientist (such as those involved in the design of computers), are most useful and creative when studying at Ph.D. level, and then become intellectually obsolescent. But as each young Form-Giver is replaced by a younger, fresher Form-Giver, the suspicion emerges that architecture is not so much form-designing as fashion-designing.

Of the 520 designs submitted in competition for the first stage of the Toronto City Hall in April 1958, only seven were selected for the final stage. One was by a graduate student at Harvard. Another was by a graduate student at M.I.T. who had been given special authorization to do the final design as his M.Arch. thesis. The design submitted by the former was described by the judges as having 'an exotic appearance that would look not less exotic in Buffalo or Boston'. The latter design was described as 'a dignified, and in many ways, a workable building; its faults were those of judgement rather than of taste'. But whatever their defects, both de-

[1] R. Banham, *Guide to Modern Architecture* (1962), p. 20.

signs had been judged better than the 513 designs which were not selected at all for further study. The question therefore arises: Is there something peculiar to the nature of the architectural profession which makes an architect's period of greatest competence coincide with the conclusion of his academic studies? Or would we expect that—all things being equal—a gifted student will become creatively more and more adept as he gains more and more experience?

The question takes on some fascinating facets when we study the careers of the paradigmatic Form-Givers recommended for our emulation by art-historians. Was Le Corbusier, who had no formal academic architectural training whatsoever, a better Form-Giver when he was twenty-five than when he was sixty-five? He was seventeen when he designed the villa at Chaux-de-Fonds, thirty-nine when he designed the League of Nations Headquarters, fifty-eight when he designed the Unité d'Habitation at Marseilles, and sixty-three when he designed the initial plan for Chandigarh. Did Walter Gropius design better buildings before he formed the Bauhaus or after? What radical differences are there between the way Mies van der Rohe was designing buildings in 1929 and the way he was designing them in 1969, at the age of eighty-three, and to what extent were those differences due to accumulated skills in the total experience of building each structure, from the initial sketches to the finished structure?

In sum, the procedural context of architecture has many aspects, from those involved in the evolution of a single design to those involved in the whole sequence of experiences which constitute a professional life-time. But if architecture is indeed a learned profession like other learned professions, three facts must emerge from any study of architecture as process. The first is that academic distinction can only be a beginning, and never the climax, of a professional career. The second is that infant prodigies are as alien to architecture as they are to medicine and law. The third is that spontaneity cannot *in itself* be a criterion of excellence. In painting, sculpture, music, drama, eloquence—in any art, in fact, that is a purely personal mode of emotional expression—spontaneity can impart a freshness and sense of sincerity which may justifiably be regarded as possessing an 'aesthetic' value in itself; but the music-inspired doodles of Eric Mendelsohn are still doodles, even if one of them was built as an astronomical observatory of stuccoed brickwork.

Finally, should an architect be trained and qualified as a builder? It will be remembered that the Bauhaus curriculum envisaged precisely this, and insisted that after the six-months' Preparatory Instruction (based on the type of creative exercise Froebel recommended for kindergartens) the student was expected to spend the rest of his time qualifying for his Master-Builder's Diploma.[1] But the fact that even Walter Gropius himself never insisted on this aspect of the curriculum once he reached Harvard is enough to refute it. Can one then argue that the architectural profession differs essentially from the legal and medical professions, in that its members have far more affinity with musical composers and playwrights—with the making of symbolic diagrams which the creator lacks the virtuosity to translate into reality? The answer must be that, in this respect, the architect is indeed more like the composer or the librettist, especially if we limit the analogy to those composers and playwrights who had at least some rudimentary technical competence as performers, as well as being endowed with creative skill. But in the present context, the fairest analogy today would be the distinction which has recently emerged between the older type of composer and the modern 'arranger' or 'orchestrator'. In popular music, the 'composer' is now simply the man who thinks up the tune, which he then hands over to an anonymous 'arranger' to score for full band. The novelty of this division of labour is not of course the technique but the *attribution*. When Rachmaninoff wrote his *Rhapsody on a Theme of Paganini*, no one ever thought of attributing it to Paganini. When Philip Johnson designed his house at New Canaan, only a few people thought it should be attributed to Mies van der Rohe. But when the new Federal Centre in Chicago was completed in 1965 [Pl. XXIII], the article in the *Architectural Record* was entitled 'Mies designs Federal Center',[2] whereas the architects of this thirty-story courthouse and office building are listed on the working drawings as 'Schmidt, Garden & Eriksen, Ludwig Mies van der Rohe, Naess & Murphy, and A. Epstein & Sons, Inc.' (including both the living and the dead, but omitting

[1] Walter Gropius, *The New Architecture and the Bauhaus* (1935), p. 46.
[2] *Op. cit.*, March 1965, p. 125.

their more active partners).[1] Architecture is admittedly something less than total building; but it is something more than a sketch on the back of an envelope.

[1] The letter heading used by Ludwig Mies van der Rohe up to the time of his death in 1969 states that, in addition to himself, the firm consisted of three other architects in partnership, plus five associates. The partner in charge of the Chicago Federal Centre was Bruno Conterato.

CHAPTER SIX

The context of precedent

The notion that 'precedent' is the most crucial aspect of the historical context of judgement has already been discussed in the first chapter. Attention was there drawn to the legal implications of 'precedent', as opposed to the more general concept of 'history', and to its analogical relevance to any theory of architecture which considers architecture as a professional discipline. Indeed, it was the apparent pedagogical indifference towards the study of history in medical schools and law schools (as indicated in their published curricula) which initially prompted this whole study, and led, by way of an inquiry into the professional concept of history as part of present-day medical and legal training, into an enquiry concerning the whole concept of professional judgement as a basic element of architectural design. There is no doubt in my own mind that, as far as professional training is concerned, the legal concept of 'precedent' is the key to any proper evaluation of the place of history in architectural training. But in both architecture and law, practical limitations reduce, or at any rate restrict, its efficacy, and it will be the purpose of this chapter to try to demonstrate why.

The first limitation concerns the decrease in the reliability of legal precedents as the facts they record become more remote—a limitation which has its counterpart in the study of architecture and urban environments, as anyone who has any familiarity with the history of these subjects well knows. It is almost axiomatic that the further back one searches in time, the more sparse and unreliable the documentation becomes. There are of course exceptions to this rule in architectural history, such as the occasional windfall resulting from the discovery of a complete set of original documents, hitherto lying forgotten among ancestral archives. But whatever contribution such treasure-trove may provide in increasing our knowledge of individual buildings or individual architects, this is usually so sporadic that it can just as easily distort the urban image of the age as clarify it.

Nevertheless, just as, by a curious paradox, nineteenth-century architectural theorists tended to rely on the buildings about which they knew least as a source for their criteria of architectural judgement, so a similar phenomenon is discernible in legal judgement. There can have been few *rationes decidendi* more famous in the law of contracts than Lord Chief Baron Skynner's oft-quoted opinion in *Rann v. Hughes* (1778), the leading case which supports the Common Law doctrine that unless a contract is under seal, it is only enforceable if there is a 'consideration'. Yet the only published report of *Rann v. Hughes*[1] omits all reference to his opinion. This lacuna was mainly due to the fact that before 1784 the House of Lords forbade reports of its proceedings;[2] and even when permission was given to publish them retrospectively from 1701 onward, none of the speeches of the judges were given. Thus none of their *rationes decidendi* were ever printed, and it is seldom we are even told who delivered the court's opinion. All we are told by Josiah Brown in his official report of *Rann v. Hughes* is that when Skynner[3] delivered to the Lord Chancellor the unanimous opinion of the judges, it was simply to the effect that Lord Mansfield's original judgement of 1774 (based on a jury verdict awarding the plaintiff half the damages demanded) should be reversed. The only published report of Skynner's now famous remarks is in a footnote to *Mitchinson v.*

[1] The usual reference (and that published in the Reprint Series) is 4 Brown 27; but this is the re-arranged second edition. In the original edition of Brown's Reports, it is in vol. vii, at pp. 550–558, and is in fact the last case reported.

[2] See Sir W. Holdsworth, *A History of English Law*, vol. xii, p. 104.

[3] He only became Lord Chief Baron of the Exchequer six months before the case came before the House of Lords. Until 27 November 1777 he was Recorder of Oxford. The fact is of importance, since it will be perceived that he was not a judge in the Court of Exchequer when Lord Mansfield's judgement was reversed by writ of error in the Exchequer Chamber in 1776. The House of Lords confirmed the latter decision.

Hewson (1797)[1] decided nineteen years later, and published in Durnford & East's King's Bench reports.

The dilemma of basing decisions concerning precedents on inaccurate reports is particularly evident in those few instances where the same case was reported by two independent authors. Professor A. L. Goodhart pointed out in his *Essays in Jurisprudence* that anyone who studies *Williams v. Carwardine* (1833) by reading the standard reference (Barnewall & Adolphus's Reports) would find the court's decision completely nonsensical, since this report does not state the crucial facts (which *are* stated in Carrington & Payne's Reports).[2]

An even more flagrant example is to be found with reference to *Hadley v. Baxendale* (1854), which is still a leading case on Common Carrier's liability. This particular case hinged on the fact that although Baxendale had agreed to deliver a broken piece of milling machinery for repair, Hadley (the mill-owner) had not informed Baxendale that the repair was urgent. When heard on appeal in the Court of Exchequer, one of the precedents advanced by Hadley's lawyer in support of his argument was rejected by one of the judges on the authority of a standard American text-book (*Sedgwick on Damages*),[3] since 'Sedgwick doubts the correctness of the report'.[4] But the report eventually published on *Hadley v. Baxendale* was itself wrong, since it stated, erroneously, that 'the plaintiff's servant told (Baxendale's) clerk that the mill was stopped, and that the shaft must be sent immediately'. As Lord Justice Asquith was later to point out when commenting on this report in a subsequent case: 'a crucial allegation of fact is definitely misleading. If the Court of Exchequer had accepted these facts as established, the court must, one would suppose, have decided the case the other way round.'[5]

Moreover, judicial opinion can be adversely affected by using unreliable re-editions of reports. In the New York case of *Strong v.*

[1] 7 T.R. at 350. [2] *Op. cit.*, p. 11.

[3] i.e., the *Treatise on the Measure of Damages* (1847) by Theodore Sedgwick, an American lawyer who was eventually appointed U.S. District Attorney of the southern district of New York.

[4] 9 Exch. at p. 347. The report alluded to was *Borradaile v. Brunton* (1818), published in vol. viii of 'Taunton's Reports'. As the judge (Baron Parke) pointed out, the cases in this volume were not reported by Mr. Taunton himself.

[5] *Victoria Laundry v. Newman* (1949) 2 K.B. 528, C.A.

Sheffield,[1] decided by the Court of Appeals in 1895, Chief Justice Andrews held that the general rule of law governing the case was clearly and accurately stated in a footnote to *Forth v. Stanton* (1669), which he then proceeded to quote. His opinion may well have been right; but the footnote he cited did not in fact appear until the fifth edition, and the 'rule' there stated (concerning the inadmissibility of indefinite periods of delay for forebearance to sue) was based on Henry Rolle's *Un abridgement des plusieurs Cases et Resolutions del Common Ley* (1688), published in the official Norman-French legal jargon invariably used in English Courts of Appeal up to the end of the seventeenth century—hardly the most reliable authority for deciding a point of law in the State of New York.

Random examples such as these could be multiplied indefinitely; but they do at least explain the importance of Lord Mansfield's dictum that 'precedents only serve to illustrate principles and to give them a fixed authority'.[2] Precedents are not so much a source of judicial doctrines as an aid to judicial consistency; and although, for this very reason, precedents cannot be nonchalantly jettisoned just because they seem inconsistent with a principle, the adaptation of law to the changing needs of society is inevitably facilitated by the tacit recognition that the older the report, the less reliance can be placed on its exactitude.

In architecture, consistency does not play the same rôle that it does in law; hence the sole value of architectural precedents is that they serve to illustrate principles. For this reason, it seems highly desirable to concentrate on the most recent precedents (or on recent examples which confirm older precedents) and to pay less attention to buildings constructed in ages so remote that the social customs and technical resources bear little relationship to our own. This is not to suggest that either lawyers or architects should totally disregard the more distant records of the past. On the contrary, it is only by possessing a general understanding of the evolution of both architecture and law that the reasons for the present state of these professions can be comprehended. But inasmuch as precedents illustrate principles, it will be apparent that conjectural or inaccurately reported precedents possess many dangers; and perhaps the main shortcoming of nineteenth-century architectural theorists

[1] 144 N.Y. 392.   [2] 1 Cowp. 17.

was that, by relying so heavily on conjectural restorations, they were led too easily to draw conclusions based on romantic wishful-thinking, rather than on historical facts.

The second limitation to be considered is the extent to which any historical precedent can usefully be studied out of context. Reasons why precedents should never be *applied* out of context have already been amply discussed; but it is not necessarily desirable to limit the *study* of precedents to situations where the entire context of the precedent can only be known with reasonable certainty. The current tendency among architectural historians is to insist on the necessity of studying buildings of former ages in the most complete environmental context determinable, and there is much to be said for this point of view. But one of the most striking characteristics of basic legal studies, in schools where the Harvard 'Case-Study' method is used, is the deliberate isolation of each problem from its total context. This is mainly because it is generally accepted that the most important legal problems are those decided on appeal; and since it is of the very essence of such appeals that all matters extraneous to the point of law at issue must be excluded, all the student learns of the contentions of the parties to the dispute is derived from summary descriptions of counsel's arguments. The re-printed reports thus consist only of the opinion—often even to the exclusion of the minority opinion—of the judges; and although these opinions generally begin by succinctly summarizing the facts of the case, the facts so summarized are restricted to those which the court considered pertinent to the point of law in dispute.

Now it may be argued that law students would be better educated if they were to be given *all* the facts of each case, from the transcripts of evidence recorded at the original trial to the complete documentation submitted by both parties during the subsequent hearings on appeal. But if this pedagogical technique were adopted, it seems unlikely that any student would have time to study more than two or three cases each semester, and the value of wading through several thousand pages of transcripts per case would seldom be very rewarding. There is of course nothing to stop a student from reading beyond the texts submitted to him if he so wishes; but from the point of view of mastering the legal principles he is supposed to be learning, it is doubtful if the time so allotted would have been most profitably spent if it had been devoted to the total recorded context of every case.

This point is of considerable relevance to architectural education, where there has been a tendency, ever since the Bauhaus first published its original curriculum, for those concerned with pedagogical techniques to imply that unless every aspect of a design is studied completely, from the most basic elements to the finished product, it is not worth studying at all.[1] The old 'Beaux-Arts' system admittedly went to extremes of over-simplification and superficiality. But the newer method seems to be going to the opposite extreme, rejecting any academic problem as worthless if it does not involve every aspect of design from the psychological and sociological environment to the final construction of the project *in situ*. If in fact a student had unlimited time at his disposal, and all these tasks were fulfilled, from the most elementary to the most complex, the effort involved might conceivably be justified; but since only the most elementary projects can be so dealt with in the time available (even by students working in groups), the results rarely attain the standards which those who created the Bauhaus originally envisaged.

The dilemma is by no means easy to resolve, and is well exemplified by the differences between the training of architects and civil engineers. In general, civil engineering schools adopt a pedagogical system much more analogous to the 'legal method'; that is to say, they do not start by designing an entire structure, but by studying detailed problems inherent in the design of a certain type of structure. Architectural students, on the other hand, have traditionally been expected to design total entities from the start of their career; and they still tend to pursue their studies by working on problems which get progressively larger and more complex. Initially, they may be required to actually build what they design; but one cannot expect junior architectural students to build anything very complex, so they inevitably tend to adopt the Bauhaus technique of designing chairs, or even small moving objects such as kites, using quite primitive materials and structural systems which have little relevance to the profession for which they are being trained. Senior students, on the other hand, tend to get so engrossed in programming and analysis that they seldom reach the point of designing anything at all.

[1] Walter Gropius, *The New Architecture and the Bauhaus* (1935), pp. 44–6.

It must be clear that, pedagogically, an analysis conducted on the basis of precedents considered out of their total context (in the manner adopted by law students) might also be profitably applied to architectural methodology. It would be perfectly feasible to say to architectural students: Here is an example of how a certain famous architect designed the juncture between a reinforced concrete column and a floor slab in a building constructed in 1946. Without even studying the reasons which led him to build this type of building, let us study in detail: (a) how in fact he could have justified the design of this juncture, (b) what precedents he had for such a design, and (c) whether, in the light of these and subsequent precedents, we can still accept the design he used, or devise a more appropriate alternative.

It could of course be retorted that such an academic study would be extremely boring, and that architectural students derive far more stimulation from trying to evolve urban environments or structural systems of a type and form which no one has ever before even contemplated. But this argument merely brings us back to the subsidiary theme of the whole essay, which is the question as to whether architectural design is essentially the visualization of conceptual novelties, to be transmuted by computers into full-size diagrams, or whether it is essentially the detailed conception of buildable environments which, however experimental, are nevertheless evolutionary because they are based on a clear understanding of what has been achieved in the past. If the latter, then precise knowledge of what has been achieved in the past has a real and positive relevance. If not, then such knowledge is merely a hindrance to originality. An architect who is familiar with the monuments of the past is positively inhibited in his creativity. The less he knows of precedents, the more likely he is to design a building which, in his own eyes at least, is unprecedented.

The arguments here put forward in favour of studying the details of past judgements without any detailed knowledge of their context are unaffected by disputes as to whether the purpose of architectural education is to solve problems in terms of building projects, or whether it is to study abstract design methodologies. It may well be that the aspect of methodology most effectively related to academic techniques of architectural education is the methodology of programme-analysis. It may well be that the most important thing for architectural students to learn is not how to solve problems of design (which can best be learnt in an architect's office) but how to determine what these problems really are. But it will be evident that both these pedagogical techniques bear a close resemblance to the legal 'case-study' method. Law students, after a year of the 'case-study' method, have no more practical knowledge of how to conduct litigation than they had when they started; but they are singularly well-equipped to evaluate and judge, and it is surely of the utmost significance that law students who are presumably learning to become advocates should be required to concentrate all their intellectual energies, during their first years at least, on the techniques of *judgement*.

The importance of the revolutionary change in legal education introduced by the 'case-study' method can only be appreciated by comparing modern text-books with the now out-moded 'horn-books'. In the older method, the author stated as succinctly as possible what the law was in certain circumstances, and then gave footnote references to the relevant precedents. A keen student, provided he had a well-equipped library, could, and presumably did, read the cases to which reference was made, and thus enlarged his understanding of the points at issue. But in the new method, the process is reversed. The student is simply given a sequence of leading cases, in which the opinion of the court is given *in extenso*, and the teacher, by discussion and argument, eventually stimulates the students themselves to enunciate the principle of law involved.

There may be teachers of law who regard the 'case-method' as just a new-fangled waste of time. 'Why', it may be asked, 'should a student spend hours discussing the measure of damages in breaches of contract, by reference to historical precedents, when all he needs to learn is the general rule that the measure of damages is the estimated loss directly and naturally resulting, in the ordinary course of events, from the seller's breach of contract? Why spend hours studying the difference between *Hadley v. Baxendale* (1854),[1] (where damages awarded were less than the loss) as against *Rodoconachi v. Milburn* (1886),[2] (where the damages awarded were more than the loss) or *Victoria Laundry v. Newman* (1949),[3] (where the

[1] 9 Exch. 341.   [2] 18 Q.B.D. 67 C.A.   [3] 1949 2 K.B. 528 C.A.

damages awarded were an arbitrator's conjectural assumption of what would have been a reasonable loss)?' The legal answer to these questions (like all legal answers to all legal questions) are complex and involved. But for the layman, the lesson is simple. The best way to teach a student a principle is to make him discover it himself. Dean J. E. Burchard once gave an illuminating example of this technique when explaining how he taught Hooke's Law (*'ut tensio sic vis'*) to students of engineering. He stated to his students this principle of the proportionality of a strain to the stress producing it, but carefully omitted to add that the principle only remained true within the elastic limits of the material. He then told his students to perform an experiment to verify the law. Inevitably, as soon as the stress exceeded the elastic limits of the wire being tested, each student automatically assumed that since the measurement of strain did not correspond to the law as enunciated by his teacher, he himself must have made an error of calculation; and it was only gradually that each student thus taught himself the fundamental limitation inherent in the principle.

Such physical experiments must necessarily be isolated artificially, and hence conducted out of context; and for the same reason historical experiments in law and architecture are also most effectively taught out of context. Basic principles are never so clear as when they thus proclaim themselves initially in physical or historical isolation; and in no profession is it more essential for a student to evolve his own philosophy by his own efforts than in architecture.

The literal application of the legal 'case-study' method to architectural design is undoubtedly limited, mainly because the law depends entirely on printed words, which are easily disseminated, whereas few schools of architecture have enough important buildings close at hand, and the limitations imposed by trying to pursue such studies by photographic reproductions and drawings are only too obvious. But the development of the 'case-study' method in law throws an interesting new light on the eighteenth-century pedagogical technique of Jacques-François Blondel, who made a regular habit of taking his students on weekly tours of Paris, explaining the relative merits and defects of the various buildings they visited. We have reasonably reliable reports of his method of criticism, since he published them in four enormous illustrated volumes when Jombert decided to re-issue Mariette's *Architecture Française*; and we can still read just how the juridical technique of 'case-studies' was applied by him.

Whatever the pace of change in architecture during the next fifty years, Blondel's pedagogical technique must inevitably be relevant to current architectural problems. Even political radicalism relies a good deal on the precedents established by Karl Marx over a century ago, whilst although campus revolutionaries are ostensibly 'different', the fact that Rosa Luxemburg's *The Mass Strike, the Political Party and the Trade Unions* (first published in 1906) was publicly offered for sale on the Berkeley campus when I was teaching there in 1968 suggests that radical tactics are not always as novel as they seem. However, since the point at issue is not whether precedents should be followed, but whether the techniques of studying historical judgements can profitably be studied out of context (assuming that they do possess a value of some kind), the conclusion would seem to be that if we regard architecture as a profession, we can learn most quickly and effectively by adopting this particular technique of legal education which, as far as lawyers are concerned, is of course virtually inevitable, since usually only appeal cases are officially reported in print.

A final aspect of the value of studying principles unencumbered by their total real-life context concerns research into standard building-types or building-components. Whatever the limitations of the classical use of standardized Orders in the sixteenth and seventeenth centuries, there is no doubt that in recent years industrialization has given standardization the added advantage of financial economy, whereby the impetus to exploit standardization has greatly increased. But of its very nature, such industrial exploitation demands that the initial studies be made without any reference to a specific environmental context, since it is only by establishing absolute norms and characteristics that the extent or limitations of the application of such standardized units can be objectively ascertained. And if it be argued that such contextual isolation has no relevance to the concept of historical isolation, this simply reflects a current delusion which results from the fact that, for the student of art-history, 'historical' has now assumed the same implication of remoteness as the word 'antique'. There is no implication of remoteness in the legal word 'precedent'. Whether the precedent was decided two days ago, two decades ago, or two centuries ago, it is still a precedent; indeed it is this majestic indifference to mere historical chronology which makes the legal concept of precedent so much more relevant to the theory of architecture than the art-historical concept of 'style'. For the lawyer dealing with a particular case, precedents are either relevant or irrelevant, valid or superseded. The precise moment of time in which their validity was first affirmed is a matter of complete irrelevance to their forensic worth.

In the ultimate analysis, the whole theory of appellate jurisdiction is based on this search for historical objectivity. However cautiously a judge may phrase his *ratio decidendi* to avoid misapplication to future situations never contemplated, he is also under a moral obligation to enunciate legal principles as broadly and as objectively as possible. Though ruling on a particular case, he is invariably being asked to decide that case in accordance with general principles which are not only true with respect to existing situations, but reliable when forecasting future decisions.

When a problem similar to *Hadley v. Baxendale* (1854)[1] had arisen seven years earlier[2] (the same defendant being similarly sued for loss of profits occasioned by unconscionable delays in delivering goods), it was decided by the four Barons of the Exchequer Court (including Baron Alderson) that as far as the liability of a Common Carrier was concerned, there was no rule, and that the matter must be left entirely to the jury's discretion. But by 1854, when *Hadley v. Baxendale* came up on appeal before the same Court, the judges were of a different mind, and it is a remarkable fact that the rule enunciated by Baron Alderson, though condensed into eighty-seven words, has remained good law for over a century, and was eloquently upheld in the House of Lords as recently as 1967 in the 'Heron II' case (*Koufos v. Czarnikow*).[3] Originally, the rule was intended simply as a guide to juries; but with the gradual disappearance of juries in civil cases, it has become a rule of law in a much more literal sense. And if ever there was an appellate decision worth studying for its own sake out of context, it is this masterly elaboration of what is

---

[1] 9 Exch. 341.   [2] *Black v. Baxendale* (1847), 1 Exch. 410.
[3] 1967 3 All E.R. 686.

probably the most contentious maxim which Lord Bacon ever enunciated: '*Causa proxima non remota spectatur*'.[1]

No thoughtful teacher of architecture, whether he works in the academic milieu of a university or the practical milieu of a busy office, can escape the urge to generalize his advice by reference to his own accumulated and acquired knowledge. Not all architects can summarize the experience of a lifetime with such laconic dexterity as Mies van der Rohe; but every teacher of architecture worthy of the name must have found, at some time or another, some felicitous formulation of an architectural criterion which transcended the specific problem under consideration. The enormous influence of *Vers une Architecture* probably owed less to the text itself than to the fact that the entire book was summarized at the beginning by five prefatory pages of 'Argument'. Many of these slogans are trite, many are plagiarisms, many are historically unjustifiable, but some of them are so brilliantly epigrammatic that they constitute the maxims which had, even for Le Corbusier himself, all the force of Law. He clearly did not *deduce*, from an examination of the ruins of the Athenian Acropolis during his youth, that '*la modénature est la pierre de touche de l'architecture; elle est une pure création de l'esprit; elle appelle le plasticien*'.[2] '*Modénature*' is essentially a decorative element, though Choisy noted that it resulted from '*l'analyse des jeux de la lumière*'.[3] '*Pure création de l'esprit*' is a quotation from the most famous writing of the mid-nineteenth-century art-critic, Charles Blanc, who thus describes Greek architecture in his *Grammaire des Arts du Dessin*.[4] '*Plasticien*' is a neologism that has yet to find its way into any French dictionary. Hence the precise relationship between '*l'architecte*', '*le plasticien*' and '*la modénature*', which we are told is the criterion of architecture, is only original in the sense that it is textually unclear. But in retrospect, we can

[1] 'The immediate, not the remote cause, is to be considered'. However, the decision as to what is, or is not, a 'proximate cause' is one of the most fascinating and complex problems in the law of Torts. It was by the brilliant solution of such a problem that Mr. Justice Cardozo acquired much of his fame: see *Palsgraf v. Long Island R.-R.* (1928), 248 N.Y. 339.

[2] 'Mouldings are the criterion of architecture; they are a pure creation of the mind; they call for a sculptor.'

[3] 'the analysis of the play of light', *Histoire de l'Architecture*, vol. i, p. 233.

[4] *Op. cit.*, p. 106.

see not only its power as the enunciation of a principle; we can see that Le Corbusier was describing that very principle on which, thirty years later, he was to design the functionally inept sculptural shapes which occupy the bleak artificial acropolis at Chandigarh.

In so far as the theoretical writings of pseudo-historians, from Le Corbusier to Robert Venturi, are occasionally misleading, it is because their historical 'precedents' are often seen, on closer inspection, to have little genuine relevance. This is presumably because they deduced the precedents after elaborating their theories, rather than proceeding the other way round. But their writings are stimulating and valuable because they recognized intuitively the validity of Lord Mansfield's assertion that 'precedents serve only to illustrate principles and give them a fixed certainty.'[1] The reliability of a precedent is less important than the reliability of the principle; and the importance of history to the architectural profession is thus comparable to its importance to the legal profession. History, as the only source of precedent, brings to light truths which serve to illuminate higher truths; and though ten thousand precedents are incapable of producing one *infallible* judgement, they are the only guides we have to making judgements of law and judgements of taste.

[1] *Jones v. Randall*, 1 Cowp. 17.

PART TWO

The Synthesis of
Professional Judgement

I hold every man a debtor to his profession; from the which as men of course do seek to receive countenance and profit, so ought they of duty to endeavour themselves, by way of amends, to be a help and ornament thereunto. This is performed in some degree by the honest and liberal practice of a profession, when men shall carry a respect not to descend into any course that is corrupt and unworthy thereof, and preserve themselves free from the abuses wherewith the same profession is noted to be infected. But much more is this performed if a man be able to visit and strengthen the roots and foundation of the science itself; thereby not only gracing it in reputation and dignity, but also amplifying it in profession and substance.

Lord Bacon: *Elements of the Common Laws of England*, Preface

CHAPTER SEVEN

The value of scientific criteria

When Russell Sturgis published *How to Judge Architecture* in 1903 he evidently considered that the most effective way to explain the appropriate judicial technique was simply to provide his readers with a concise history of architecture from 460 B.C. to 1895. 'The reader must feel assured', he asserted before embarking on the well-trodden path from Paestum to Westminster Cathedral, 'that there are no authorities at all in the matter of architectural appreciation: and that the only opinions, or impressions, or comparative appreciations that are worth anything to him are those which he will form gradually for himself'.[1] Nevertheless, despite this liberal and encouraging generalization, he began by asserting dogmatically that Greek temples built before 300 B.C. were 'the most perfect thing that decorative art has produced',[2] and ended with the lament that the clients of the architects of his own generation were concerned only with heating, lighting, ventilating and plumbing, and 'do not care about design'[3]—a term which he later indicated was to be understood 'in its artistic sense'.[4]

It would nowadays be a waste of time to embark on an evaluation of Russell Sturgis's attitude, since although it must have seemed relevant to his contemporaries, it has little relevance to us. By the middle of the present century, there had emerged a growing dissatisfaction with the archaeological approach to architectural criticism; and although the majority of architects still favoured traditional ornamentation, those who opposed it increasingly resented any form of historicism. Even so, it was not until after 1950

[1] *Op. cit.*, pp. 11–12.   [2] *Ibid.*, p. 13.   [3] *Ibid.*, p. 212.   [4] *Ibid.*, p. 213.

that architects can be said to have grappled seriously with the problem of 'how to judge architecture' by non-archaeological criteria. Before 1950, those who favoured traditional ornament had no cause to question traditional methodologies, whilst those who opposed traditional ornament enthused indiscriminately about any structure which appeared sufficiently eccentric to be classified as '*avant-garde*'. It was not until after World War II, when the champions of the New Architecture emerged as undisputed victors of the ideological battlefield, that criticism based on the realities of the architecture itself was dimly perceived as having a vital and immediate rôle to play. It was not until the 1960s that the methods and criteria upon which such criticism was to be based were the subject of systematic scholarly research.

The periodical literature of the 1960s dealing with architectural theory, and the curricula of schools of architecture, show two distinct tendencies characteristic of this change. Firstly, there is the tendency exemplified by Sir Herbert Read's lecture to the Architectural Association in 1960 on 'The Aesthetics of Architecture',[1] whereby the spiritual qualities of architecture are relegated more and more to the realm of an all-embracing system of philosophical abstractions. Secondly, there is the rapidly growing preoccupation with the measurement and appraisal of building performance, and of 'building design decisions', stimulated by the establishment of the Pilkington Research Unit at Liverpool University in 1959 and by the continuation of its work after 1967 at the University of Strathclyde. As a result of the latter, no doubt, the curriculum of the newest school of architecture in Canada shows a zeal for scientific omniscience unrivalled since Vitruvius wrote the preface to his treatise. According to the published announcement, students in the first two years draw their ideas from 'the disciplines of physiology, biology, ecology, physics, psychology, psychiatry, geography, sociology, anthropology, history, literature and architecture, etc.'[2] No indication is given concerning the delimitation of 'architecture, etc.'; but the impression is conveyed that this is more in the nature of a doxological peroration than an assertion that architecture is the

[1] *Journal of the Architectural Association*, May 1960, pp. 202–209. The lecture was repeated in New Zealand in 1963.

[2] *Carleton University Calendar*, 1969–70, p. 85.

discipline which predominates, and which possesses the distinctive criteria on which all professional judgements must ultimately be based.

The extent to which 'aesthetics' is or should be relevant to the problem of architectural judgement will be discussed in the next chapter. This present chapter will be concerned only with the natural sciences; with assessing the extent to which the terms 'design decisions' and 'architectural judgement' are synonyms for each other, and with the criteria by which 'Building Performance Research' is normally evaluated.

As regards the distinction between 'design decisions' and 'architectural judgement', it is clear that 'design decisions' can only refer to those aspects of architectural judgement involved in the *creation* of an architectural environment. But it seems equally clear that there do exist, and must exist, other types of architectural judgement, such as laymen's judgements of finished buildings, or juries' assessments of competitive designs, which, to have any validity, must not only have many criteria in common with Building Performance Research, but many other criteria as well.

What these criteria are is of course the crux of the whole complex and at times frustrating problem. Indeed, the purpose of this essay is an attempt to make some useful contribution towards solving it. At this stage it will suffice merely to draw attention to some of the more obvious limitations which confront those who specialize in 'scientific' architectural research. The first concerns the extent to which their methodology can appropriately be applied to the whole field of architectural judgement. The second concerns certain contradictions implicit in the stated aims of such research, whereby the establishment of exact norms for architectural design seems at variance with the insistence that criticism and judgement are integral parts of the design process. The third concerns the extent to which architectural ideals can or should be expressible mathematically. The fourth concerns the limitation on the number and character of building types to which these new research techniques seem restricted.

As regards the degree to which the methodology of such research can appropriately be extended to the whole field of architectural judgement, it can hardly be denied that such methodology inevitably tends to be limited to the standard cybernetic concept of 'feed-back'. Indeed, it is by this term that it was specifically described in the Royal Institute of British Architects' *Handbook of Architectural Practice and Management* (1967).[1] In other words, it seems inevitable that those involved in such research will have a tendency to concentrate exclusively on those aspects of existing buildings or building-components which determine *precedents* for the design of future buildings. Such concentration is, in itself, by no means reprehensible. On the contrary, I have already attempted to show the importance which precedent must play in all true professional judgements. But precedent, as Karl Llewellyn has ably demonstrated,[2] can be catastrophic in the legal profession if it is divorced from the various creative impulses which contribute equally essential ingredients to the judicial process. Hence even the most sophisticated experiments in Building Performance Research may also be vitiated unless the criteria they establish are seen within the framework of a wider concept of professional judgement.

As regards the contradictions in the aims of such research, these are implicit in the R.I.B.A.'s 'Design Morphology'[3] sequence which asserts that the transition from the 'outline proposals' to the moment of signing the contract is a continuous evolutionary process which, in theory, admits of no revision. Admittedly, full recognition is given by the University of Strathclyde's Building Performance Research Unit to the fact that 'the design process is characterized by its iterative and cyclic character. It has vital feed-back loops and demands that the task is repeated as often as necessary within the limits of design resources available at any phase'.[4] But as Professor Markus observes, the authors of the 'Design Morphology' sequence also make it clear that the structure of the morphology is sequential and not iterative, and hence 'any retracing of steps from a later phase to an earlier is seen as a *design failure*. In a major project, involving design teams, it would mean either collapse of the project or *gross over-spending of design resources*'.[5] But this exacting standard

---

[1] Cited by T. A. Markus in *Architects' Journal*, 20 December 1967, pp. 1567–8.

[2] Karl Llewellyn, *The Common Law Tradition: Deciding Appeals* (1960).

[3] *Architects' Journal*, 20 December 1967, p. 1567.

[4] Ibid., p. 1569. [5] Ibid., p. 1568.

of professional judgement would seem to lead analogically to the conclusion that every judicial error in a court of law is also a 'failure', an example of 'gross over-spending', or both.

Without questioning the desirability of getting the right answer every time, it must be apparent that in those professions where professional skill lies precisely in the ability to make judgements, fallibility is not and cannot be synonymous with failure. In law, the reversal, by an appellate court, of the judgement of a trial court with respect to a difficult point of law is not regarded either as a criticism of the trial judge or as proof of the inefficiency of the legal system. Nor is the reversal (by a State Supreme Court or the House of Lords) of an appellate decision a slur on the initial Court of Appeal. Indeed, as I hope to demonstrate, appellate courts have in fact made far more positive and valuable contributions to the healthy evolution of our legal system than have ever been made by uncontested decisions.

The extent to which the results of Building Performance Research can or should be expressible mathematically raises more agonizing questions, since the notion that architecture is a branch of mathematics goes back at least to Vitruvius, whilst the notion that architectural harmony is based on simple mathematical ratios probably goes back to Pythagoras, and has been elaborated upon by an impressive sequence of writers from Alberti to Le Corbusier. This attitude has naturally been reinforced by the invention of electronic computers: technological devices which, among today's humanists, possess an academic prestige similar to that held by palaeography in the early Renaissance.

No one would deny that, insofar as architectural values are mathematically measurable, they should be measured with the greatest accuracy that research techniques can devise. The problem is in the qualifying phrase: 'insofar as'. Unless *every* architectural value is accurately measurable, the computer will be fed an unbalanced diet which may be so unbalanced as to be deleterious; for it could well be that it is the incommensurate qualities of a design which are the most vital to our environmental well-being.

The problem is well exemplified in the design of concert halls, where despite the enormous progress achieved during the present century in the correlation of qualitative and quantitative analyses, it is still possible for disastrous blunders to be made. The acoustics of the Philharmonic Hall in New York, which was opened in June 1962, could hardly have been studied more conscientiously. Indeed, the extensive preparatory research on fifty-four famous concert halls was so thorough that it was published as a five hundred and forty page book by the consultants.[1] But within two years, complaints of acoustical defects in the Philharmonic Hall became so insistent that a wooden enclosure was built behind the orchestra, and, when this modification proved ineffectual, the hall was closed for radical changes which cost $800,000.00.[2]

The significance of these events, in the present context, is firstly, that the defects were detectable only by the human ear; secondly, that the sole acoustical factor then calculable was the reverberation time;[3] and thirdly, that when alterations were effected in 1965, the reverberation time was changed from 1.6 seconds to 2.1 seconds.[4] There was never any suggestion that the original selection of 1.6 seconds was unwise, or that the original reverberation time differed radically from that of the famous concert halls previously studied. The mistake seems to have been due to the error of confusing diagnosis with design—an error which can be detected at the root of many architectural theories which stem from analogies with the natural sciences.

At the risk of reiterating the obvious, it may be useful to consider the significance of the relationship between qualitative analysis and mathematical accuracy in medical diagnosis. Such mathematical accuracy has undoubtedly increased enormously in recent years with advances in analytical research; but even quite basic criteria have little pathological significance other than the fact they *are* phenomena which can be measured by relatively simple apparatus. The invention of the sphygmomanometer at the end of the nineteenth century, whereby physicians could henceforth determine the blood-pressure in the brachial artery both accurately and simply,

[1] L. L. Beranek, *Music, Acoustics and Architecture* (1962).

[2] When these radical changes also proved ineffectual, another consultant was engaged, and the interior was rebuilt at an additional cost of $1.3 millions (*New York Times*, 24 September 1969).

[3] P. H. Parkin & H. R. Humphreys, *Acoustics, Noise and Buildings* (1958), p. 98.

[4] *Progressive Architecture*, 1965, News Report, p. 62.

I. Toronto City Hall International Competition (1958): some of the 520 models submitted

II. Toronto City Hall International Competition (1958): the winning project by Viljo Rewell

III. Toronto City Hall International Competition (1958): one of the six rejected final projects (Architects: Gunlogsson & Nielson)

IV. Marin County, California: County Centre (1958–61) (Architect: Frank Lloyd Wright)

V. Marin County, California: County Centre under construction (Architect: Frank Lloyd Wright)

VI. London: South Bank Arts Centre (1967) (Architect to the G.L.C.: Hubert Bennett).
View from across the Thames

VII. London: South Bank Arts Centre (1967) (Architect to the G.L.C: Hubert Bennett). Detail

VIII. Dublin: Trinity College. International Competition for an extension to the library
(1961) (Architect: Paul Koralek)

IX. Ottawa. National Competition for a City Hall (1956) (Architects: Rother, Bland & Trudeau)

X. Amsterdam City Hall International Competition (1968): the winning project by Wilhelm Holzbauer

XI. Amsterdam City Hall International Competition (1968): one of the six rejected final projects (Architect: L. J. Heijdenrijk)

XII. London: Royal Courts of Justice. Limited competition (1867): E. M. Barry's project

XIII. London: Royal Courts of Justice. Limited competition (1867): G. E. Street's project

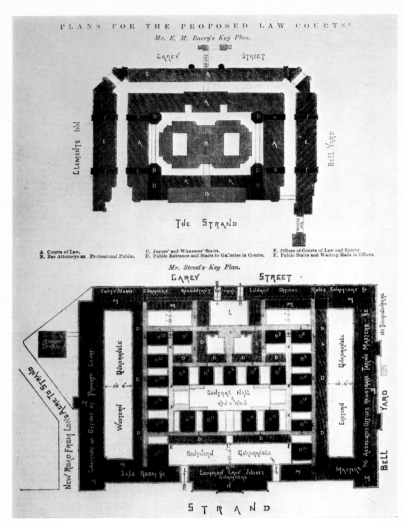

XIV. London: Royal Courts of Justice. Barry's and Street's compositions
compared (1867)

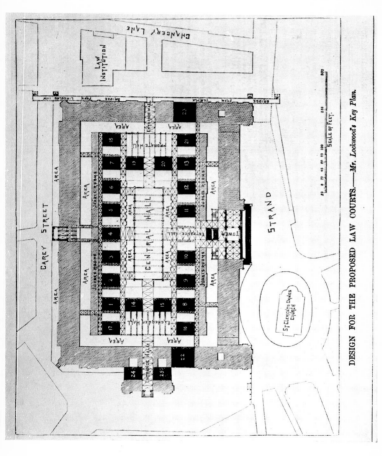

DESIGN FOR THE PROPOSED LAW COURTS.——*Mr. Lockwood's Key Plan.*

XV. London: Royal Courts of Justice. Limited competition (1867): H. F. Lockwood's project

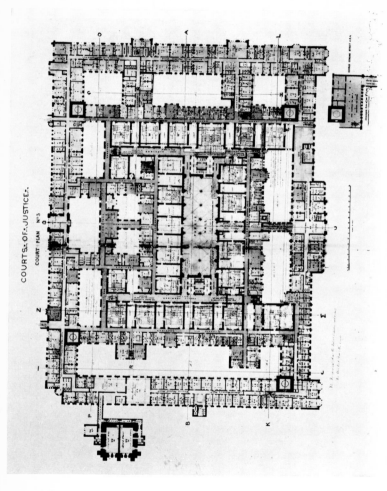

COURTS. OF. JUSTICE.

COURT PLAN Nº 3

XVI. London: Royal Courts of Justice. Limited competition (1867): G. E. Street's plan

COURTS OF JUSTICE

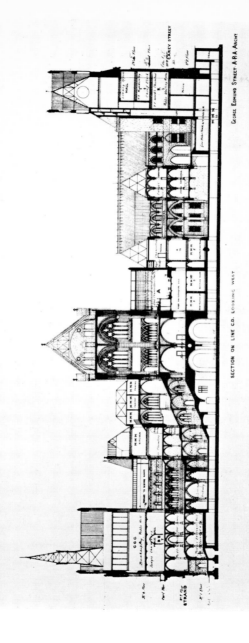

XVII. London: Royal Courts of Justice. Limited competition (1867): G. E. Street's section

XVIII. London: Royal Courts of Justice (1871–82): Carey Street façade (Architect: G. E. Street)

XIX. London: Royal Courts of Justice (1968): The Queen's Building (Ministry of Public Buildings and Works: project architect, John Masson)

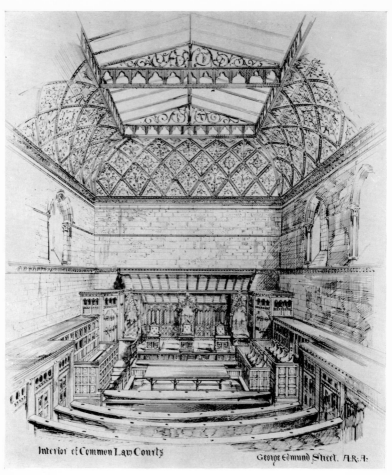

Interior of Common Law Courts

George Edmund Street. A.R.A.

XX. London: Royal Courts of Justice (1871–82): sketch of a Common
Law Court by G. E. Street

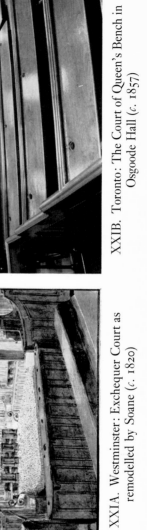

XXIB. Toronto: The Court of Queen's Bench in Osgoode Hall (*c.* 1857)

XXIA. Westminster: Exchequer Court as remodelled by Soane (*c.* 1820)

XXII. London: Royal Courts of Justice: new courtroom (1963) occupying part of the basement of the original building (1871–82) by G. E. Street (Ministry of Public Buildings and Works: project architect, John Masson)

XXIIIA. Chicago: Federal Centre (1965). One of the courtrooms (Office of Mies van der Rohe in conjunction with Schmidt, Garden & Erikson; C. F. Murphy Associates and A. Epstein & Son. Partner in charge, Bruno Conterato)

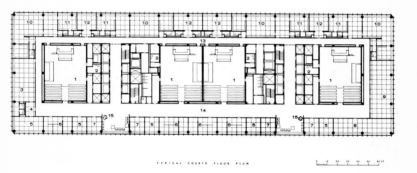

TYPICAL COURTS FLOOR PLAN

XXIIIB. Chicago: Federal Centre (1965). Typical floor plan

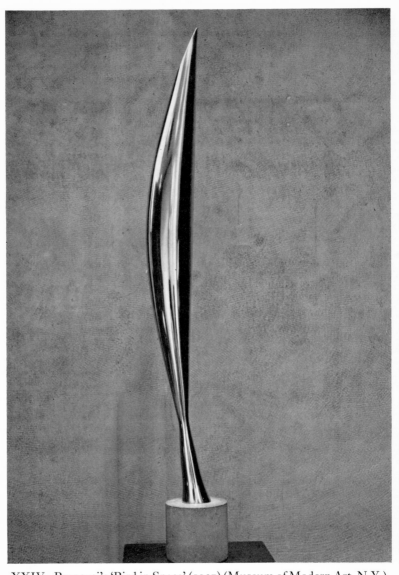

XXIV. Brancusi's 'Bird in Space' (1927) (Museum of Modern Art, N.Y.)

undoubtedly enhanced the reliability of many diagnoses; but apart from the fact that pathologists are still unclear as to the causes or even the significance of variations in human blood-pressure, and still argue as to what in fact is meant by 'normal' blood-pressure in terms of millimetres of mercury in a manometer tube, it is obvious that such data would be of little help in designing and building a novel living organism. The fact that surgeons are not required to create novel organisms tends to disguise this limitation of the 'organic' theory; but recent inter-disciplinary research relating cybernetics and biology seems to be demonstrating that, whatever analogies between computers and human brains may exist, no surgeon or electrical engineer is ever likely to build a three pound computer capable of emulating his own creative mind.

This problem is fundamental to the whole theory of modern architecture, as is evident if we compare the two widely-differing professions of civil engineering and law. In civil engineering analysis, every value can be expressed numerically, even though some of the most fundamental values, such as the magnitudes of the design loading, are as fictitious as the legal supposition that Mrs. Bumble acted under Mr. Bumble's direction.[1] For example, once a loading pattern has been postulated and adopted, all values can be precisely calculated to several decimal places. But this exactitude is quite illusory. If the loading pattern is revised, it will produce equally precise analytical design-results, even though the revision itself may have been relatively arbitrary. The Forth Bridge was designed for wind-pressures of 50 lbs. per square foot, though it is now recognized that 20 or 30 lbs. per square foot would probably have been adequate. Contrariwise, after the Quebec Bridge collapsed during construction in 1907, the new design provided two and a half times as much steel as its submerged predecessor.[2]

In legal analysis, mathematics are virtually useless as a factor for apportioning blame or exonerating the blameless; and even the most brilliant mathematician might find difficulty in solving the standard

[1] C. Dickens, *Oliver Twist*, ch. 49. It was this assertion which prompted the oft-quoted retort by Mr. Bumble: 'If the law supposes that, . . . the law is a ass—a idiot!'

[2] D. B. Steinman & S. R. Watson, *Bridges and Their Builders* (New York 1957 ed.), pp. 253, 309.

third-degree equation of the Canadian Criminal Code: 'not more than five hundred dollars or imprisonment for six months or both'. Yet the lack of mathematical precision does not mean that there is no precision at all, or that the failure of a badly framed indictment is not as easy to forecast as the failure of a badly framed bridge. Judgement is at times facilitated by mathematical analysis, but it is not rendered impossible whenever mathematics can play no part.

There may well of course come a day when the prophesy of the drunken solicitor in Henry Cecil's novel *Much in Evidence* will be fulfilled: ' "Automatic judges, my dear sir. No barristers or solicitors. You just put down your statement of the case, the other side puts down his, push 'em in the machine—pull the lever and, after a few minutes' calculation, the answer comes out on a ticket".'[1] If judges are superseded by computers in courts of law, the nature of the analogy between law and architecture will undoubtedly change accordingly. But it seems safe to assume that there is no immediate prospect that litigation will be settled by business machines, and, by the same token, that there is little likelihood that conscientious architects will shortly be able to base every single design-decision on computerized data-processing.

These distinctions have been emphasized at some length because if one accepts the thesis that architecture is a profession, and if it be admitted that some heuristic value is to be drawn from analogies with other professions, it is important to study all professions whose problems resemble those which architects are called upon to solve. It may be argued that since the whole basis of Building Performance Research rests on the belief that the architectural profession is essentially analogous only to applied sciences, it would be futile to try to assimilate the philosophy of architecture to any disciplines which are non-mathematical. Admittedly, it would be foolish to try to persuade psychologists, physicists, operational research scientists, and other technical experts involved in such work that architecture is fundamentally unscientific. But surely no one has ever seriously claimed that a person holding the degree of Juris Scientiae Doctor is less scientific than a Doctor of Philosophy; and though my suggestion that 'science' is not exclusively mathematical may well be unfashionable, it has yet to be proved untrue.

[1] H. Cecil, *Much in Evidence* (paperback ed.) p. 83.

The fourth major dilemma posed by the emphasis on Building Performance Research concerns the limitation on the number and character of building-types to which its techniques are applicable. We can all see how opportune it is to give research priority to schools, offices, housing, factories, and hospitals. It is also evident why, in the formative stages of this new type of research, the decision should have been made to concentrate initially on the design of schools. But it has yet to be proved that *all* other building-types would indeed be susceptible to this kind of analysis, even assuming that the funds, personnel and research-equipment were fully available.

According to Dr. Peter Manning, who was in charge of the Pilkington Research Unit at Liverpool University, 'the design of the few exceptional buildings that are needed from time to time—like the concert halls, embassies, cathedrals and other prestige buildings that really have some unique requirement—can (from the point of view of this study) be left to themselves. Numerically, at least, they are only a small problem'.[1] But is it the whole truth to say that such buildings '*can* be left to themselves'? Might it not be truer to say that they *must* be left to themselves, because the experts in performance research can envisage no effective means of analyzing them with their mathematical techniques? Does a concert hall in fact have unique requirements? Does a cathedral have unique requirements? Surely the standardization of antique Greek and Roman theatres, and the fact that churches built during virtually every epoch of the last thousand years are still in use without major alterations might suggest that the *requirements* of the drama and the liturgy are probably more standardized and more enduring than almost any other human activity. Finally, what exactly are we to understand by the term 'prestige building'? Is a 'prestige building' to be *defined* as 'a building which has some unique requirement'? If so, what are those unique requirements, and by what criteria are they to be assessed? If some other definition is more apt, what exactly are those qualities which authorize us to declare when a building is a 'prestige building' and when it is not?

The word 'prestige' has recently acquired many new and emotional overtones, some of which go to the very root of architectural

[1] 'Appraisal of Building Performance' in *Architects' Journal*, 9 October 1968, p. 794.

judgement. For the radical social reformer, 'prestige' presumably indicates the proletariat's hereditary moral superiority to capitalism, paternalism, fascism, and other soul-destroying ideologies, and hence his automatic right to make all decisions. For the Industrial Public Relations Executive, 'prestige', on the contrary, means increased sales, lavish advertising, distinctive luxurious packaging, 'graphic symbols' (i.e. the American equivalent of Corporate Heraldry) and all the other enviable attributes of affluence. For the tax assessor, a 'prestige' building is simply a building which cost far more than usual, and also far more than the rents seem to justify.[1] Now admittedly the difference between an ordinary office building and a 'prestige' office building is susceptible to mathematical analysis in terms of the return on investment. But then the whole function of Building Performance Research can be stated in terms of the return on investment. When an insurance company requests a revision of the zoning regulations in Copley Square, Boston, so that it can construct a 'prestige building' in such a way that it will, in some people's minds, be detrimental to the environment of Trinity Church and the Boston Public Library,[2] the mathematical computation of both 'prestige' and 'efficiency' appears singularly inadequate to constitute the sole or even the predominant criterion of architectural judgement.[3]

The advantages of being able to assess 'efficiency' with mathematical precision are incontestable. But when attempting to assess 'prestige', it is worth remembering that, originally, the word meant illusion, deception, or imposture, and derived from *praestigiae*, meaning 'jugglers' tricks'. Few architectural theorists would accept the idea that the essence of a concert hall or of an embassy is illusion, deception or imposture; and whilst anarchists or atheists might cheerfully apply these adjectives to a cathedral or a court of law, they would do so, not because they believed this to be the way

[1] The legal implications of 'prestige architecture' are discussed below, p. 199 by reference to the Seagram Building in New York (See also Appendix A).

[2] A whole essay could be written about the various attempts to have the height restrictions round Copley Square declared unconstitutional. See esp. *Williams v. Parker* (188 U.S. 491) of 1899 and *Welch v. Swasey* (193 Mass. 365) (Petition for writ of mandamus filed 21 December 1905).

[3] Cf. *The New Hancock Building; an example of public and private decision-making* (Boston Architectural Centre, 1968).

cathedrals and courts of law should be built, but, on the contrary, because they believed cathedrals or courts of law should not be built at all.

In the last resort, then, it must be seen that the value which Dr. Manning describes as 'prestige' is really nothing more or less than a lop-sided interpretation of that traditional classical value which Vitruvius called *decorum*,[1] which Perrault translated as *convenance*, and which M. H. Morgan translated as 'propriety'. That propriety, with respect to mass-housing, factories, schools and hospitals, demands qualities different from those appropriate to concert halls or embassies, is as obvious to us as it was to our ancestors, even though the *nature* of those qualities and the *degree* of that difference may well have changed too much to allow for qualitative and quantitative comparisons. But it would be as misleading today to isolate or dismiss any group of building-types by lumping them into a category labelled 'prestige buildings', as it was misleading a century ago to isolate and dismiss 'utilitarian buildings' as unworthy of the architectural historian's attention—an attitude tellingly exemplified by James Fergusson's criticism of the Crystal Palace (which he so enthusiastically admired): 'It has not a sufficient amount of decoration about its parts to take it entirely out of the category of first-class engineering, and to make it entirely an object of Fine Art.'[2]

Nevertheless, despite all these various expressions of misgiving concerning the adequacy of Building Performance Research as a total philosophy of architecture (an adequacy which, it must in all fairness be emphasized, has never been claimed by its leading practitioners), its techniques do seem to have one specific over-riding merit, as compared with the techniques of judgement exemplified by Russell Sturgis's treatise on *How to Judge Architecture*: they are undoubtedly professional techniques in a way that Sturgis, though a professional architect himself, could not have even begun to understand in the era in which he lived. Indeed, when the American periodical *Progressive Architecture* published its special issue on 'Performance Design' in August 1967, it went so far as to claim that 'Performance Research' is a profession in itself. According

[1] Book I, ch. 2.
[2] J. Fergusson, *A History of Architecture* (1862), vol. iii, p. 483.

to the editorial staff, 'a new profession has grown up in the last thirty years whose members, variously titled "systems analysts", "systems engineers", and "operations researchers", claim to have developed a unique methodology for problem-solving far superior to older methods used in other professions',[1] and the article went on to claim that the term 'Performance Design' (defined as 'design based on a scientific method of analyzing functional requirements, including the psychological and aesthetic needs of people') had actually been coined by the editorial staff of the magazine.[2]

The idea that such research is a professional technique seems to be one of the healthiest developments of current architectural thought. Yet the question still remains as to the *extent* to which it contributes toward fulfilling the needs of a total architectural philosophy suited to the needs of the present age. Are mathematical criteria, of some kind or another, ever likely to be *totally* adequate to judge architectural quality? If not, is there any alternative to so-called 'aesthetic' criteria—to all the interchangeable epithets of art criticism derided by Viollet-le-Duc (whereby music is praised for its colour, and painting for its rhythm)[3] and to nebulous terms of architectural praise like 'crisp'? Can non-mathematical architectural judgements be intimately related to reason, to the extent of being explicable by reasoned argument, or do they all occur in some separate psychological limbo half-way between brute sensation and the highest levels of rational thought?

The question as to whether architecture can be solely a matter of rational judgement may appear futile to those who contend that since architecture has long been recognized as both a science *and* an art,[4] its criteria of judgement must inevitably be a mixture—

---

[1] *Op. cit.*, pp. 104–5.   [2] *Ibid.*

[3] Cf. Viollet-le-Duc, *Entretiens*, i, 19: 'Pourquoi dison-nous tous les jours: "Ce morceau de musique est d'une fraîcheur ravissante"? . . . Malheureux sont ceux qui ne peuvent sentir la réalité de ces non-sens du langage des arts.'

[4] The confusion made possible here by the ambiguity of the word 'art' is well exemplified by the definition of 'architecture' in the *Century Dictionary* (1914 ed.), where Viollet-le-Duc is quoted, in translation, as follows: 'Architecture, the *art* of building, includes two elements, theory and practice. The former comprehends *the fine-art side proper*, the body of general rules inspired by taste and based on tradition, and the science, which admits of demonstration by means of absolute formulas. Practice is the application of theory to particular

perhaps even an inextricable mixture—of both reason and sentiment. Such a criticism would indeed be conclusive if the theme of
this essay were based on the tenet that emotional criteria are totally
irrelevant; but it is in fact based on an entirely different premise,
namely, that those aspects of 'artistic' judgement which are relevant
to architecture are equally relevant to other professions, such as
law. It is not claimed here that creativity, elegance, originality and
other values associated with 'the Fine Arts' have no place among the
criteria of architecture, but simply that a proper understanding of
the way these values exist in other professions can provide us with
an integrated set of criteria, as opposed to criteria which oscillate
between two contradictory scales.

---

needs; it is practice which causes the art and the science to conform to the
nature of materials, to climate, to the customs of a period, or to the necessities
of the occasion.'

But in the original text (*Dictionnaire*, vol. i, p. 116), the second sentence
begins 'La théorie comprend: l'art proprement dit, les règles inspirées par le
goût, issues des traditions, et la science, qui peut se démontrer &c. . . .', which
might more accurately be translated as: 'The former comprises (i) art properly
so called, rules inspired by taste and born of tradition, and (ii) science, which
admits of demonstration &c. . . .'

CHAPTER EIGHT

The value of artistic criteria

In March 1891, a century-old debate as to whether architecture was a profession or an art suddenly erupted into public controversy. Its immediate cause was a Bill introduced into the British parliament for making architecture a closed profession of architectural practitioners, 'accessible only by passing examinations and obtaining diplomas as in the case of the professions of Law and Physic'.[1] On the day before the formal introduction of this Bill,[2] *The Times* had published the text of a vigorous dissenting statement (addressed ostensibly to the President of the Royal Institute of British Architects, but addressed in fact to the public at large) which was signed by forty-six architects and twenty-four 'other artists'. The list of signatories included fifteen members of the Royal Academy, and several other celebrities, such as Ford Maddox Brown, Holman Hunt and, most notable of all, William Morris. Norman Shaw (one of the few architects who was also a full-blown Royal Academician) together with T. G. Jackson (elected to the Royal Academy in 1892) led the dissent. Their architectural following included such 'Pioneers of the Modern Movement' as A. H. Mackmurdo and Philip Webb. Perhaps it was because of this vigorous protest that the Bill was not even given a second reading in the House of Commons. In any event, no similar statute was to become law in the United Kingdom until 1938.[3]

In retrospect, it is perhaps difficult to see what all the fuss was

[1] T. G. Jackson (ed.), *Architecture, a Profession or an Art?* (1892), p. xxx.
[2] i.e. 3 March 1891.
[3] F. Jenkins, *Architect and Patron* (1961), pp. 222–7.

about. The French Government has been awarding architectural diplomas to graduates of its Ecole des Beaux-Arts since 1867,[1] and although initially there were only four successful candidates, by 1891 the total had grown to 238.[2] In America the regulation of the practice of architecture was evidently not regarded as a threat to civil liberty, since it was during this same era that laws were first enacted to this effect in the United States.[3] Nevertheless, it should be noted that in France it was not until 1940 that the government deemed it necessary to restrict the practice of architecture *exclusively* to those holding diplomas (clients having hitherto been considered adequately protected against technical incompetence and malpractice by Article 1792 of the Napoleonic Code) whilst the early United States legislation did not in fact prevent unqualified persons from preparing plans and specifications for buildings; it merely insisted that the absence of proper qualifications should be expressly known to the client,[4] under penalty of either a fine of from $50 to $500, or one month in jail.[5]

Though the issue which ostensibly aroused antagonism to the Bill of 1891 was the implied arrogation by government of the power to limit the practice of architecture to persons having passed an examination, the real issues were made manifest by the polemic with which the attack was conducted. This is enshrined in thirteen essays written by the leading opponents of the scheme; essays which were eventually published in a volume entitled *Architecture: a Profession or an Art?* From this book it is clear that the resistance to the proposed legislation was not so much a challenge to those who wished to establish a closed profession, as a formal assertion that architecture was not really a profession at all. The letter published

---

[1] Arrête ministériel of 27 November 1867, articles 70–75. See also J. Guadet, *Conférence sur le Diplôme d'Architecte* (Orleans 1892).

[2] *Annuaire, S.A.D.G.* (1962): 26e Promotion, (p. 227).

[3] The first three States to pass such laws were Illinois (1897), Arkansas (1901) and California (1901). See T. C. Bannister, *The Architect at Mid-century* (1954), vol. i, p. 357.

[4] See, for example, *Laws of New Jersey, 1902*, ch. 29, sec. 14.

[5] *Ibid.*, sec. 13. In 1957 the New Jersey law was amended, whereby contravention became a civil instead of a criminal offence, and imprisonment was no longer a penalty. However, it is still a criminal offence in Connecticut (one year in jail).

in *The Times* had merely claimed that 'architecture has for some time been less constantly associated with the sister arts of Painting and Sculpture than, in our opinion, is desirable, and we think that examinations and diplomas, by raising up artificial barriers, would have the tendency still further to alienate these branches of art'. But in the introduction to the thirteen essays, written by T. G. Jackson, he stated the real issue without ambiguity. 'Legislation has at last reached the domain of Art; and it has been seriously proposed to charge Parliament with the duty of providing the public with good architecture and properly qualified architects. It is not likely that anyone, whether artist or amateur, who knows what Art really means, will be taken in by this chimerical project. *To a true artist his art is an individual matter purely between himself and his artistic conscience. . . If architecture is ever to live again amongst us, the professional idea must disappear*'.[1]

Whether architecture is a profession or an art, or whether it is both a profession *and* an art, has by no means been settled even today. Architectural institutes naturally tend to concentrate on what are indisputably organizational aspects of architectural practice. Art historians, in general, tend to see architecture solely as a visual art, and would probably accept Nikolaus Pevsner's assertion that 'what distinguishes architecture from painting and sculpture is its spatial quality. In this, and only in this, no other artist can emulate the architect.'[2] The view that architecture is both a profession *and* an art is accepted by sociologists, but regarded by them as its chief eccentricity. Barrington Kaye considers the peculiarity of architecture, as compared with other professions, to be that 'the architect thinks of himself, and claims to be, not only a skilled technician, but also an artist', and he quotes with obvious approval the assertion by A. M. Carr-Saunders and P. A. Wilson that 'architecture differs from every other profession . . . in that the technique contains an aesthetic element'.[3]

---

[1] *Op. cit.*, pp. vii, xxviii.

[2] N. Pevsner, *Outline of European Architecture*, Introduction, first paragraph (1942 ed., p. 10).

[3] B. Kaye, *The Development of the Architectural Profession in Britain* (1960), p. 23. This assertion is well supported by American legislation. For example in 1961, the Indiana Architectural Act (1929) was amended, whereby the

We thus find, intermingled in Professor Kaye's analysis, four terms which seem to require different sets of criteria: 'profession', 'technique', 'art' and 'aesthetics'. Some of them may have criteria of excellence in common; but they may, on the contrary, have criteria which not only differ, but conflict. I therefore propose to examine each of these concepts briefly in turn, with the aim of arriving at some preliminary conclusions as to any fundamental notion of art on which a theory of architectural judgement can logically and reliably be based.

Professional arts

When Roscoe Pound, a former Dean of the Harvard Law School, lectured to the Massachusetts Medical Society on 'The Professions in the Society of Today' in 1949, he defined a profession as 'an organized calling in which men pursue a learned *art* and are united in the pursuit of it as a public service'.[1] Few members of the architectural profession are likely to disagree with this definition, even though it was intended for an audience of physicians and surgeons; but since it cannot be assumed that all architectural theorists will interpret the key words of this definition consistently and uniformly, it may be useful to study each in detail.

In the present context, the most important term in this definition is obviously the word 'art'; but since its architectural implications are so complex and so controversial, it will be best treated later under a separate sub-heading. On the other hand, the assertions that a profession must be 'organized', 'learned' and 'a public service' can profitably be considered together, since differences of opinion as to the nature of a profession will usually hinge on variations in emphasis on these three qualities.

The notion of a profession as a public service is the most difficult

---

original definition of the practice of architecture was rewritten to include the word 'aesthetic'. The original section (1929, ch. 62, §17) referred only to 'the planning, designing, specifying or supervision &c.', whereas the modified text (1961, ch. 331, §6) used the phrase: 'the safe, healthful, scientific, *aesthetic* or orderly coordination of the planning, designing, &c.'.

[1] *New England Journal of Medicine*, 8 September 1949, vol. 241, No. 10, pp. 351–7.

of the three. For example, the legal profession has, since the dawn of history, consistently and fervently asserted that its main purpose is to serve the ends of justice. Yet there have been few more popular comic rôles in the traditional stock-in-trade of the satirist than the corrupt lawyer, and even St. Ives, the patron saint of lawyers, who was canonized in 1347, was honoured because he was '*advocatus et non latro, res miranda populo*'.[1] In English law, barristers (unlike solicitors) are not even officers of the court,[2] so that although they can be suspended by the benchers of their Inn for misconduct, their standards of public service are, in fact, governed only by rules of etiquette, which inevitably diminish in force as the size of the profession increases, and which have almost disappeared on the other side of the Atlantic.[3] Indeed, Dean Pound goes so far as to suggest that in the United States, where there has never been any traditional disciplinary organization comparable to the Inns of Court, such a concept of professional etiquette was originally regarded as positively un-American. 'The idea of a profession seemed repugnant to rising American democracy . . . Some states that retained a requirement of admission to the bar provided that anyone was to be admitted with no other qualification than lack of a conspicuously bad character. All the states, by legislation or by increasingly lax administration of their requirements and lack of public or professional interest in the matter, made entrance upon practice easy with a minimum of qualification. As population increased, and large numbers of lawyers were admitted in great urban centres, discipline became lax, and many forensic abuses, such as offensive conduct toward witnesses and abuses in the fomenting of litigation, grew up . . . The feeling was strong that all callings should be on the same footing, namely, the footing of a business—of a money-making calling'.[4]

[1] The text is given in the *Catholic Encyclopaedia*. St. Ives (1253–1303) is more familiar to architectural historians as S. Ivo, to whom Borromini's chapel of the Sapienza in Rome is dedicated. The doggerel verse asserts that St. Ives was 'an advocate and not a robber, something singularly astonishing to the populace'.

[2] 3 *Halsbury's Laws of England* 35.

[3] In the United States, advocates *are* officers of the court, since there is no distinction between barristers and solicitors.

[4] *New England Journal of Medicine*; reference cited above.

However, since the arguments in this book are concerned with analogies between the legal and architectural professions, it should perhaps be re-emphasized here that the analogies sought are concerned with *judgement*, rather than advocacy. Whatever may be the varying ethical standards of individual members of the bar, it can safely be asserted that even in the United States, where judges are appointed by political elections, and for relatively short periods of tenure, the judiciary is still 'professional' as regards its concept of the primacy of public service.

In contrast to the legal profession (where the distinction between judges and advocates is clearly defined) or the medical profession (where the interests of the public and those of individual patients seldom conflict), architects find themselves in an embarrassingly ambiguous situation when called upon to make judgements in the public interest. Unlike surgeons, they cannot justify an abortion on the grounds that it is necessary for their patient's health. Unlike High Court judges, they cannot rely on their competence, integrity and scrupulous regard for public duty to ensure for themselves an adequate and regular stipend. Even the general nature of an architect's public service is more difficult to ascertain (and is certainly far more controversial as regards its specific application) than that of the legal or medical professions, where at least the lowest standards of public service are relatively easy to define in law, and relatively easy to justify in public.

This architectural dilemma is not insoluble; but it can more conveniently be discussed further in the context of Professional Ideals, so it will be more profitable to confine ourselves now to a consideration of the other two characteristics listed by Dean Pound, namely the concept that a profession is necessarily both 'learned' and 'organized'. The emphasis on the educational standards of a profession has usually (though not always) been given primacy whenever disputes as to what is or what is not a profession have involved litigation. Such problems of legal definition usually arise out of disputes on the interpretation of tax laws, and hence the most characteristic decisions and opinions are to be found in such cases as *Currie v. Inland Revenue*,[1] *Teague v. Graves*,[2] and *Wright v. Borthwick*.[3] The latter case, decided in 1937 by the Supreme Court

[1] 1921, 2 K.B. Appeals, 332.   [2] 27 N.Y. Supp. 2d., 762.   [3] 34 Hawaii, 245.

of Hawaii, involved a number of plaintiffs, only one of whom was an architect; but the opinion of the court significantly rejected the definition of a profession given in Webster's dictionary, and relied on that given in the old *Century Dictionary*, according to which a profession is 'a vocation in which a professed knowledge of some department of *science* is used by its practical application to the affairs of others, either in advising, guiding or teaching them, or in serving their interests or *welfare* in the practice of an *art* founded on it'. The court thus deliberately rejected, as unhelpful and inaccurate, a definition which not only omitted the idea of 'welfare', but accepted any 'principal calling, vocation or employment' as a profession. Yet both definitions, it should be noted, insist that professional advice, guidance or teaching is concerned with an art, though only the *Century Dictionary* insisted that it also involved a knowledge of some department of science.

Teague v. Graves et al. (State Tax Commissioners) is of particular importance in the present context, because apart from ruling on the extent to which a profession must be 'learned', it established the right of 'industrial designers' to be classified as professionals for taxation purposes. It thus seems to have authorized a practice at variance with one of Dean Pound's ideals; for whereas Dean Pound insists that 'what a member of a profession invents or discovers is not his property, it is at the service of the public',[1] the Court clearly saw nothing objectionable in the idea of a professional designer patenting what he had designed, in addition to holding the normal copyright.[2] The plaintiff was Walter Dorwin Teague (1883–1960), a pioneer of streamlining, who testified that he had designed photographic equipment, meteorological instruments, mimeograph machines, motor cars, gas ranges, cash registers, vacuum cleaners,

---

[1] Cf. *supra.*, p. 123.

[2] To avoid doing an injustice to Mr. Teague, it should be emphasized that in United States law the copyright to a design (such as that automatically possessed by architects in English Law) is called a 'Design Patent'. Nevertheless, it seems doubtful whether the assignment to an industrial firm of the copyright of an architectural design would be regarded as ethically desirable by the architectural profession. According to information kindly supplied to me by the Texaco Development Corporation, Walter Dorwin Teague assigned at least four design patents to Texaco Inc. (then the Texas Co.) between November 1935 and December 1937.

and many other appliances,[1] and was also responsible for the
Texaco service stations which still give a sense of national homo-
geneity (if not of identity and grace) to several thousand street
corners throughout North America. He also claimed authorship of
three pavilions for the 1939 New York World Fair, and designed a
project for rebuilding San Francisco based on Le Corbusier's *Ville
Radieuse* (a commission from the United States Steel Corporation).[2]

When giving judgement for the plaintiff in 1941, the Appellate
Division of the New York Supreme Court took the view that since
the activity of 'industrial designer' was recognized as a profession
in many universities and colleges, it could justifiably conclude that
although Mr. Teague himself possessed no degree, the fact that he
lectured on the topic at universities created a presumption that he
was fully qualified. There was, however, a powerful dissenting
opinion from Mr. Justice Heffernan, who emphasized that the
plaintiff's formal education consisted only of a High School course
followed by three and a half years' training in the Art Students'
League, that he made no claim to be authorized to practise as a
licensed architect or a graduate engineer, and that he had never had
any extensive course of specialized instruction and study in a given
field of science. 'A background of practical training and education',
Mr. Justice Heffernan concluded, 'does not of itself raise the dignity
of his occupation to that of a profession'.[3]

Whatever the merits of Mr. Justice Heffernan's opinion in the
context of *Teague v. Graves*, it clearly raises important issues regarding the mystique attached to the criteria of the Bauhaus and of
Le Corbusier. The records of the Bauhaus show that it was essentially
a school of industrial design; and although Walter Gropius graduated from the Technische Hochschule in Berlin, his biographers
take pains to emphasize that his *real* training was gained by collabor-
ating with Peter Behrens (a painter whose energies extended to every
aspect of industrial design, from typography to building), and that
his real achievement is to be measured as much by his design of a
diesel locomotive in 1913, and of an automobile in 1930, as by his
designs for buildings and furniture. Similarly, the biographers of

[1] 27 N.Y. Supp. 2d. at 765–7.
[2] Illustrated in W. D. Teague, *Design this day* (1940), *passim*.
[3] 27 N.Y. Supp. 2d. at 765–7.

Le Corbusier (an architect who left school when he was thirteen, and had no subsequent formal education apart from an apprenticeship in engraving watches) emphasize that his architectural training was derived from touring the Balkans with a sketchbook, and by working as a part-time draftsman in Paris for Perret Frères (who at that time were engaged mainly as building contractors for buildings designed by others). The latest edition of *Space, Time and Architecture* has had the grace to delete the assertion made in the original edition that 'Le Corbusier's spirit was never ground to a smooth specialization at a university';[1] but it still pointedly insists that 'architectural creations came easily to him, although he continued always to struggle with painting'.[2] Hence however much teachers in schools of architecture may encourage those intellectual pursuits which prompted Roscoe Pound to define a profession as a 'learned art', the prestige of Gropius and Le Corbusier is such that there still remains a subconscious belief that in some undefined way, architectural studies are not, and should not be, 'academic' in the manner implied by other professional curricula.

Currie v. Inland Revenue (1921), though a dispute concerning the alleged professional status of an accountant who specialized in 'advising' on Income Tax evasion, is of relevance to the present inquiry because, in contrast to these American decisions, the opinion stated by Lord Justice Scrutton placed all the emphasis on professional organization. 'In my view', his Lordship asserted, 'it is impossible to lay down any strict legal definition of what is a profession, because persons carry on such infinite varieties of trades and businesses that it is a question of degree in nearly every case whether the form of business is, or is not, a profession . . . To determine whether an *artist* is a professional man again depends, in my view, on the degree of artistic work that he is doing[3] . . . If I were invited to define exhaustively what a profession was, I should find the utmost difficulty in doing so . . . But I myself am disposed

---

[1] *Op. cit.* (1941 ed.), p. 407.   [2] *Op. cit.* (1967 ed.), p. 520.

[3] Lord Justice Scrutton was here referring to the case of *Cecil v. Inland Revenue* 1919 (36 Times L.R. 164) where the plaintiff had (unsuccessfully) claimed that though a commercial photographer, his work was so artistic that he could be considered, for taxation purposes, as a professional artist. Giving judgement, Rowlatt J. said that 'he (the appellant) did not, as it appeared (to his Lordship), do anything in law beyond what an ordinary photographer did'.

to attach some importance in findings as to whether a profession is exercised or not to the fact that the particular man is a member of an organized professional body with a recognized standard of ability enforced before he can enter it and a recognized standard of conduct enforced while he is practising it.'[1]

Now this notion that the essence of a profession is 'membership of an organized professional body' constitutes the definition generally favoured by sociologists; but whereas Lord Justice Scrutton took care to re-emphasize that he was merely 'disposed to attach some importance' to this aspect, and hastened to add that 'he did not for a moment say it settled the matter', Sir Alexander Carr-Saunders and P. A. Wilson assert categorically that 'a profession can only be said to exist when there are bonds between the practitioners, and these bonds can take but one shape—that of formal association'.[2]

It is true that a number of sociologists, such as Roy Lewis and Angus Maude, have rejected this concept as too narrow and oversimplified, and have emphasized the importance of professional *ethics*, and the primary need to contribute toward the public good.[3] But the very nature of the sociologist's specialization orients him automatically towards concepts involving social organization, so it is not surprising that Professor Kaye, in his *Development of the Architectural Profession in Britain*, should not only follow the lead given by Carr-Saunders and Wilson, but should define a profession, for the purpose of his study, as 'an occupation possessing a skilled intellectual technique, a voluntary association and a code of conduct'.[4]

To avoid the historical inaccuracy which would result from including 'voluntary association' as an *essential* ingredient of a profession, Professor Kaye takes the view that architecture only gradually became a profession; indeed, the most brilliant aspect of this splendidly written book is the dramatic way in which he leads the reader along the evolutionary path to the time when 'true' professional status was ultimately obtained by the establishment of

[1] 1921, 2 K.B. Appeals 332 at 340–1.
[2] A. M. Carr-Saunders & P. A. Wilson, *The Professions* (1933), p. 298.
[3] R. Lewis & A. Maude, *Professional People* (1952), pp. 54–6, 58–64.
[4] *Op. cit.*, p. 17.

an Architectural Institute. But even if we accept his viewpoint (which is less plausible historically with respect to the evolution of the architectural profession in the United States and on the continent of Europe), it helps little towards resolving the kind of dispute which aroused such animosity in 1891, namely whether architecture is a profession or an art. The fact that half the architects who signed the protest were *not* members of the Royal Institute of British Architects (or later resigned their membership) emphasizes the irrelevance of a 'voluntary association' as compared with compulsory registration. Moreover, the fact that no code of conduct is enforceable without some form of delegated statutory authority—which again implies compulsory registration—also emphasizes this irrelevance. We are thus left with the notion of a 'skilled intellectual technique', which sociologists rightly reject as adequate by itself to define a profession. Indeed, this problem is particularly well illustrated in *Professional People* by Lewis and Maude, who cogently argue that it is impossible to accept the claims of the advertising industry to professional status because 'the function of producing half-truths and bogus scientific terminology to sell products (however "ethical" they may be) cannot be professional'.[1]

It is therefore difficult to escape the conclusion that the best sociological definition of a profession was also the earliest, namely that enunciated by Sidney and Beatrice Webb in 1917: 'A profession is a vocation founded upon specialized educational training, the purpose of which is to supply disinterested counsel and services to others, for a direct and definite compensation, wholly apart from expectation of other business gain'.[2] Nevertheless, even this definition seems vitiated by two defects. Being sociological, it is concerned only with how a professional person should behave, and not with what he is or does (since the expression 'A profession is a vocation' avoids the problem of defining the nature of the 'counsel and services' rendered). Perhaps the Webbs had good reason to avoid stating, as the dictionaries state, that such counsel and services constitute an *art*. But it seems clear that specialized educational training must, in this context, involve something more than the performance of mere mechanical operations; and once we are in the

[1] *Op. cit.*, pp. 68–9.
[2] 'Professional Associations', *The New Statesman*, 21 April 1917.

realm of intellectual skills, the implicit demand for creativity and intuition cannot be ignored.[1]

If Dean Pound, the *Century Dictionary* and the *Oxford English Dictionary* are all correct in asserting that professional practice is indeed the practice of an *art*, it seems likely that the fundamental criteria of each art must, when considered in their totality, be regarded as *sui generis*. This is not to deny that many or even all professional arts can have criteria in common. Indeed, the whole thesis of this essay is based on the assumption that 'art' cannot be a generic term unless they do have criteria in common. But decisions as to which criteria are identical, which are only analogically similar, and which are peculiar to a particular profession, can only be determined accurately if one begins by assuming that at least some criteria must be peculiar to each professional art. This assumption, therefore, constitutes the basis of the ensuing comments on the nature of art in its professional sense, and on the relationships and distinctions between 'art' and 'technique'.

Art and Technique

Semantically, 'art' and 'technique' would seem to have essentially identical meanings, since their only etymological difference is that the former originates from Latin and the latter from Greek. But the implications of these words are quite distinct; indeed, the noun 'technique' was deliberately introduced into the French and English languages to create the verbal distinction required in the mideighteenth century by new theories of 'the Fine Arts'. Whether or not this verbal distinction is admissible is, after two centuries of use, an academic question of interest only to lexicographers. Whether or not it is ever objectively real depends very much on the context, as is well demonstrated by comparing its use by critics of the 'performing arts' and its use by critics of painting and sculpture. Whether or not it has any valid place in the theory of architecture goes to the root of the whole controversy as to whether architecture is a profession or an art.

[1] See also M. L. Cogan, 'The Problem of Defining a Profession' in *Annals of the American Academy of Political and Social Science*, vol. 297, pp. 105–11, (1955) at p. 107. Also in *Harvard Educational Review*, vol.2 3, pp. 33–50 (1953).

The chief dilemma in discussing this latter question is, of course, the very ambiguity in the term 'art' which the introduction of the word 'technique' sought to eliminate. Those who, in 1891, argued that architecture was an art rather than a profession clearly conceived of 'art' as synonymous with 'the Fine Arts'—a view explicit in Gerald Horsley's essay on 'The Unity of Art' which constitutes part of T. G. Jackson's symposium. But advocates and surgeons at that time also contended (as they still contend) that they practised an art (even though they might have been bewildered had they been referred to as 'artists')[1] for the obvious reason that 'art', in most languages, is still used indiscriminately to denote both 'the Fine Arts' and technical creative skill.[2]

This dilemma is not resolved by Bruce Allsopp's assertion that 'Art is *creation* (which is making in a non-technical sense) in which the thing made is not an artifact and may not even exist except in imagination. Technique is, properly, the skill by which a craftsman achieves his end, and we have seen that craftsmanship and art are quite different things'.[3] Neither a lawyer's cross-examination nor a surgeon's appendectomy are artifacts; nor can either activity proceed unless it has previously existed in the mind of the lawyer or the surgeon respectively. Admittedly, the 'creativity' of both professions is limited by the fact that both these arts are subject to certain rules. The lawyer proceeds in accordance with the rules of law, just as the surgeon proceeds in accordance with the rules of therapy. But this reliance on a *corpus juris* or a *corpus humanus* no more allows us to distinguish between art and technique than the fact that real architecture presupposes what the French building trade terms '*les règles de l'art*'. Indeed, it is precisely this factor which differentiates real architecture from the type of drawing that used to win the *Grand Prix de Rome*, and which prompted Julien Guadet to assert that 'the laws of construction are the first laws of architecture'.[4]

[1] However, Mr. Justice Cardozo referred to judges as 'artists' in *The Nature of the Judicial Process* (Paperback edition), p. 36.

[2] In German, *Kunst* does not seem to be used with reference to law, but *kunstgerecht* (literally: 'in accordance with the rules of art') means 'technically correct', in the French sense of '*selon les règles de l'art*'. The equivalent of 'medical art' is '*Heilkunst*'.

[3] B. Allsopp, *Art and the nature of architecture* (London 1952), p. 27.

[4] J. Guadet, *Elements et Théorie de l'Architecture*, vol. i, p. 174.

Nor is the dilemma resolved merely by typographical or grammatical distinctions. The introduction to *The Encyclopaedia of the Arts* tells us that 'The Arts, in English usage, is a term that covers more than the single substantive word "art". Though this single word can be used to denote skill in any kind of human activity, its proper use is restricted to spheres in which utility is not the first consideration'. But such a distinction, however strenuously asserted, evades the root of the whole problem, which lies in the obvious reluctance, rather than the inability, of the Ancients to see any need to distinguish clearly between the two ideas. The etymological basis of the English word 'art' is succinctly expounded by Lewis and Short in their *Latin Dictionary*: 'With the advancement of Roman culture' they write, '*ars* (meaning skill in joining something, combining, working it, etc.) was carried beyond the sphere of the common pursuits of life, into that of artistic and scientific action, just as, on the other hand, in mental cultivation, skill is applied to morals, designating character, manner of thinking, so far as it is made known by external actions'. The same evolution also took place in the German word *Kunst* (which originally meant 'knowledge' or 'skill', and derived from *können*),[1] and presumably occurred in all Indo-European languages. Now whether or not 'art' in the limited sense of the 'beautiful arts' is in fact generically distinct from 'art' in its wider sense of skilled craftsmanship; whether or not 'beauty' is philosophically to be distinguished from 'goodness' (an idea only formally introduced into philosophy in the early nineteenth century by Victor Cousin's book *The True, the Beautiful and the Good*), it is indisputable that the belief that the art of architecture is generically allied to painting and sculpture, and hence generically distinct from the medical arts and the legal arts, is of quite recent origin, and forms part of a theory which only emerged after the Renaissance, when the doctrines of Vasari were later reinforced by two centuries of theorizing about 'aesthetics'.

If 'Art' is to be regarded as essentially only a matter of aesthetic perception, the new classification is inescapable. Neither the most accomplished laparotomy nor the most daring stereotomy is likely to gratify the lay eye with the same voluptuous emotions as those aroused by the Leaves of Southwell or the Stones of Venice. Nor is

[1] M. O'C. Walshe, *A Concise German Etymological Dictionary*.

the forensic rhetoric of a Lord of Appeal in Ordinary likely to be included in an anthology of contemporary English prose. Nevertheless, the arts of the surgeon, the architect and the lawyer have at least one life-enhancing quality in common: they are all necessary humanitarian skills, performed in the service of specific social ideals. And whether or not the most outstanding achievements of justice, health, and environmental amenity can ever be described in modern circumstances as 'beautiful', rather than as merely elegantly successful, is a verbal distinction which would have presented little difficulty to the philosophers of ancient Greece, however perplexing it may be to the philosophers of the present day.

At the time of the controversy in 1891, the notion that the quality called 'Fine Art' elevated a basic technological skill by means of an ineffable but essential *je ne sais quoi* had, admittedly, a certain plausibility, in that although photography had then been invented, painting and sculpture were still imitative. But today, when anyone with a rudimentary urge to throw paint around can call himself an artist, and when professorships in musical composition are awarded to experts in random computer programming, the earlier implication that 'Art' implies and included some inherent technical virtuosity must, of necessity, be jettisoned. For this reason one must be particularly cautious of evaluating assertions that 'Art is essential to architecture' out of their context. For example, Burchard and Bush-Brown, in their prologue to *The Architecture of America*, claim that 'a building which serves practical functions well, and is eminently durable, but lacks art, is not architecture at all'.[1] Yet it is clear from the rest of their dissertation on 'The Nature of Architecture' that 'art' is here equated with the quality which Sir Henry Wotton called 'delight', so the authors are simply expressing the traditional view that *firmitas*, *utilitas*, and *venustas* are three essential and interdependent ingredients of any architectural composition. The crucial assertion which Burchard and Bush-Brown are really making is to be found a few pages later in their book, in the sentence: 'Architecture as a social art is doomed to the imperfection that is at once its limitation and its glory';[2] a point more fully elaborated at the end of the first chapter, where the seventh section begins: 'Architecture, as we have now seen, must meet so many criteria

[1] *Op. cit.*, p. 3.   [2] *Ibid.*, p. 4.

that there never has been a perfect building. To meet the demands of commodity, solidity, and aesthetic satisfaction, a building must not compromise in any area. Unfortunately that is impossible, for the several measures, as we have said, make contradictory demands and often cancel each other. Perfection in formal design tends to be sacrificed to expression or utility, structure impinges on utility and elegance defers to expression in an endless round of concessions'.[1]

Aesthetics

In his book on *The Development of the Architectural Profession in Britain*, Barrington Kaye devotes the first part of his second chapter to the problem of 'The Architect as Technician and Artist', and eventually decides that 'for theoretical purposes, a work of art is defined here as a product of human activity intended by its maker to be judged according to aesthetic criteria'.[2] The tautology implicit in such a definition is patently obvious; but it has the merit of leading directly to two questions which are crucial to the present topic, namely (1) is there in fact such an entity as 'aesthetics' and (2) if so, are the criteria of architecture substantially based on aesthetic theories?

As regards the first question, there have in fact been scholars, such as Professor W. E. Kennick, who have had the temerity to repudiate traditional aesthetics by asserting that it rests on two fundamental mistakes. The first error, he claims, is the necessary implication that 'despite their differences, all works of art must possess some common nature, i.e., some distinctive set of characteristics which serves to separate Art from everything else'.[3] The second error, which he sees as closely related to the first, is 'the view that responsible criticism is impossible without standards or criteria universally applicable to all works of art'.[4] In the course of his argument he makes a casual remark which (though incidental to his own thesis) is peculiarly relevant to the present enquiry. 'There

---

[1] *Ibid.*, pp. 35–6.   [2] *Op. cit.*, p. 26.
[3] W. E. Kennick, 'Does traditional architecture rest on a mistake', in C. Barrett (ed.), *Collected Papers on Aesthetics* (1965), p. 3.
[4] Ibid., p. 11.

is also a gratuitousness in aesthetic criticism', he asserts. 'Moral appraisal, like a legal judgement, is a practical necessity; aesthetic appraisal is not'.[1]

It is unlikely that Professor Kennick's views will be generally accepted in the present age, even though the dogmatic attitude toward 'aesthetics' characteristic of the era from 1750 to 1950 has now given way to a far more liberal and modest approach. Nevertheless, since about a thousand departments of philosophy in various universities and colleges include 'Aesthetics' in their curricula, and since at least six journals of aesthetics and art criticism are published by Societies for Aesthetics in the United States, Britain, France, Italy, Spain and Japan respectively, the vested interest in the maintenance of the discipline makes the discipline itself hazardous to contest. Fortunately there is no need to prejudice any reader of this book by vigorously supporting Professor Kennick's views. The question he specifically raises (namely: 'Does traditional aesthetics rest on a mistake?') is not the basic problem raised in the present context, which is rather: 'Does the view that architectural criteria are basically identical with those of the other visual arts rest on a mistake?' It will thus be clear that the answer to this question does not necessarily challenge the validity of 'aesthetics' in other contexts, but is concerned only with the application of 'aesthetic' criteria in one particular field.

Similarly, none of the arguments which will be put forward in this chapter are intended to imply that architects can learn nothing from art-historical studies of the psychology of perception. They will merely suggest that no art-historical study of the activities of painters and sculptors *proves* anything about the creative activities of architects; and scholars who have written authoritative works about the relationship between the way painters depict natural objects, and the natural objects themselves, would undoubtedly be the first to subscribe to this limitation. For example, E. H. Gombrich, in *Art and Illusion*, deals specifically with the relationship between what a painter depicts, or how he depicts it, and what a painter either sees or knows. He makes no attempt to grapple with the problem as to why, given certain environmental requirements and a wide choice of structural systems and materials, an architect judges

[1] Ibid., p. 18.

it appropriate to build one kind of abstract composition rather than another. Indeed, Professor Gombrich takes pains to demonstrate his ignorance of this type of problem by referring, in one of his more telling metaphors, to a 'coping stone' when what he really means is a keystone.

A lengthy analysis of all the controversial issues involved would defeat the purpose of this study by giving the question itself undue prominence. I shall therefore simply list five points for consideration, without even discussing their respective merits. If the reader concludes that the fundamental criteria of architecture *are* basically identical with those of the other visual arts, the ensuing arguments will not necessarily be vitiated.[1] If, on the other hand, he concludes that the fundamental criteria of architecture are *not* identical with those of the other visual arts, the ensuing arguments are likely to be more plausible.

The first point concerns the place of architectural criticism within the totality of writings on aesthetics. Even the most cursory and random glance through standard authoritative works published in the last century and a half will show how infrequently their authors choose buildings to exemplify their theories. Now where an author implies, or specifically asserts, that his theory of aesthetics *is* valid for architecture, the least that can be expected of him is that he should include architectural examples. Yet Benedetto Croce discusses ornament solely with reference to rhetoric,[2] Taine avoids both architecture and music by disassociating them from painting, sculpture and poetry,[3] whilst Herbert Read, who begins *The Meaning of Art* by asserting that 'the architect must express *himself* in buildings which have some utilitarian purpose',[4] gives no verbal or pictorial evidence of this phenomenon whatsoever. He remarks that 'the Greek architect was always striving to avoid the impression of hollowness',[5] and makes casual allusions to the ornamental glories of mediaeval architecture and the architectural ineptitude of

---

[1] There are some legal scholars who consider the traditional theory of aesthetics relevant to law. For their views, see the excellent article by R. F. Wolfson, 'Aesthetics in and about the law' (1944), in 33 *Kentucky Law Journal* 33.

[2] B. Croce, *Aesthetic* (Paperback edition, 1965), pp. 426–36.

[3] H. Taine, *Philosophie de l'Art* (Paris, n.d.) (1865).

[4] H. Read, *The Meaning of Art* (1936 ed.), p. 18.   [5] *Ibid.*, p. 50.

the Baroque. But the only reference to specific buildings, apart from the names of two rococo interior decorations by Robert de Cotte, is the assertion (now disproved by Professor Ackerman) that the vestibule of the Laurentian Library in Florence contains columns which fulfil no structural purpose, and is therefore 'an architectural composition obeying the laws, not of architecture, but rather of painting and sculpture'.[1] Yet surely here, more than anywhere, Michelangelo could be said to have been 'expressing himself in a building which had a utilitarian purpose'.

The second point concerns the validity of the whole concept of 'the Fine Arts'. Professor P. O. Kristeller[2] has demonstrated that the theory does not appear before the mid-eighteenth century, though it stemmed initially from the foundation of the French Academy in Rome in 1666. The idea of an academy for teaching the 'arts of drawing' (i.e. painting, sculpture and architecture) was of course already common in Italy by that date. Indeed, it was the Italophile faction at the French Court, led by Colbert, which was responsible for taking the initiative in establishing this French Academy in Rome. But the Italians never at that time used any phrase equivalent to 'Beaux-Arts' (a term which was invented by Colbert's secretary)[3] and hence it was in France that the decisive step towards a system of 'the Fine Arts' was taken when the Abbé Batteux published his famous, influential, and confusing treatise, *Les beaux-arts réduits à un même principe*, in 1746.[4]

The French origin of the term is worth noting, because it has led to the erroneous assumption that the term corresponds to a traditional national attitude, whereas in France itself the disciplines of painting, sculpture and architecture were never conjoined until the Napoleonic era. Not only was the pre-revolutionary Royal Academy of Architecture (founded in 1671) entirely distinct from

[1] *Ibid.*, p. 146.

[2] P. O. Kristeller, *The Modern System of the Arts*, first published in vols. XII and XIII of the *Journal of the History of Ideas*, and now reprinted as the ninth essay in *Renaissance Thought II* (Paperback ed., 1961).

[3] i.e. Charles Perrault, in the second dialogue of his *Parallèle des Anciens et des Modernes* (1688–96) and in his *Cabinet des Beaux-Arts* (1690).

[4] As I pointed out in *Changing Ideals in Modern Architecture* (p. 174), Batteux specifically excludes architecture from his theory because, like eloquence, it has a practical purpose.

the Royal Academy of Painting and Sculpture (founded in 1648), but even during Colbert's lifetime it remained quite aloof. Thus the values and criteria established by the Royal Academy of Architecture were totally distinct from those of the Royal Academy of Painting and Sculpture, and were at times outspokenly at variance. On 7 March 1678, for example, the Academy of Architecture was 'unable to avoid reflecting how capricious sculptors and painters are when given responsibility for ornament, and how little they bother to subject themselves to the proportions of the architecture and of the various parts of the building'.[1] In the eighteenth century, the professor of architecture was particularly distressed by his students' infatuation with pictorial techniques.[2]

When, after the French Revolution, 'the Fine Arts' were united into a single academy, as a result of the machinations of Quatremère de Quincy and the prejudices of the painter J. L. David, it was inevitable that the criteria of architecture, sculpture and painting should become intermingled and confused. This confusion still persists, though the 'Beaux-Arts' system of architectural education has been nominally abandoned, even in France; and it can only be dispelled by a deeper understanding of the professional nature of architectural judgement as it existed in an earlier age.

The third point concerns the limitations of 'aesthetics', which, historically, have proved so difficult to define. If we trace the development of the general idea, from the invention of the concept of the Nine Muses (which represented astronomy, history, various types of music, poetry and drama) to the most recent text-books written by philosophers who specialize in this topic, it is apparent that there is not, and never has been, a consensus of opinion as to which activities are the concern of 'aesthetics', and which are not. It seems reasonable to suggest, therefore, that there may be creative activities requiring the exercise of judgement in which general theories of aesthetics play no part. The operative word here, of course, is *general*. My intention here is not to exclude special theories about some particular 'Fine Art' which have obvious relevance to architectural criticism. It is to dispose of the popular view

---

[1] *Procès-Verbaux* (ed. Lemonnier), vol. i, p. 161.
[2] J. F. Blondel, *Cours d'Architecture* (1771), vol. iii, 'Observation XV' (p. xlviii).

that 'if all people who write and talk about art would constantly remind themselves that the particular art they happen to be talking about is one kind of art, and that whatever principles they may believe apply to it must fit into a theory of art as a whole, then a great deal of trouble would be avoided. First come the principles of art, and then come the principles of the separate arts'.[1] This theory, far from avoiding a great deal of trouble, is the procrustean bed which has tortured architectural criticism for nearly two centuries. The sooner we forget about it the better.

The fourth point, which concerns the rational element in criticism, will be dealt with in detail later; but since reference has just been made to the difficulty of deciding which activities can be regarded as 'aesthetic', attention may appropriately be drawn here to the difficulty of deciding which 'aesthetic' activities can be regarded as 'professional'. Talcott Parsons points out in the *International Encyclopaedia of the Social Sciences*, that 'over the whole range of technical competence, including the early reference points of law and medicine, there are serious limits to, and possibly inherent limitations on, the extension of the process of professionalization, a process which, in one aspect is almost synonymous with that of *rationalization*'.[2] Now however one defines rationalization, there is clearly a conceptual distinction to be made between a rational art and an irrational art, though authorities may differ as to which is best or which is which. The Fine Arts may be Apollonian or they may be Dionysian; but a Dionysian profession would be hard to reconcile with the lexicographic assertion that professional arts are based on 'some department of learning', even if the process of learning is defined in terms of psychological experiments on rats and mice.

Finally (and this is the fundamental difficulty posed by Croce's theory of aesthetics): whilst we may all agree that true architecture should be 'expressive', and that the quality which an architect expresses involves a relationship between his personality and the products of his specific skill, few architectural theorists would agree with T. G. Jackson's statement, quoted at the beginning of this chapter, that architecture is an individual matter purely between

[1] B. Allsopp, *Art and the nature of architecture* (1952), p. 68.
[2] *Op. cit.*, vol. xii, p. 545.

the architect and his artistic conscience,[1] or that personal expression should be as uninhibited as that of painters, sculptors, musicians or poets. Architectural integrity can no longer be identified (assuming that it ever was) with the expression of the individual architect's personality, untrammelled either by the needs of society or by the needs of a client as he conceives them, to the extent that an architect's self-loyalty becomes his supreme moral code. It is this consideration which, more than any other, brings architectural criteria into line with those of the other learned professions; for whatever the merits of Art for Art's sake, there is clearly no value in advocacy for the sake of advocacy, or surgery for the sake of surgery, except as academic exercises. If the practice of law and medicine are not in every respect social arts, they are not arts at all; and the same may be said of architecture.

[1] See note (1) above, p. 122.

CHAPTER NINE

Professional criteria of judgement

The traditional argument against regarding architectural judgement as an aspect of professional judgement (rather than as an aspect of art-criticism) may be summarized as follows: 'the criteria of architecture cannot be compared analogically with those of law or medicine, because legal and medical criteria are essentially far more objective. Social groups may disapprove of particular techniques; osteopaths, natureopaths, chiropractors and Christian Scientists may challenge the academic supremacy of traditional medicine;[1] but the arts of healing and litigation are nevertheless firmly based on the same universal concepts of natural justice and normal health which have existed unchanged for centuries. No controversy comparable to 'the Battle of the Styles' has ever shaken the legal or medical professions. No modification in popular views concerning the absolute right to enjoy personal property has ever seriously threatened the Fifth Amendment, nor have the remarkable statistical changes

[1] The history of the legal recognition of osteopathy, chiropractic and natureopathy forms in itself an instructive commentary on the legislation's attitude towards professional registration. In 1915 a chiropractor was successfully prosecuted for illegally practising medicine (*Commonwealth of Massachusetts v. Zimmerman* [221 Mass. 184]), and in the same year the New England College of Chiropractic was convicted of issuing spurious degrees (221 Mass. 190); but chiropractic is now officially recognized in most States, and is listed in the *General Statutes of Connecticut* under Title 20 ('State Board of Healing Arts').

In March 1897, the Iowa State Legislature enacted a Medical Practice Act which specifically excluded osteopaths unless they had passed the same examinations as those required of physicians; but as a result of effective lobbying, an *Act to Regulate the Practice of Osteopathy* passed the Iowa Legislature in the following year (27 G. A. 1898, ch. 69).

in the incidence of pock-marks or infant mortality affected our ideas as to what constitutes a normal complexion or a normal duration of life. If such absolute criteria existed in architecture, there might be some parallel between architectural, legal and medical criteria. But judgements as to whether or not a building is a masterpiece, or even whether or not it is architecture, bear no comparison with judgements as to whether a building is a danger to health or contravenes the Building Code. The latter type of judgement is indeed analogous to professional judgement, since it is based on medical or legal factual evidence. But the former type of judgement is more akin to the judgements we make about painting and sculpture, a sphere of connoisseurship in which norms vary in complex unpredictable ways, and depend on sensibility as well as reason.

It is indisputable that the more obvious diseases are now easy enough to diagnose by uncontrovertible factual evidence, just as the more flagrant offences against society can be settled by courts of law without judicial dissent. But when a biographer of Baron Pollock describes the opinion delivered by that eminent jurist in *Egerton v. Brownlow* as a 'judicial triumph',[1] it can be assumed, even by those who have never read the case, that this legal opinion was not only as dependent on the complexity and unpredictability of the norms involved as any judgement about painting or sculpture, but was expressed with the same kind of outstanding oratorical felicity which obliges us to classify the parliamentary speeches of Lord Macaulay as 'literature'.

It must here be emphasized that, in this context, the words 'complexity and unpredictability' are used to refer only to the *problem* involved. Few theorists would suggest that the *solution* to a professional problem must be complex in order to be brilliant. On the contrary, it is usually the simplicity of the solution which causes it to be so clearly recognized as a masterpiece. Although a simple answer can often be found to complex problems, there is no merit in finding simple solutions to simple problems, and considerably less merit in solving simple problems with elaborately complex solutions.

These points are emphasized for two reasons. The first is that

[1] (1853, 4 H.L. Cas. 1). The statement occurs in the 1938 edition of the *Encyclopaedia Britannica*, but has been deleted in more recent editions to make room for an article on Jackson Pollock.

the judicial assertion, 'My Lords, the principles on which this case must be determined appear to me to be extremely simple' (a phrase which acquired great popularity among British High Court Judges in the last century),[1] must not be construed as a claim that the problems in the case are simple, but as a modest but subtle euphemism intended to persuade his Lordship's brethren that his own solution is the more correct. Secondly, it seems to me that a major defect of Robert Venturi's *Complexity and Contradiction in Architecture*[2] lies precisely in its insistence on the intrinsic virtue of complex solutions, regardless of the problems to be solved. Despite the book's many cogent arguments, its theme is undisguisedly derived from the notion of 'Mannerism' as conceived by Italian painters and sculptors in the sixteenth century; and although Professor Venturi ostensibly bases his argument on the thesis that complex functions require complex forms,[3] it seems clear from his discussion on what he calls 'the rhetorical element',[4] and from the historical illustrations which he selects, that he not only finds a positive architectural merit in arbitrary sculptural and pictorial complexities, but that he is little concerned with whether such visual complexities really do correspond to the functional complexities and contradictions necessitated by the programme or the existing environment.

In contradistinction to this architectural philosophy, based largely on theories of painting, I would contend that the essential difference between 'professional' judgement and 'aesthetic' judgement cannot be that one is simple and mechanical, whilst the other is complex and intuitive. It must be that whereas the complexity and unpredictability of 'aesthetic' judgements—that is to say of

---

[1] It occurs, for example, in the Lord Chancellor's opinion in the famous leading case of *Rylands v. Fletcher* (1868, 3 H.L. at 338). This case took seven years to settle. In 1862 the Liverpool Assizes referred it to an arbitrator. In 1865, the case was argued in the Exchequer Court, where judgement was given for the defendant (Rylands) by a 2:1 majority (3 H. & C. 774). In 1866, on appeal to the Exchequer Chamber, it was decided that the dissenting judge in the Court below (Baron Bramwell) had been right, and judgement was given for the plaintiff. In 1868, Rylands brought a writ of error to the House of Lords, but the judgement for the plaintiff was affirmed.

[2] Published as vol. i of *The Museum of Modern Art Papers on Architecture* (1966).

[3] *Ibid.*, p. 38.   [4] *Ibid.*, p. 44.

judgements about the expression of personal emotions—derive from the fact that almost every work of painting or sculpture nowadays depends, for its inception and execution, on the personal initiative of its creator, the complexity and unpredictability of legal and medical judgements result essentially from extraneous conditions over which the practitioner has virtually no control.

The important implications of this argument with regard to architectural judgement will be readily apparent if one reflects on the types of building which, in the nineteenth century era of 'art-architects', enjoyed the greatest critical acclaim. It was the isolated Greek temple; the single-cell ruin of indeterminate purpose, which was most admired by the architectural historians, whilst the intact and complex elements of their own intricate urban environment were virtually ignored. Russell Sturgis, it will be remembered, asserted in *How to Judge Architecture* that 'there is no serious dispute as to the standing of the Greek architecture previous to the year 300 B.C. as the most perfect thing that decorative art has produced',[1] just as Nikolaus Pevsner's *Outline of European Architecture* still begins its first chapter with the sentence: 'The Greek Temple is the most perfect example ever achieved of architecture finding its fulfilment in bodily beauty'. Yet even Viollet-le-Duc had pointed out why such a monument must 'échappe à la critique',[2] and Sturgis himself, after noting with regard to such temples that 'nothing of this complete beauty is now to be seen above ground', warned his readers that 'it is extremely important to consider the probable ancient surroundings of the building in question'.[3] The illustrations he provided can have contributed little towards this consideration; for it was characteristic of the age in which he lived that, as soon as he began to deal with buildings which *could* be studied in relationship to their purpose and surroundings, his enthusiasm evaporated. Just as mediaeval cathedrals and renaissance palaces are discussed as if they existed in a vacuum, so he described the commercial buildings of his own century as if they were isolated monuments in some vast urban desert. No wonder that he concluded his book (published in 1903) on a pessimistic note by lamenting that 'The nineteenth century was not, and the twentieth century is

[1] *Op. cit.*, p. 13.　　[2] Viollet-le-Duc, *Entretiens* (1863), vol. 1, p. 93.
[3] *Op. cit.*, p. 16.

not as yet certain to be a great day of art in the decorative or artistic sense'.[1]

Such pessimism was perhaps inevitable in an age obsessed with the problem of avoiding stylistic imitation; but this obsession was really only a minor symptom of the basic ailment, which, as we can now see, consisted in the delusion that new social needs were obstructions to the progress of good architecture. It must be insisted, despite all the art-historical assertions to the contrary, that programmatic complexity and contradiction are the *essential prerequisites* of any architectural masterpiece, just as they are the essential prerequisites for any demonstration of outstanding surgical or forensic skill.

If this premise be granted, it will readily be admitted that architectural criticism is not something which can be limited to the contemplation of a finished artefact, but is impossible without a full knowledge of the problems to be solved and of the limitations imposed. This does not mean that a critic is obliged to pronounce every building satisfactory unless he is able to envisage a better solution. But it does mean that he should be wary of acclaiming any building as a masterpiece if the requirements of those who commissioned it, and the difficulties confronting those who designed it, have not been, or cannot be, evaluated and correlated with the resultant architectural forms.

Phases of Architectural Judgement

Architectural judgements usually relate to one of four main categories which may be classified, for the sake of discussion, as (1) the design process, (2) competitive assessments, (3) control evaluations and (4) journalism. In the design process, judgement constitutes one of the integral creative components, in that it is the mechanism by which the relationship between intuitively imagined forms and intellectually apprehended data is continually assessed.[2] For reasons stated earlier, this aspect of judgement can be most con-

---

[1] *Ibid.*, p. 213.

[2] Cf. J. Guadet. *Eléments et Théorie de l'Architecture* (1904), vol. i, p. 101: 'Le raisonnement, la critique, viendront à leur tour pour contrôler votre conception, car après avoir imaginé, il faut que vous sachiez être les propres juges de votre imagination'.

veniently considered in terms of 'decision-making', because although, in theory, it would be possible for an architect to complete several different projects for any one building, and then 'judge' which is the best, in practice the process of selection can usually be effected most efficiently at embryonic stages in the course of the design, whereby only one final project is produced.

At the opposite extreme is architectural criticism in its journalistic sense; an activity which, despite its many merits, may be regarded as the antithesis of design. Whether enunciated by architects, art historians or laymen, it can have no possible effect on the building under review. It may educate the public. It may publicize the architect, ulcerate the client or help overthrow the municipal government. But its *immediate* influence on the environment is nil. Whatever it creates, it creates for the future; and the most sagacious evaluation of this kind of judgement was probably the cartoon published in a recent issue of the *New Yorker* where a workman, assembling the foundation steelwork of a sky-scraper, remarks laconically to his mate: 'I see in *The Times* that Ada Louise Huxtable already dislikes it'.

Competitive assessments and control evaluations thus remain the only two categories which can offer a sound basis for the study of architectural judgement by analogy with other forms of professional judgement. Their procedural techniques certainly suggest *prima facie* evidence as to their potential suitability. Unlike journalistic criticism, they both play a decisive rôle with respect to the environment under immediate consideration. Unlike the design process, neither of them is potentially vitiated by the possibility that the judge's own personal involvement will play a decisive rôle in reaching conclusions.

Competitive Assessments

The merits and demerits of architectural competitions have been hotly debated for centuries, and this is no place to discuss further the many different methods of organizing them. It seems clear, however, that the main causes of disagreement (apart from mundane problems concerning fairness, remuneration and so on) usually revolve round the question as to whether the purpose of a competition is to choose an ideal design, or to choose an ideal designer. If it is to choose an ideal project, there is usually an outcry if an inexperienced winner makes some major alteration. If it is to choose an ideal architect, there are good grounds for the layman's assertion that only competitions limited to a few well-established practitioners will produce the most reliable results. But such controversies (which usually centre round the theme of 'giving opportunities to undiscovered talent')[1] do not get to the heart of the kind of problem with which this book is concerned, namely: how can any group of judges afford the time to give due consideration to an unlimited number of entries? In a court of law, it sometimes takes several years to decide between two parties; and even with only two parties to the dispute, the judges of the final court of appeal are sometimes fairly evenly divided. How would a Court of Appeal react to a complicated case involving five hundred and twenty separate litigants,[2] each pleading his own special cause? Can we imagine a suit for the Specific Performance of a contract, where five hundred and twenty separate plaintiffs, each claiming that his own distinctive product fully complied with the stipulated requirements, demanded that judgement be given in his favour?

Thus stated, it seems self-evident that the idea of having large international competitions, open to anyone who pays a modest fee,

---

[1] Compare the following comment in the *Architectural Review* on the Trinity College Library Competition: '. . . the winner, Paul Koralek (a British architect —product of the A.A.—of Austrian origin) is exactly the kind of person everybody likes to see as the winner of such a competition, a young architect just embarking on independent practice' (August 1961, p. 77). A century ago, the débâcle of the Foreign Office Competition (so amusingly described by Sir Kenneth Clark in *The Gothic Revival*) prompted the President of the R.I.B.A. to tell the House of Commons that unlimited competitions 'now stink in the nostrils of the House', though he was sorry it should be so. Speaking as M.P. for Stoke-upon-Trent, during the debate on the New Courts of Justice, he deplored the 'tricked-out, burnished pictures of architects' artists', and asserted that they should obtain 'just so many designs and no more, and just so roughly done as would enable competent judges to decide who was the best man; for the competition was not meant to enable them to decide on the building in all its details, but to discover the man best competent to create the final structure' (*Hansard*, 22 March 1866, cols. 779–82).

[2] This number has been chosen because there were 520 entries for the Toronto City Hall Competition.

never emanated from any theory of professional judgement. On the contrary, it seems more likely to have developed from the type of judgement exemplified by the annual Salons of academies of painting.

The evolution of such Salons has been well summarized by Ernest Short,[1] who points out that whereas, in the mid-eighteenth century, the Salons of the French Academy of Painters only displayed about a hundred canvases, the nature of the Salon was completely changed after the French Revolution, when J. L. David insisted that every citizen had a democratic right to make submissions. As a result, the Salon of 1833 displayed 3,318 exhibits by 1,190 exhibitors, and in 1848 (when the judges only met fourteen times for about four hours at a session to examine five thousand canvases) the average time allotted to the examination of each submission was approximately thirty-six seconds.[2] In England, conditions became even worse. The number of paintings submitted for the Royal Academy's Summer Exhibition increased in the 1930s to an average of from ten to twelve thousand.[3] Even so, it is important to note that the selection committees of these exhibitions were not attempting to decide which painting was the *best*; they were simply judging in accordance with what, in today's academic jargon, would be called a 'pass/fail' basis. Moreover, they were passing judgement on finished articles, rather than on preliminary diagrams. To equate this type of selection with that of an international architectural competition, one would have to assume a hypothetical situation whereby, for example, the commission for decorating the interior of an opera house would be awarded on the basis of the best anonymous thumb-nail pencil sketch selected from over five hundred submissions, each made by artists residing in distant lands, and unfamiliar with the carcass of the building to be adorned.

Several analyses of the problem of architectural judgement, as exemplified by international competitions, have already been given. For the present, it will be sufficient to remark that the comments made are in no way intended as adverse criticisms of the manner in which the judges of international competitions have grappled with

---

[1] E. Short, *The Painter in History* (1948), pp. 353-4.　　[2] *Ibid.*
[3] S. C. Hutchinson, *The History of the Royal Academy, 1768-1968* (1968), p. 172.

their task. On the contrary, the point at issue is not whether recent international competitions have been judged as well as possible in the circumstances, but whether such competitions are in fact susceptible of any valid professional judgements whatsoever; and from what has been said, it would seem indisputable that competitions restricted to half a dozen nominated competitors are, from the judicial point of view, the most likely to produce reliable results.

Control Evaluation

As regards 'control evaluation' (a term used here to mean those kinds of judgements which confront a statutory commission when asked to approve a specific design in a particular location), the authority, terms of reference and procedure of such commissions vary considerably from country to country. But their tasks usually have certain basic features in common, and these are of particular relevance to the present study, since they correspond more closely than any other kind of architectural judgement to the processes of legal judgement.

First, they are concerned, like courts of law or arbitration tribunals, only with two parties to a dispute, that is to say the architect (who together with his client may be considered as the plaintiff) and the general public (whose interests are being ostensibly safeguarded, and who therefore plays the rôle of defendant). When a dispute arises, it usually takes the form of an appeal against some decision by a subordinate official vested with delegated authority. Hence the settlement of the dispute tends to have more in common with an arbitration tribunal than with a court of law, in that whereas, in an ordinary trial, a court would have to weigh its conclusions in the light of expert testimony produced by the two parties respectively, in tribunals of the type we are now considering, the expertise is assumed to reside in the judges themselves. Nevertheless, whether the procedure for dealing with the dispute be by arbitration, or by a civil action in an ordinary court of law, expert testimony of some kind of another is essential.

The possibility of settling 'aesthetic' disputes about a project by means of expert witnesses is certainly questionable; but it would be unwise to assume that other forms of expert testimony are necessarily more reliable.[1] Judicial expressions of scepticism on this subject were uttered as long ago as 1843, in an exchange between the Solicitor-General and Lord Campbell in the *Tracy Peerage* case.[2] In reply to the Solicitor-General's assertion that expert witnesses *must* be reliable (since they clearly had no vested interest in the matter in dispute) Lord Campbell retorted: 'they are witnesses on one side, and I am sorry to say that respectable witnesses are apt to form a strong bias'. A similar view was expressed in an American court in 1870, when Judge Temple, in the California case of *Grigsby v. Clear Lake Water Co.*,[3] commented: 'It must be painfully evident to every (legal) practitioner that these witnesses (i.e. the expert witnesses) are generally but adroit advocates of the theory upon which the party calling them relies, rather than impartial experts, upon whose superior judgement and learning the jury can safely rely'.

As compared with such tendentious witnesses, the reliability of a tribunal of experts is naturally greater, since whereas 'expert witnesses' are usually selected separately by each party to the dispute, the impartiality of a tribunal of expert judges acceptable to both parties is easier to ensure. But even here, the problem is less simple than it looks. Let us take, as an example, a tribunal established to settle a labour dispute. However impartial the members of such a labour tribunal may strive to be, and however acceptable they may be to the parties involved, each member, by the very fact that he *is* an expert in labour relations, will presumably have certain definite theories which might well—however subconsciously—tend to favour one party to the detriment of the other as the precise nature of the dispute becomes apparent. Thus whereas, in the traditional Anglo-American 'adversary system', the bias of the two opposing teams of experts is at least manifest to both the litigants and the

---

[1] The unreliability of this type of 'scientific' expert witness is particularly obvious when evidence involves predictions. Judgements awarded on the strength of erroneous predictions have caused considerable procedural trouble in American Courts. Cf. *Wagner v. Loup River Public Power District* (150 Nebraska 7) where expert testimony as to what would happen to riparian lands as a result of the diversion of water by the defendant was proved wrong by subsequent events. The trial judge granted a new trial, but the appellate court reversed the motion.

[2] 10 Clark & Finnelly 177.   [3] 40 California 405.

judges, in tribunals where the experts are themselves the judges, the bias is not only harder to detect, but harder to challenge effectively during the course of the hearings without the risk of antagonising those who will have to make the final decision.[1]

Such difficulties are increased when the tribunal does not even have statutory authority. Anyone at all familiar with the work of the American Institute of Architects' 'Committee on Aesthetics' will recognize its scrupulous regard for judicial integrity, and its indefatigable zeal in the collection and examination of relevant evidence. But whenever the conclusions of this Committee differ from those held by a local Chapter (which may well claim prior jurisdiction over the issue in dispute), the American Institute of Architects Committee's lack of statutory authority tends to nullify any effective appellate function which the national character of the Institute might, at first sight, seem to confer. There is never in fact any enforceable hierarchical distinction, among voluntary tribunals, of the kind which exists in courts constitutionally established by the State; and there are several good reasons why such a distinction could never be brought about by positive law.

The most obvious reason, in the architectural profession, is that it is not possible to make the distinction between judges and practitioners which evolved naturally and necessarily in the legal profession. Whatever may be the various systems used in different countries to appoint judges, it is clear that they must all be based on the assumption that no judge can be permitted to act as a part-time attorney.[2] It may of course be presumed that when an architect is made a member of an Architectural Commission, a sense of delicacy would preclude him from accepting an invitation to replace the architect whose design his Commission had rejected. But whereas in the architectural profession, it would only be 'ethically reprehensible' to act otherwise, in the legal profession it would be physically impossible, since no judge can appear in court as an advocate.[3] Even in England, where the fraternal atmosphere of the

---

[1] See J. H. Beuscher, 'The Use of Experts by the Courts', in *Harvard Law Review*, vol. liv, p. 1105.

[2] These lines were written at the time of the events which obliged Mr. Justice Fortas to resign from the U.S. Supreme Court.

[3] Cf. *Halsbury*, vol. iii, pp. 62–3 (Part 7, Sect. 2, para. 94).

Inns of Court might seem to create the closest bonds between the Bench and the Bar, the dividing line between judges and advocates is unequivocally distinct. In some countries, such as France and Holland, judges and advocates constitute virtually two separate professions. Hence the idea of giving busy practising architects statutory authority to assess the merits of other practising architects is untenable, as is the thought that the public might be prepared to pay a number of distinguished architects princely salaries to abandon their practices, and devote their time exclusively to judging the projects of their confrères.

Nevertheless, there is a branch of the architectural profession which might to some extent fulfil this rôle, and which, in fact, frequently *has* been called upon to fulfil it, namely, the teaching staffs of architectural schools. The lists of names of the judges of international competitions during the last decade demonstrate that many, if not most of them, are in fact so selected. Arguments against basing such selection on purely academic qualifications are of course numerous, and some of them are incontestable. But it is worth noting that although few British High Court Judges now start their careers by holding professorships in law (as Sir William Blackstone did two centuries ago) the same prejudice is not so marked in the United States. Oliver Wendell Holmes was by no means the only lawyer to be promoted to the Bench on the strength of a distinguished academic record, though he is still probably the most illustrious.[1]

[1] For a brief but eloquent statement of the influence of academic scholars on judicial decisions, see B. N. Cardozo, *The Growth of the Law* (1966 ed.), pp. 11–16.

CHAPTER TEN

The laws of architecture

Although the art of building, like any other human activity, is subject to various statutory requirements and legal restrictions of the kind which increasingly regulate the complexities of modern life, it should be clear by now that any 'laws of architecture' relevant to this study will be of quite a different order. The question which will here be considered is not: 'what obligations are imposed on architects by the Common Law or by the Legislature?' but rather: 'what obligations are imposed on architects by the nature of architecture itself?' Is an architect absolutely free to create anything whatsoever which comes into his mind, provided it is not expressly forbidden by Building Codes or Zoning Ordinances? Or is he limited in some additional way, and if so, why and how? The answers to these questions are simple only if we are to be satisfied with generalizations which every architect and architectural critic can interpret as he himself sees fit. But to clarify the issue as much as possible, it will be convenient to pretend, for the sake of argument, that all official Building Codes and similar regulations correspond with reasonable fidelity to social realities and to the most up-to-date concepts of optimum stress, ideal methods of analysis, and other scientific data or techniques.[1] In this way, we can omit all reference to those architectural laws which were defined by Viollet-le-Duc as: 'purely mathematical', and concentrate solely on the laws which he defined as belonging to 'abstract art'. These, he asserted,

[1] Cf. J. Burchard and A. Bush-Brown, *The Architecture of America* (1961), p. 6: 'Modern building codes prohibit some interesting architectural possibilities . . .'

154

concern 'proportion, the observance of effects, decoration, and fitness deduced from the requirements, purpose, and available means.'[1]

Disregarding, for the moment, Viollet-le-Duc's interesting use of the term 'abstract art' (probably the earliest published text in which it is to be found) the first question which seems to arise is: if these alleged 'laws of abstract art' really *are* laws, how is the term 'law' to be defined? Here we are confronted immediately with a conundrum which is either so abstruse as to be unanswerable, or so mundane as to be self-evident, but which in any event has baffled legal scholars for centuries. As Hugh Gotein wrote in the 14th edition of the *Encyclopaedia Britannica*, 'Jurisprudence is the name given to those studies, researches and speculations which aim primarily at answering the plain man's question: What is Law? But because the law is a thing of so many aspects, those inquirers who keep that object foremost do not necessarily come quickest at the answer. Indeed the more promising the method pursued, the farther the goal recedes'.[2]

Since the problem has vexed so many jurists, and produced whole libraries of treatises, it is unlikely that a direct answer, however felicitously phrased, will meet with universal legal approval. But some answer must be given here, and it may be that in this context, brevity will be less repugnant to architects than it is to practitioners of the law.

The extent, if any, to which Viollet-le-Duc's notion of 'the laws of architecture' can be interpreted as analogous to legal rules, can only be determined if three juridical aspects of 'the rules of law' are first explained in an architectural context. Otherwise any argument will be irretrievably lost in ambiguities. The first aspect concerns the semantic ambiguity whereby 'laws' can mean either scientifically *observed* uniformities of action or socially *imposed* uniformities of action; the second aspect concerns the linguistic ambiguity whereby 'law' is equivalent both to the French word '*loi*' and the French word '*droit*'; the third aspect concerns the now obsolescent distinction between law and equity. All three distinctions involve, in different ways, the basic distinction between 'rules' and

[1] E. E. Viollet-le-Duc, *Entretiens* (1863), vol. i, p. 488.
[2] *Op. cit.*, vol. xiii, p. 197.

'principles', and hence all must affect our concept of architectural laws.

As regards the first distinction, it is of the utmost significance to the present enquiry that the word 'law' does not seem to have been applied to the observed uniformities of nature until 1668, when the Rev. John Wallis described his astronomical theories as 'Laws of Divine Providence'. Hence his phrase 'the general laws of motion', used in a discourse to the Royal Society in that year, implied that since the observed uniformities of nature were the imposed uniformities of the Almighty, the distinction between rules imposed by an earthly sovereign and rules imposed by the King of Kings was a distinction only of degree, not of kind: 'the Laws of Nature and of Nature's God', as the author of the Declaration of Independence puts it.

The romantic fallacy inherent in the concept of 'natural law', insofar as it implied a 'social contract', was exposed over a century ago by Sir Henry Maine,[1] who demonstrated that, however appealing such a theory might be to the egalitarian temper of the Enlightenment, it was totally unsupported by historical facts. Moreover, even in the natural sciences, where 'natural laws' are simply a convenient way of stating measurable relationships between cause and effect, such 'laws' assert only that the relationships described have never been disproved.[2] Viollet-le-Duc was undoubtedly correct in asserting that the laws of construction are purely mathematical; but the history of structural analysis, even during the last quarter of a century, has demonstrated that these laws of nature are no less vulnerable to radical reinterpretation than the laws of man.

It is unlikely that the term 'laws of nature' came into general use before it was popularized by Voltaire, who used it to describe Newton's *Principia*.[3] Hence it will be apparent why the architectural theorists of the seventeenth and early eighteenth centuries seldom used the word 'rules' and never apparently used the word 'law', despite their nominal servitude to Vitruvian authority. Like Justinian, they spoke of *praecepta*, implying principles exemplified by

---

[1] H. Maine, *Ancient Law* (1906 ed.), pp. 319–56.

[2] Karl R. Popper, *Logic of Scientific Discovery* (1959), esp. pp. 109–11, where he compares the methods of Law and Science.

[3] Voltaire, *Eléments de la Philosophie de Newton* (1738).

precedents.[1] Like Newton, they thought of such laws as *principia*, meaning 'beginnings'; and although we do find occasional references to 'rules' in the architectural text-books of the period (as for example in d'Aviler's preface to his *Cours d'Architecture*) no reference to architectural 'laws' seems to have appeared before J. F. Blondel published his *Cours d'Architecture* in 1771. Even here, the use of the term is confined to the phrase: 'the laws of unity'[2] (where unity is defined as the art of reconciling *firmitas*, *utilitas* and *venustas* without any of these three elements being destroyed) and to a general warning concerning the danger of following the precepts of architecture too rigidly, whereby 'too great an attachment to its laws often prevents an architect from showing any freedom of composition'.[3]

If then we consider the word 'law' in its current usage, as applicable either to a uniformity of action which has been observed (whereby the law *follows* the uniformity), or to a uniformity of action which is *imposed* by authority, it seems clear that when Viollet-le-Duc wrote of the laws of architecture, his idea of laws (being based on biological and mechanical analogies) might more aptly have been referred to as 'principles'. Indeed, in the most eloquent summary which he made of his philosophy, this is precisely the word he does use. 'The architecture of the lay school of the thirteenth century is true', he asserted in his seventh *Entretien*, 'because its *principles* derived from a process of reasoning rather than from a form'; and he went on to make his famous assertion: 'I cannot give you the *rules* imposed on the form because the quality proper to that form is to lend itself to all the necessities of the structure; impose upon me a structural system, and I will find for you naturally the forms which should result from it'.[4] Law, for Viollet-le-Duc, was thus perceived primarily as the source of

---

[1] e.g. the celebrated remark in the *Institutions* (I.i.§3) taken from Ulpian's *Digest* (I.i.10.§1): 'Iuris praecepta sunt haec: honeste vivere, alterum non laedere, suum cuique tribuere'. The second chapter of J. F. Blondel's *Cours d'Architecture* is entitled 'Préceptes de l'Art'. See also in vol. i, pp. 405, 452, 459 etc., and in vol. iii, 'Observation XVI' (p. lxx) which begins: 'La théorie qui a pour base les préceptes de l'Art . . .'

[2] *Op. cit.*, vol. ii, p. 399; vol. iii, p. lxj.

[3] *Ibid.*, vol. iii, p. lxvi ('Observation XII').

[4] E. E. Viollet-le-Duc, *Entretiens* (1863), vol. i, pp. 248–5.

variety[1] (as opposed to artificial uniformity); and in emphasizing the notion of laws as evolutionary, he was following biological theories, rather than legal theories, current in his age.

For the age which saw the birth of architectural Rationalism also saw the reorganization of the French legal system, whereby the '*droit*'[2] of the *ancien régime* (i.e. regional laws based on 'custom') was transmuted and codified by legislators inspired by the Civil Code of the Roman Empire. The essential differences between Common Law and Codified Law are no longer as clear as they used to be, because many ameliorations of the Napoleonic Code during the last century and a half have been effected by processes more characteristic of the Common Law, whilst many ameliorations of the Common Law, during this same period, have been effected by Statutes (i.e. partial codification).[3] But the essential difference between Codified Law and Common Law is the difference between a relatively rigid but concise body of rules established without possibility of variation except by the legislature (i.e. Codified Law) and an adaptable but infinitely complex body of rules which can be modified in accordance with the needs of justice by the judicature (i.e. the Common Law). Admittedly, when the original stipulation of the Napoleonic Code (to the effect that modifications could only be made by the legislature) proved unworkable, its rigours were diminished by recognizing the binding force of certain types of decision of the French Supreme Court (Cour de Cassation). Hence the analysis of cases (known in French as *jurisprudence*—a homonym which is an inevitable source of ambiguity when discussing the philosophy of law) became as essential to Codified Law as it is to the Common Law. Indeed, one authority has pointed out that 'it is

---

[1] *Ibid.*, p. 87: 'Ils (les Grecs) observent la nature et procèdent comme elle; si elle a ses lois, elle est variée à l'infini'.

[2] The word derives from *directum*, meaning in Latin 'straight' or 'straight-forward'.

[3] The modern system of statutory codification is familiar to all; but it is not always realized that, even in the distant past, many statutes were often regarded simply as the codification of common law crimes. Cf. *Rex v. Norris* (96 Eng. Rep. 1189) (1758), where Lord Mansfield called a contractual monopoly a crime, on the grounds that it was a conspiracy, pointing out that statutes forbidding monopolies (such as 21 Jac. I, c. 3) specifically stated that they were consonant to the ancient and fundamental laws of the realm.

common knowledge that articles 1382 and 1383 are too general to tell us much about the French law of civil responsibility, which must be found in the text-books and reports; and on perusing these, we find that the actual solutions of particular cases are not so very different from those of English law'.[1] Nevertheless, it seems likely that such classic English cases as *Rylands v. Fletcher*[2] (discussed in Chapter five) might have proved easier to solve in France, Louisiana[3] or Quebec, where art. 1053 lays down that 'Every person capable of discerning right from wrong is responsible for the damage caused by his fault to another, whether by positive act, imprudence, neglect or want of skill', and where art. 1055 lays down that 'The owner of a building is responsible for the damage caused by its ruin, where it has happened from want of repairs or from an original defect in its construction.'

The important implications of this difference with respect to architectural theory is that 'law', considered as a general body of rules imposed by authority, has been less congenial to architectural theorists during the last two centuries than the idea of 'law' as a general elaboration of principles adaptable to each case by judicial reasoning and interpretation. Thus, if we situate the French nineteenth-century theory of Rationalism in its historical context, we can see not only why Viollet-le-Duc should have preferred the concept of 'law' in its 'organic' sense, but why, a century later, it is now permissible for English-speaking architectural theorists to interpret those same ideals of law in a juridical sense.[4] However alien the spirit of architectural Rationalism might have been to that of the Napoleonic Code, it is perfectly compatible with the philosophy of Anglo-American Common Law as it exists today.

The current philosophy of the Common Law has been admirably expounded by Ronald Dworkin in a thirty-three page article published in 1967 in the *University of Chicago Law Review*.[5] After

[1] *Tulane Law Review*, vol. xxii, p. 118.

[2] 3 H. & C. 774 and L.R. 3 H.L. 330 (1868).

[3] Articles 2315, 2316 & 2322. In the 1952 edition of the Louisiana Civil Code, the 'jurisprudence' on article 2315 is summarized in six hundred and twenty-six sections! (vol. ix, pp. 107–285).

[4] Cf. his *Entretiens* (1863), vol. i, p. 88: 'Certes ils (les Grecs) avaient des lois, mais pour les interpréter et non pour s'y soumettre comme un troupeau de moutons marchant dans le même sillon, sous la houlette du berger'.

[5] *Op. cit.*, vol. 35, pp. 14–46.

challenging the Positivist doctrines expressed by John Austin and elaborated upon by H. L. A. Hart (Dworkin's predecessor in the chair of Jurisprudence at Oxford), he refutes the idea that the Common Law is based on 'rules', and claims that, on the contrary, it is based on 'principles' which are the ultimate source for deciding which rules are to be followed when they conflict, and which rules are to be over-ruled when their strict application would be unjust.

The credibility of Professor Dworkin's lengthy arguments and conclusions is undoubtedly enhanced by the fact that they were succinctly stated in three sentences by Lord Mansfield in *Jones v. Randall*[1] in 1774. 'It is admitted by the counsel for the defendant,' said Lord Mansfield, 'that the contract is against no positive law; it is admitted too, that there is no case to be found which says it is illegal: but it is argued, and rightly, that notwithstanding it is not prohibited by any positive law, nor adjudged by any precedents, yet it may be decided to be so upon *principles*; and the law of England would be a strange science indeed if it were decided upon precedents only. Precedents serve to illustrate principles, and to give them a fixed certainty. But the law of England, which is exclusive of positive law, enacted by statute, depends upon principles; and these principles run through all the cases according as the particular circumstances of each have been found to fall within the one or other of them'.

Professor Dworkin's philosophical position is probably only tenable today because of the gradual fusion of Law and Equity during the nineteenth century,[2] as exemplified by the New York State Code of 1848 and, in England, the Judicature Act of 1873. But in the present context it will be profitable at this stage to keep these two ideas initially distinct, because although it has generally been held (as Lord Chancellor Ellesmere asserted in 1615 in *The Earl of Oxford's Case*)[3] that law and equity have both the same end,

---

[1] 1 Cowper 37, at 39.

[2] The attempt to create a fusion between law and equity in the Anglo-American Common Law seems to have been initiated largely by Lord Mansfield, but it was first achieved in the State of New York in 1846. The beneficial results of this fusion are probably self-evident; but there were in fact a number of bad effects, which are concisely stated by Sir William Holdsworth in his *History of English Law*, vol. xii, p. 547.

[3] Cf. *Halsbury's Laws of England*, vol. xiv, p. 465, note (q).

which is to do right, whereby in some matters equity follows the law implicitly, the evolution of the Common Law concept of judgement has been greatly influenced by the original separation of the two types of Court.

The nature and evolution of Equity have been the subject of many lengthy treatises, so it is unlikely that anyone could summarize adequately the distinction between Law and Equity in the space which the present context reasonably permits. Moreover, the retention by several States in North America of the procedural and jurisdictional distinctions between Law and Equity, which were abolished in England a century ago, makes any generalization virtually impossible. But insofar as the *origin* and fundamental justification of the distinction are concerned (as opposed to the developments which ultimately caused Law and Equity to bear increasing resemblance to one another) 'Equity' can be defined as the means either of limiting the literal interpretation of laws when their strict application would be manifestly unjust, or of providing a remedy for injustice when no legal remedy could be found.[1] Whereas the mediaeval Common Law was generally required to adjudicate strictly upon each transaction as presented by the litigants, Equity, under the influence of Christian notions of *caritas*, insisted upon the *conscientious* obligations of the suitors. It could, for example, compel the specific performance of a contract, where the law would only give damages for the breach of it. Moreover (and this is perhaps the only other essential aspect of the distinction) the administration of Equity was originally based on the doctrine that the merits of each individual case were to be assessed without any reference to previous decisions.[2] The authorities recognized that hard cases made bad law, but they also recognized that, in a few cases of particular hardship, *justitia* required that the law be set aside. Inevitably, however, the lawyers who attended suits in courts of Equity ultimately pleaded their clients' causes by reference to *precedents*. Thus the original freedom to judge every case in Equity solely on the basis of principles of individual fairness was gradually limited in such a way that suits in Equity eventually bore little

[1] This definition is essentially a paraphrase of the relevant entry in Lord Jowitt's *Dictionary of English Law*.
[2] Cf. Blackstone's *Commentaries*, pp. 61–2.

difference from actions in Common Law, except as regards the types of remedy which were sought.

The relevance of these basic distinctions to the theory of architecture will be apparent to anyone familiar with the Rationalist theories of Viollet-le-Duc which, as John Summerson has observed, provide the firmest starting point for any theory of modern architecture in harmony with the conditions of thought prevailing today.[1] When Viollet-le-Duc wrote of laws, he was not concerned with the letter of the law, but with the spirit of the law.[2] It was moral equity rather than legal prescription which constituted the basis of his idea of architectural law; a concept more comparable to the equitable ideals of justice than to the kind of justice achievable by codified rules. Similarly, although Julien Guadet condemned Vitruvian 'rules', he asserted that 'although architecture has no rules, it has laws which cannot be violated with impunity'.[3] Now that all branches of the English Supreme Court are empowered to administer Equity, the distinction has admittedly little practical significance for lawyers; but it has considerable practical significance for architects, whose instinctive distrust of any theory of judgement which claims to be systematic is almost certainly inspired by the misapprehension that the rational interpretation of architectural laws must imply the mechanical application of pre-conceived rules.

If we exclude such eccentricities as Adolf Loos's essay on 'Ornament as Crime',[4] it is obvious, from all that has been written on architectural theory during the last century, that insofar as architectural judgement concerns the relationship of the architect to society, its most relevant equivalent in law is to that branch of the Rights of Property which in Roman Law is termed 'Obligations'. These are nowadays of two kinds: voluntary reciprocal obligations (which usually take the form of 'contracts'), and obligations derived from rights implicit in the structure of society (the non-observance of which the Common Law classifies as Torts).

[1] J. Summerson, *Heavenly Mansions* (1963), p. 158.

[2] E. E. Viollet-le-Duc, *Entretiens* (1863), vol. i, p. 193.

[3] J. Guadet, *Elements et Théorie de l'Architecture* (1904), vol. i, p. 97 and p. 146.

[4] Translation published in: L. Munz and G. Kunstler, *Adolf Loos* (1966), pp. 226-31. (First published in 1908.)

To avoid any misunderstanding at this point, it should be emphasized that these assertions are not intended to suggest that the Law of Obligations is to be regarded as the criterion of architectural excellence, but simply that the techniques which the law uses for adjudicating upon obligations may be useful in indicating the most efficacious way of *judging* the criteria of architectural excellence. These latter criteria will always, in my opinion, be essentially reducible to 'commodity, firmness and delight', however abstrusely these qualities may be re-phrased by translation into the latest pseudo-scientific jargon. And if this is so, the most pressing problem of contemporary architectural criticism must necessarily concern the method of assessing them. The contention here put forward is that, if we keep foremost in our minds the idea that commodity, firmness and delight are indeed *obligations*, our judgement will be more realistic, and hence both more accurate and more tolerant.

The architect's contractual obligations are easy enough to enumerate with respect to any particular design, since they require only that he satisfies his client. The architect's environmental obligations to society are far more difficult to establish, since they often involve factors which are either impossible to ascertain in advance, or so impermanent as to render any deep concern with them futile. But once the architect's task is accepted as essentially a social obligation, it is clear that, insofar as he also has obligations towards himself, these are the professional obligations of moral integrity, which differ fundamentally from the moral duties of contemporary painters and sculptors, who are under no obligation to a client, and whose creations are rarely intended for any specific location.

The main difficulty in defining an architect's obligations to society involves a problem where legal analogies would seem, at first sight, to provide the least assistance, namely the distinction between minimum and optimum obligations. The laws of God require us to love our neighbour; but the laws of man only require that we do him no injury, and there is no law on earth which can compel a man to be a public benefactor, except by confiscating his property and instructing the State to perform these benefactions on his behalf. The machinery of Equity can issue an injunction, preventing a man from doing his neighbour an injury. The machinery of law can oblige a man to compensate his neighbour for any injury he may have inflicted, even unwittingly.[1] Yet despite the persuasive writings of Richard Neutra,[2] environmental injury is as difficult to define legally as any other kind of injury, and in the whole law of Torts there are few injuries more difficult to prove than those which are essentially emotional.[3]

Nevertheless, Richard Neutra's determination to demonstrate the positive injury inflicted by poorly designed environments probably indicates the soundest approach to this vexing problem. We all admire benevolence. We are all prepared to support demands for social benevolence, especially if someone else will be made to pay for it. But in the last resort, judgements in architecture, as in law, must be with respect to minimum obligations rather than optimum obligations, and it is clearly the professional duty of every architect to do his best to minimize the gap.

At this point, exasperated aesthetes may be goaded into an attempt to refute the whole notion of a legal analogy of judgement by bringing jurisprudential arguments to their support. 'There is at least one eminent legal scholar', they may say, 'who specifically asserts the incompatibility of legal and aesthetic criteria. In his book, *The Morality of Law*, Professor Lon Fuller shows that much of the confusion about the relationship between morality and law results from a failure to distinguish between "duty" and "aspiration". In a section entitled "The Vocabulary of Morals and the Two Moralities", he criticizes the term "value judgement" on the grounds that persons who couple these two terms (instead of referring more correctly to "the *perception* of value") are guilty of suggesting not a striving towards perfection, but a conclusion about obligations. Thus, he says, a subjectivism appropriate to the higher reaches of human aspiration spreads itself through the whole language of moral

[1] The justification for imposing 'absolute liability' for injury is one of the more contentious problems of the law of Torts, but there are many situations, both in the Common Law and in the Napoleonic Code, where absolute liability is held to exist.

[2] R. Neutra, *Survival through Design* (1954).

[3] The problem as to whether, or in what circumstances, emotional injury is actionable in the absence of physical injury, constitutes another complex controversy of the modern law of Torts.

discourse and we are easily led to the absurd conclusion that obligations obviously essential for social living rest on some essentially ineffable preference. "The morality of aspiration", Professor Fuller asserts, "shows its close affinity with aesthetics. When we seek to comprehend some new form of artistic expression, our effort —if it is well-informed—will direct itself at once to the purpose pursued by the artist . . . Norman T. Newton has demonstrated, in his book, *An Approach to Design*, how aesthetic judgements of architecture can be distorted by the effort to find some verbal formula that will seem to justify the judgement passed".'[1]

These assertions, if truly applicable to architecture, would undoubtedly be fatal to the arguments so far put forward. But is Professor Fuller indeed correct in implying that what architects call 'judgements' are really only aesthetic perceptions which have nothing to do with those obligations which are essential for social living? Even if it is true that architectural criticism and decision-making can only be concerned with 'the purpose pursued by the artist', the most respected architects today would certainly contend (however hypocritically) that the purpose they are pursuing *is* concerned primarily with the obligations essential for social living. Hence the only real element of controversy is thus reduced to the interpretation of the word 'essential'. Professor Fuller naturally uses it in its legal sense, as meaning 'minimum'. Indeed, one of Walter Gropius's essays on 'Minimal Housing' was published in a magazine called *Die Justiz*.[2] Most architects—especially the more idealistic architects—would interpret it as meaning 'optimum'; but once we accept the idea that architectural criticism is not primarily concerned with the artist's own private purpose but with his obligations towards society, the whole problem appears in its proper perspective. Decisions as to where to draw the dividing line between minimum and optimum are admittedly difficult; but once they are perceived as being at the very root of architectural criticism, the whole theory of architecture is removed from the artificial celestial heights of visual and symbolic euphory to the more commonplace but more realistic plane of social co-existence. For whatever may be the distinctions between minimum obligations and optimum obligations;

[1] *Op. cit.* (Yale University Press, 1964), pp. 13–14.
[2] Cf. bibliography in J. M. Fitch, *Walter Gropius* (1960), p. 121.

whatever may be the sacrifices necessary to achieve a viable compromise; it is clear that such distinctions and adjustments are as dependent on the circumstances of the case, and on the principles of justice, as any decision in a court of law. And it is this fact which, I contend, has hitherto vitiated so much architectural criticism. Ideals are as necessary to architecture as they are to law. But the continued glorification of Greek temples as the quintessence of architectural perfection is but one symptom of the persistent incapacity of so many architectural theorists to see why the shackles increasingly imposed on an architect's imagination in recent years by the nature and location of the site, by economic restrictions, or by the limitations of time and resources, cannot be brushed aside as irrelevant to the final assessment. An architect's obligations to twentieth-century society can no longer be based on conjectural romantic interpretations of Antique or Mediaeval life. However much the Parthenon may have infused a sense of purpose into those who dwelt in the Periclean hovels which originally surrounded the Acropolis; however spiritually satisfying the sight of St. Nicaise may have been to those living in the mediaeval slums of Rheims, the fact remains that even if we could actually see these buildings in their entirety, and fully comprehend the emotions of these remote peoples for whom they were built, those emotions would have little relevance to architectural criticism today.

For too long, the history of architecture (despite the admirable examples set by such scholars as Eduard Sekler and Bruno Zevi) has been little more than a history of tourist attractions, of buildings and ruins which are valued essentially in terms of fleeting visits and coloured postcards. The fact that Robert and Denise Venturi evidently regard Las Vegas as the most significant contemporary urban conglomeration in North America[1] demonstrates only too clearly how tenaciously this attitude persists. For if we ask ourselves how characteristic of modern society were the *obligations* of those who designed Las Vegas, either as regards their obligations to their clients or their obligations to the general public, we can see that such obligations are on a par with those which inspired the

[1] The results of a research project conducted at Las Vegas by Professor and Mrs. Robert Venturi was the subject of a lengthy and well-publicized seminar at the Yale School of Architecture on 10 January 1969.

166

creation of all the exhibition pavilions which figure so prominently in histories of modern architecture. In other words, although the architectural influence of such prototypes may well have been enormously beneficial, as elements of a social environment they offer *in themselves* very limited criteria on which architectural judgement can realistically be based.

To avoid misunderstanding, it must be emphasized that the foregoing remarks are in no way intended to denigrate all buildings implied by the term 'tourist attractions'. On the contrary, there are many advantages to be gained from visiting a sequence of examples of this building-type; and it would be hard to find any buildings more inspiring than the Rococo pilgrimage-churches in the area stretching from Franconia to Lake Constance and beyond (including Le Corbusier's church at Ronchamp). But the meaningful character of such a study must reside precisely in the fact that these buildings *were* specifically designed to be visited by pilgrims, and hence their character can only be fully appreciated if they are seen as they were intended to be seen, namely as sacred visiting-places set prominently in the countryside.

The nature of this problem was well understood by Vincent Scully, and it is for this reason that *The Earth, The Temple and the Gods* is probably the greatest book on Greek architecture to be published in the last hundred years. But few of our more eminent art-historians have emulated Professor Scully by studying religious shrines primarily in accordance with their function. One of the best of such analyses is that of the church of the Vierzehnheiligen given by Nikolaus Pevsner in his *Outline of European Architecture*. But even he was unable to resist singling it out as an example of 'architects' architecture', and then contradicting this assertion by commenting on the pleasure it gives to 'rustic worshippers'[1] (as compared presumably to urban atheists).

Sigfried Giedion treats the church of the Vierzehnheiligen simply as a development of Italian Baroque architecture, which, he asserts, 'does not continue the complicated constructional treatment of Guarini's domes, nor has it Borromini's plastic intensity'.[2] Unlike Professor Pevsner, he shows no comprehension of the *programmatic*

[1] 1963 paperback ed., pp. 267–71.
[2] S. Giedion, *Space, Time and Architecture* (1967 ed.), p. 133.

reason for avoiding a dome at the crossing, so as to place the emphasis over the shrine, which is in the nave;[1] and he concludes his analysis by saying, somewhat inconsequentially, that 'it should perhaps be remembered that these magnificent churches were created just at the time when the Protestant workmen of Birmingham and Manchester were inventing their first cotton-spinning machine'.[2]

Sigfried Giedion may well be right in asserting that 'the principal force at work in this church is not pre-eminently architecture—as in the constructions of Borromini and Guarini—but rather a magnificent balance between architecture, sculpture and painting', and hence 'a most effective unification of all the arts'.[3] But the assertion provides an unwitting but eloquent commentary on his reluctance to discuss the merits of Notre Dame du Haut at Ronchamp. His unusual decision to postpone commenting on one of Le Corbusier's most celebrated buildings was prompted, he tells us, by the conviction that 'we have to wait before it is possible to evaluate the complete significance of Le Corbusier's work. We need historical perspective in order to make a final assessment of his buildings'.[4] But anyone who visits both the Vierzehnheiligen church and the Ronchamp chapel within the same week will have little difficulty in evaluating both buildings reciprocally, provided he has the privilege of witnessing a throng of Bavarian villagers marching in procession round the shrine of the Vierzehnheiligen in the train of their brass band, and has also sat in the Ronchamp chapel whilst a group of youthful pilgrims were singing an unaccompanied polyphonic hymn in honour of the Virgin Mary.

There is no need to wait until these buildings become ruins, or until the religious rites connected with them are no longer ascertainable, before trying to evaluate their architectural merits. But it will be obvious that the criteria for judging such buildings must be as untypical as the criteria for judging Las Vegas, and that a non-Catholic must find as much difficulty in comprehending the signifi-

[1] The whole significance of the position of the dome of St. Peter's, Rome, is of course that it was centred on the saint's shrine. In the Paris Panthéon, the central dome was similarly designed by Soufflot to indicate the intended position of the shrine of St. Geneviève.
[2] S. Giedion, *Space, Time and Architecture* (1967 ed.), p. 133.
[3] *Ibid.*, p. 133.   [4] *Ibid.*, p. 554.

cance of the church of the Vierzehnheiligen as an impecunious
student would find in comprehending the real meaning of the Las
Vegas strip. Yet whereas architects have long been aware that the
social merits of mass-housing can best be assessed by the residents,
they seem less ready to accept the view that the merits of a theatre
can best be assessed by theatre-goers, or that the merits of a courtroom can best be assessed by judges, advocates, and those who
know what it is like to be a litigant, a witness or a juror.

The genius of some of our greatest judges was due to their
perception that any new field of law can only be valid if those
directly involved are given a voice in formulating judgement upon
it. Lord Mansfield's right to the title of 'the father of modern Contract Law' is based on his awareness that, in the last resort, the just
settlement of the new type of commercial disputes which emerged
in the mid-eighteenth century could only be achieved after con-
sultation with the merchants most familiar with the type of obligations involved. For this purpose he even instituted 'special juries'.
Relatively little attention is given to this fact by Sir William
Holdsworth; but Cecil Fifoot convincingly suggests that it was
crucial to Lord Mansfield's success, and quotes, for example, his
remark in *Hamilton v. Mendes* (1761)[1] to the effect that the daily
negotiations and property of merchants ought not to depend upon
subtleties and niceties, but upon rules easily learned and easily
retained, because they are the dictates of common sense, drawn from
the truth of the case.[2] The phrase 'the dictates of common sense
drawn from the truth of the case' not only illustrates how Lord
Mansfield anticipated the fusion of law and equity by more than a
century, but also illustrates in what sense the Common Law, as
practised today, relates both in its achievements and its dilemmas to
the problems confronting those obliged to make judgements about
architecture.

Nevertheless, just as Lord Mansfield made clear to the merchants
that, in the last resort, it was he, a lawyer, who would ultimately
have the duty of deciding points of law, so, in the last resort, it must
be the architect who decides points of architecture. Whatever the
merits of Street's project for the Law Courts competition—as
compared with Barry's—might have been, judicial witticisms about

[1] 2 Burrow, at 1214.   [2] C. H. S. Fifoot, *Lord Mansfield* (1936), p. 85.

the inadequacies of the Royal Courts of Justice which have enlivened dull cases during the last hundred years suggest that the competition judges—composed mainly of politicians—might have been wise to accept their architectural advisers' assessment concerning the superiority of Barry's plan. Though in both architectural competitions and litigation, justice must be manifestly seen to be done, architectural judgement, like legal judgement, is in the last resort a matter for experts. It is often as hard for a layman to interpret architectural draftsmanship as it is for him to interpret legal draftsmanship; but for this very reason he must accept the fact that real justice is often based on technicalities which, though incomprehensible to him, are quite apparent to those of good faith trained in the profession.

CHAPTER ELEVEN

Affinities between architectural and legal judgement

The affinity between the judicial criteria of architecture and law was first noted by Professor Karl Llewellyn, a leading authority on the nature of the judicial process. In an article published in 1940 in the *University of Chicago Law Review*, he wrote: 'The aesthetic phase of a legal system is cognate to architecture as it is not, for instance, to painting, and as it rather rarely is to music. Architecture and engineering strike most closely home—perhaps because both look so directly and so inescapably to use'.[1] It may be useful, therefore, to enumerate briefly certain aspects of legal judgement which seem to have a close affinity with architectural judgement, yet far less affinity with the current 'aesthetic' criteria of art criticism.

First, there is the concept of 'territorial jurisdiction' or, to use the better-known corollary of this concept, the legal problem of 'the conflict of laws'. The history of legal institutions makes abundantly clear that the validity of laws has usually been closely associated with specific localities, whereby the modern notion of International Law is as alien to the theory of the Common Law as the notion of an International Style is alien to the Rationalist theory of architecture.[2]

[1] K. N. Llewellyn, 'On the Good, the True, the Beautiful in Law' (1942), *University of Chicago Law Review*, vol. ix, p. 230.

[2] The term 'International Style', invented by Henry-Russell Hitchcock and Philip Johnson in 1932, with reference to the architecture of the previous decade, is so closely associated with their famous book that one can easily overlook the fact that the *idea* of an 'International Style' was a product of the Renaissance. In fact, the so-called 'battle of the styles' might be more realistically and

In political confederations (where individual states, each with its own judicature, legislature and constitution, are politically subordinate to a federal government and a federal constitution), conflicts of law frequently affect dealings between ordinary citizens. Elsewhere, such conflicts are usually limited to problems of international trade, and they are quite exceptional in countries where jurisdictions are coextensive with national boundaries.[1]

If we consider the notion of territorial sovereignty as it affects architecture, and then as it affects *objets d'art*, it seems clear (or at any rate, it seemed clear to nineteenth-century Rationalists) that the idea of a *genius loci* must have a more formative influence on the former than on the latter. Although both architecture and the other 'Fine Arts' have emerged from the social, topographical and climatic environments which have nourished them, *objets d'art* are, by their physical nature (particularly their smallness) transportable and transposable, whereby a modern Japanese vase in a European house seems no more incongruous than a modern European bracelet on an oriental wrist. In architecture, however, it is a noticeable fact that whenever exotic styles have been transplanted, they have been adapted to their new environmental conditions.

Furthermore, this *adaptation* of exotic tectonic forms is particularly pertinent to any analogy between architecture and law. Though the general improvements to English law made by Lord Mansfield were not a little due to his early mastery of Roman law (just as his special contribution to mercantile law was facilitated by his familiarity with the then novel studies in International law) these improvements were due to the rational interpolation of alien juridical elements whenever they seemed congruous; and it would

---

meaningfully interpreted as an attempt to refute the concept of an 'International Style', rather than as a conflict between 'Gothicists' and 'Classicists'. This was certainly the essence of the philosophical position taken by Viollet-le-Duc and James Fergusson.

[1] One of the most fascinating lawsuits involving this problem was *The Duke of Brunswick v. The King of Hanover* (6 Beavan 1), argued in Chancery in 1844, when the exiled Duke of Brunswick was able to sue the King of Hanover (i.e. Queen Victoria's uncle, who had become King of Hanover on the death of William IV) on the grounds that, as descendants of the Electress Sophia, they were both British subjects by virtue of the statute 4 Ann, c. 4!

never have occurred to Lord Mansfield to abandon the basic law of England or Scotland in favour of some extraneous system simply because of its titillating novelty. And so it has been in the recent history of architecture. For example, those elements of traditional Japanese timber architecture which suggested rational means of exploiting the newest developments in steel and glass technology are now a part of our own architecture; but the kind of building represented by the Royal Pavilion at Brighton is best regarded as an eccentricity, rather than as a 'key monument'[1] of the age in which it was built.

Secondly, there is the concept of 'social acceptability', whereby laws are virtually unenforceable unless acceptable to the general public. Obnoxious statutes will either become dead letters or will be formally repealed. Obnoxious procedural rules will either be abandoned, revised, or transmuted into legal fictions. Obnoxious judgements will either be over-ruled on appeal, or deprived by statute of their binding force as precedents.

Whether or not social acceptability is a criterion of contemporary architecture is perhaps debatable; but it is certainly not a criterion of modern painting and sculpture. On the contrary, the less acceptable such works are to the masses, the more respected they are by the *cognoscenti*. Ever since the French Revolution, the incomprehension of the bourgeoisie has, among painters and sculptors, been regarded as the supreme evidence of artistic genius; and the mystique of aristocratic connoisseurship seems so persistent that even in this democratic age, nothing condemns a novel painting or novel work of sculpture so devastatingly as immediate popular acclaim.

Thirdly, the concept of law is intimately associated with social stability, whereby it is recognized that ordinary citizens cannot be expected to know, understand and obey the law if it is constantly changing. The corollary of this doctrine is that the law should only be modified if the needs of society make such changes essential; and indeed, one of the dilemmas of the legal system is that its powerful mechanism for maintaining stability frequently resists every attempt made to adjust its equilibrium when the ballast of precedents needs to be moved.

[1] See H. A. Millon, *Key Monuments of the History of Architecture* (New York, n.d.).

In the history of the last two centuries, few phenomena are more fascinating than the interplay of legal permanence and legal change. The latter is of course well documented; but less attention has been given to the element of permanence, which is nowhere better exemplified than in the United States. One might have thought, for example, that once having successfully repudiated British sovereignty, and established a new Constitution, the liberated colonists would have had no other thought than the construction of a legal system more in conformity with their new political and social ideals. But in fact the very opposite occurred. So insistent were the State Courts on observing the traditional legal precedents (except of course as regards the Treaty Rights of the defeated Loyalists) that no one reading American law reports of the period 1770 to 1810 would ever suspect, from the texts, that a revolution had occurred. The courts not only applied British precedents established in England prior to 1776; they continued to rely on British precedents long after the political independence of the United States had been acknowledged;[1] and although such decisions were no longer regarded as binding in the strict sense, it is still common to find British decisions cited in United States Courts of Appeal, just as it is common to find prominent attention given to American decisions by the House of Lords.[2]

[1] A good example is *Leonard v. Vredenburgh* (6 Johns. 28), decided by the New York Supreme Court in 1811. When delivering the opinion of the court, Chief Justice Kent stated: 'The case appeared to me then (i.e. at the original trial) to be governed by the decision in *Wain v. Warlters* (5 East 10), which was recognized by this court in *Sears v. Brink* (3 Johns. 210)'. *Wain v. Warlters* was an English case decided in 1804, and *Sears v. Brink* was decided in 1808. In justification of the court's decision to allow this appeal, Chief Justice Kent relied on *Stadt v. Lill*, an English case decided in the Court of King's Bench in 1808 (9 East 348).

[2] The relationship was felicitously expressed by Lord Buckmaster in 1932 in the leading case of *Donaghue v. Stevenson* (1932 A.C. at 576): 'One further case mentioned in argument may be referred to, certainly not by way of authority, but to gain assistance by considering how similar cases are dealt with by eminent judges of the United States. That such cases can have no close application and no authority is clear, for though the source of the law in the two countries may be the same, its current may well flow in different channels. The case referred to is that of *Thomas v. Winchester* (6 N.Y. 397) (1852) . . . In another case of *MacPherson v. Buick Motor Co.* (217 N.Y. 382), where a manufacturer of a defective motor-car was held liable for damages at the instance of a third party,

Whether or not a stable architectural environment is as important as a stable legal environment will be considered later; but it is clear that the concept of social stability is totally irrelevant to contemporary theories of the Fine Arts outside the Soviet Union. In Western Europe and America, the criteria of painting and sculpture necessarily give prime consideration to *originality* and *individuality*, whereby even in the contemporary attitude towards symbolism (with which several modern theories of architecture are associated), there is a complete rejection of the notion that symbolic forms are, by their nature, essentially reliant on some fixed association of ideas.

It has long been debated whether or not our attitude towards originality and individuality in architecture should be similar to that of painters and sculptors. But even the most passionate devotee of architectural originality must find it difficult to accept the implications of the view expressed by Peter Moro, in his assessment of the Queen Elizabeth Hall in London, that 'in matters connected with architecture the layman seems easily irritated by the unfamiliar, and his qualitative judgement is often confused when confronted with a new experience . . . Only buildings with architectural significance seem to invite public scorn and abuse.'[1] What is bewildering about this remark is not its allegation about the layman's scorn of significant new architecture, but Mr. Moro's scorn of the layman's qualitative judgement. Perhaps he is right in asserting that 'immediate public acclaim often is a sign of lack of architectural significance' in a building;[2] but if so, architecture must be a very curious profession indeed. Immediate public acclaim is seldom a sign that a new law, or a new surgical operation, lacks significance; and whilst it may possibly be true that the immediate public acclaim of painting and sculpture is nowadays a sign of lack of artistic significance, it was not so in the late middle ages and early Renaissance when (if we are to believe Vasari's account of the

---

the learned judge appears to base his judgement on the view that a motor-car might reasonably be regarded as a dangerous article'. The second of these New York cases was one of Judge Cardozo's more famous judicial triumphs; and Cardozo himself, in the course of this opinion, cited at length the opinion of the Master of the Rolls in *Heaven v. Pender* (1883, 11 Q.B.D. 503 C.A.).

[1] *R.I.B.A. Journal*, June 1968, p. 252.   [2] *Ibid.*

Madonna of the Rucellai chapel at S. Maria Novella): 'The people of that day considered this work so marvellous that they carried it to the church from Cimabue's house in a stately procession with great rejoicing and blowing of trumpets'.[1]

But perhaps the legal concept of social stability is more relevant to urban design than to the design of individual public buildings. Admittedly it is difficult, in the age of the bulldozer, to attach much importance to the maintenance of a stable environment, and to regard environmental stability as a fundamental architectural quality which should only be modified radically when absolutely necessary; but recent critics of mid-century town-planning theories now lay increasing emphasis on the importance of continuity in urban character, and are clearly becoming more and more disillusioned with the town-planning techniques which Edmund Bacon has aptly described as 'painting on a clean canvas'.[2] In the 1969 Discourse to the Royal Institute of British Architects, Vincent Scully was particularly bitter about the changes contemplated at Dayton, Ohio, as it now stands. 'Its Redevelopment Agency', Professor Scully commented, 'would like to see it bombed out, with no streets, no people, nothing left but a kind of amusement park for suburbanites on wheels. Cataclysmic, automotive and suburban, such are the principles which have formed the architectural concept here'.[3]

In law, there is another concept, closely related to the concept just described, which may be termed 'historical continuity', and which postulates that revolutionary principles should never be introduced if it is possible to adapt existing principles to a new purpose. One of the most striking examples of how this works in practice is the development of law in relationship to new mechanical inventions. The developments in commerce which resulted from the

[1] Vasari, *Lives* (Everyman ed.), vol. i, p. 25. Art-historical research has demonstrated fairly conclusively (by reference to the State Archives in Florence) that the painter commissioned to paint the Rucellai Madonna was the Siennese artist Duccio, and not Vasari's compatriot Cimabue. Nevertheless, it has frequently been pointed out that Vasari's apocryphal anecdotes often give a clearer indication of the artistic theory of his *own* age than any biographical 'facts' he catalogues.

[2] E. Bacon, *Design of Cities* (1967), p. 219.

[3] V. Scully, 'A Search for Principle between Two Wars', *R.I.B.A. Journal*, June 1969, p. 240.

Industrial Revolution and from the invention of railroads, auto-mobiles and aircraft, all raised legal problems which at first seemed incapable of solution by laws based historically on feudal tenure. But although it proved necessary, in a few instances, to make radical changes to the law by legislative action, such devices were, in general, only used as a last resort, and the necessary adjustments were usually accomplished by the skilful adaptation of existing precedents.

Similarly, though present-day architectural historians generally argue that the true pioneers of reinforced concrete architecture were those who immediately abandoned all traditional masonry forms, Auguste Perret may well be justified by later historians for limiting his inventiveness to such modifications as were required by the new constructional techniques. But such arguments are of less impor-tance than the fact that this type of controversy does not even have a place in controversies about painting and sculpture, where historical continuity is seen only in terms of outmoded 'styles' struggling in vain against the *Zeitgeist*. Art-historical scholarship still indulges with undiminished enthusiasm in the hunt for pre-cedents, but only to prove that there is nothing new under the sun. Practising painters and sculptors react vigorously to such impugn-ments of their creativity, and it is more than likely that the modern craze for eccentricity in the plastic arts is simply the frustrated artist's frantic attempts to beat *kunstwissenschaft* at its own game.

The fifth concept is that of 'functional conformity', by which I mean that a law is, for all practical purposes, a dead letter unless it fulfils some practical use. This idea, which has already been referred to in a different context, is generally accepted by practising architects, though it tends to be blurred by architectural historians, who are so used to studying buildings in terms of the function for which they were originally constructed that they seldom pay atten-tion to the extent to which these functions have now changed. But the distinction was very apparent to architectural historians of the nineteenth century, who became so irritated by the adoption of obsolete prototypes for new buildings that they sometimes referred to them all as 'stuffed specimens'.[1]

[1] J. Fergusson, *An historical inquiry into the True Principles of Beauty in Art, more especially with reference to Architecture* (1849), p. 403.

Such views are seldom forcefully held today, since, with the rehabilitation of Victorian architecture (and hence its newly acquired respectability as a source of historical monuments), the architectural predilection for putting new wine into old bottles, criticized by such authors as James Fergusson, is now no longer condemned. Whether or not Fergusson was right is still debatable; but one advantage accruing from this change of attitude is that architects can now have more sympathy with the juridical concept of a 'legal fiction', and see how this relates to the history of architectural development. A legal fiction is simply an obsolete legal form adapted to a new and immediate practical purpose, just as a 'stuffed specimen' was also an obsolete architectural form adapted, however ineptly, to new architectural needs. Eventually the more ludicrous legal fictions were abolished by radically new statutes, in the same way that the more ludicrous architectural fictions were abolished by radically new tectonic shapes. But just as the new procedural forms introduced by the Judicature Act of 1873 are (despite subsequent legislative revisions) occasionally adapted to functions for which they were never intended, so many of the forms introduced by the Pioneers of the Modern Movement are now used for purposes which their original inventors could never have anticipated.

Moral scruples as to the extent to which old architectural forms and spaces can legitimately be adapted to novel uses are easy to dispel, now that so many distinguished modern buildings have been converted to serve purposes for which they were never originally designed; but whatever the merits or demerits of either legal fictions or architectural fictions, it is clear that although such scruples may have some significance to architects and lawyers, their relevance to contemporary painting and sculpture is far less apparent. 'The Fine Arts', by popular definition, serve no material function. They may fulfil an invaluable social purpose by expressing or stimulating specific emotions; but this subtle function is so easily disregarded, that no museum director would see anything ludicrous, or scandalous, in juxtaposing a mid-eighteenth-century altarpiece with Boucher's painting of *Vénus à sa toilette* (now in the Metropolitan Museum in New York, but originally commissioned for Madame de Pompadour's bathroom). Indeed, with the growth of abstract art, the original communicative function of all paintings, whether representational or not, has tended to be subordinated to their decorative qualities. In art galleries, the size, chronological sequence, or stylistic classification of the canvases may have some influence on their arrangement; but this is merely dictated by the needs of students of Art History. The type of moral scruple which faces architects and lawyers does not even suggest itself.

The sixth concept which relates architectural judgement to legal judgement, but has no place in the idea of judgement as it concerns painting or sculpture, is the notion that all judgement must have a rational basis which can be intelligibly explained. The need for rational judgements in law—however the word 'rational' may be precisely defined—is sufficiently obvious to require no further comment at this stage. The need for rational architectural judgement is a topic which is at least debatable. But the need for rational judgement with respect to works of painting and sculpture is not (according to Gilbert and Kuhn's *History of Aesthetics*) recognized by any modern theory of aesthetics. The Semiotic school, following the lead given by Benedetto Croce, situates the critical faculty 'in that obscure middle realm between immediate biological experience of the human animal and the thinner air of reason'.[1] The Semanticists, who are also classified by philosophers as belonging to the 'rational' school, only assert that every person is entitled to find aesthetic excellence wherever his own thoughts lead.[2] No other aesthetic theories even apparently claim to be 'rationalist'.

It may of course be argued that philosophical rejections of 'rationalism' in theories of aesthetics do not prove that contemporary painters and sculptors create irrationally, or even that they think that they create irrationally. Indeed, numerous examples could doubtless be given of non-representational painters and sculptors who spend months of anxious thought deciding intellectually the correct place for each stroke of their palette-knife, or each blast of their welding-torch. But in this present context, the issue is not so much whether an artist or connoisseur can justify rationally the relative merits of works of art, but whether the distinction between art and non-art is capable of being rationally defined in the way that a judge decides what is, and what is not, the law. It is true that when

[1] K. Gilbert & H. Kuhn, *A History of Aesthetics* (1954), p. 563.
[2] *Ibid.*, p. 566.

painters or sculptors compete for prizes or commissions, the judges of the competition often use elaborate verbal explanations to justify their choice; but only because it is tacitly assumed that all the entries are really works of art of some form or another; and subsequent announcements by a prize-winner that his entry was simply the top of his work-bench, or had been created by tying a paintbrush to a donkey's tail, are unlikely to affect the judges' decision, or even enrage the unsuccessful competitors.

The problem of defining a work of art is well exemplified by the famous case of *Brancusi v. United States*[1] which was tried in 1928 before three judges of the United States Customs Court. In 1926 Brancusi had despatched a piece of abstract sculpture in polished metal, entitled 'Bird in Space' [Fig. XXIV], to an American purchaser, after having declared it to be a work of art (and thus entitled to duty-free entry). But the New York customs officers asserted that, on the contrary, it was not a work of art, and they accused Brancusi of trying to smuggle bronze into the United States in the form of a 'manufactured metal object' which, as such, was liable to 40 per cent duty; and they assessed this on the basis of the market value of the raw metal (i.e. $210.00 as opposed to the $600.00 which Brancusi declared to be its value as a work of art).

Considerable testimony was produced by Brancusi, whose witnesses included one practising sculptor (Jacob Epstein), the Director of the Brooklyn Art Museum, and a number of art critics. The defendant's witnesses comprised two practising sculptors, R. J. Aiken and T. H. Jones, who 'pronounced the importation to be neither a work of art nor sculpture'. But the written opinion of Mr. Justice Waite stated that 'there is no question in the mind of the Court but that the man who produced this importation is a professional sculptor',[2] and he insisted that 'while some difficulty might be encountered in associating it with a bird, it is nevertheless

[1] 54 T.D. 428, and C. Giedion-Welcker, *Brancusi* (1959), pp. 212–13.
[2] Note that Mr. Justice Waite describes Brancusi as a '*professional*' sculptor. In view of the decisions and quotations cited in Chapter eight, it is by no means certain that Brancusi would have been regarded as practising a 'profession' in accordance with the New York Income-Tax Laws, or in accordance with those sociological definitions which rely on membership of 'Professional Associations' as an essential feature of professionalism.

pleasing to look at and highly ornamental'. Judgement was therefore entered for the plaintiff.

Mr. Justice Waite's *ratio decidendi* is not included in standard anthologies on abstract art; nor do Dictionaries of the Fine Arts ever include, among their art-historical definitions, section 1704 of the United States Tariff Act of 1922, which specifies that the term 'work of art' shall be understood as *excluding* any article of utility. But in combination, these seem to offer a reasonable definition of what most laymen probably understand by a 'work of art', and would seem to suggest convincing reasons for refusing to accept Norman Shaw's assertion that 'We hold that the art of architecture is on precisely the same footing as painting and sculpture'.[1]

The final, and most important legal concept to be considered in this present context is the notion of dissent. The dissenting opinions of courts of appeal would seem to have little relevance to problems of architectural judgement, since although in architectural competitions, dissenting opinions are occasionally written and even published (as for example in the Toronto City Hall Competition), the judges tend to think of themselves as 'juries', and hence bound by the tradition that a jury's final decision must be terse and unanimous. But even if we concentrate on the more controversial competitions, in which dissenting opinions have been published, we can immediately see a striking difference between judicial dissent in law and judicial dissent in architecture which, I would contend, results from the distortion of architectural criteria by the misguided, though subconscious, influence of the criteria of 'The Fine Arts'.

The difference is this: that whereas in law it is generally accepted that the minority decision is wrong, in architecture the presumption seems to be that it must be right. As an example, let us take the famous competition for the League of Nations Headquarters. Henry Russell Hitchcock tells us in *Architecture, Nineteenth and Twentieth Centuries* (which is surely the most objective book of its kind ever written) that 'Le Corbusier's project for the Palace for the League of Nations came very close to winning the competition of 1927. Moreover, the totally undistinguished scheme jointly produced by the elderly Frenchman P. H. Nénot and various other architects from several different countries eventually executed in Geneva

[1] *Architecture, a Profession or an Art?* (1892), p. 9.

never received the attention or the flattery of world-wide emulation and imitation which Le Corbusier's project did'.[1] Le Corbusier tells us in his *Oeuvre Complète 1910–1929* that the executed building was 'directly inspired by the design of MM. Le Corbusier and Pierre Jeanneret', and that they took legal steps to vindicate their rights 'in the form of a printed document of thirty-six pages drawn up on the advice of Maître Prudhomme, Professor of the Faculty of Law at the Sorbonne'.[2] Sigfried Giedion (who, it will be remembered, had been appointed secretary of C.I.A.M. by Le Corbusier when that organization was founded in 1928) tells us in *Space, Time and Architecture* that the design 'remained a project', though he insists that among the three hundred and thirty seven projects[3] submitted for the competition, only one—the work of Le Corbusier and Pierre Jeanneret—'was peculiarly important and significant[4] . . . The outstanding fact about the scheme submitted by Le Corbusier and Jeanneret is that they found the most compact and best-conceived solution to these needs[5] . . . In the requirements of the Secretariat simply as an office building, in the need for making it possible to hear from every bench in the Grande Salle, in the traffic problems that arose at General Sessions—in the needs of *contemporary* life that is—Le Corbusier and Jeanneret found incentives to artistic creation. But it was exactly those requirements which proved stumbling blocks to the architects who adopted the familiar monumental routine. *As a consequence there is no need to consider which of these compositions was, as a whole, the best—for all alike were incapable of functioning'.*[6]

Giedion then continues: 'All the architectural fashions of the late nineteenth century are represented, together with all the experimental developments in contemporary architecture[7] . . . from various countries the most radical experimentalists sent plans—not always ripe for execution—of structures imbued with Russian constructivism or of dream fantasies in glass . . . In fact, the state of architecture in each of the European countries appeared in its choice

[1] *Op. cit.* (1958), p. 373.   [2] *Op. cit.*, p. 161.

[3] *Ibid.*, Le Corbusier points out that if the drawings had been placed end to end, they would have extended for eight miles!

[4] *Op. cit.* (1941), p. 417.

[5] *Ibid.*, p. 418.   [6] *Ibid.*, p. 421.   [7] *Ibid.*, p. 422.

of a distinguished man to represent it on the jury . . . Berlage, Hoffmann and Moser made up the group favouring the choice of a work in the modern spirit; with the support of Horta they would have constituted a clear majority . . . Horta joined the advocates of the conventions and made it impossible for a non-academic project to be selected for execution. Le Corbusier's project was one of these[1] . . . As a last compromise, the creators of four schemes in the established international monumental style were selected to collaborate in a final version[2] . . . in 1937, ten years after the competition was held, the building was opened and put into service. Everyone, from typists to diplomats, agreed that it was a failure'.[3]

Giedion's description has been quoted at considerable length for two reasons. The first reason is that in the introduction to *Space, Time and Architecture*, he not only insists on the importance of historical objectivity, but on the duty of judging. 'The true critique of an age can be taken from the testimony of that age. Entirely objective judgement with no trace of personal bias is, on the face of things, quite impossible. Nevertheless, the infiltration of the personal must be reduced to a minimum. The historian is not solely a cataloguer of facts; it is his right, and indeed his duty, to pass judgement. His judgement must, however, spring directly from the facts.'[4]

The second reason is that some very significant alterations were made to the original text in the last English edition to be published before the author's death. All the words in the quotation which are here printed in italics were ultimately deleted from the original version; and the following paragraph was inserted after the phrase '. . . dream fantasies of glass': 'Although no other designs for the League of Nations building had the clear-sighted rightness of Le Corbusier's plans, there were other very considerable entries, such as those submitted by Hannes Meyer and Hans Wittwer, R. J. Neutra, E. Mendelsohn, and the Polish group Prezens. The catalogue of the projects published by the awarders is even more instructive than the catalogue of the competition for the Chicago Tribune. It demonstrates that the lowest mass standards guided the judgement of the designs'.[5]

[1] *Ibid.*, p. 423. [2] *Ibid.*, p. 424. [3] *Ibid.*, p. 424, footnote. [4] *Ibid.*, p. 18.
[5] *Op. cit.* (1967), p. 536.

Enlightened criticism in law journals of the majority opinion of a court of law is neither improper or uncommon. Nor is it unknown for a minority opinion in an intermediate appellate court to become the majority opinion in the final court of appeal. But it seems clear that the forces of dissent in the architectural profession, as well as among painters and sculptors, are far more influential than in the legal profession, and it is important to decide whether such dissension is an intrinsic virtue or not.

The dilemma is well exemplified in the writings of Frank Lloyd Wright, who was not only the greatest architect of his age, but was far less influenced by contemporary painters and sculptors than most of the other Pioneers of the Modern Movement. His writings, which oscillate between passionate demands that all architects should adopt his principles, and passionate condemnations of architects who plagiarized his work, express only too plainly the recurring drama of the dedicated compulsive proselytizing reformer: the precursor so dedicated to dissent that his one obsessive, subconscious dread is that his nonconformity will become orthodoxy during his lifetime, thereby depriving him of any moral *raison d'être*.

Few architects today would deny that when Sigfried Giedion first delivered the lectures which were eventually published as *Space, Time and Architecture*, he showed a remarkable prophetic vision. But whether or not his attitude toward nonconformity—which was fashionable enough in artistic circles long before World War II—is equally justified today, is a question which must be settled before any theory of architectural judgement can be fruitfully discussed. For all its scholarly and literary merits, *Space, Time and Architecture* is nonetheless dominated by the Hegelian concept of the *Zeitgeist* as a force which attains its fulfilment only by the instrumentality of a few enlightened individuals; precursors who subconsciously steer humanity towards its unsuspected destiny.[1] As a result, Giedion's

---

[1] This is a paraphrase of the Sibree translation of that part of the introduction to Hegel's *Philosophy of History* which reads: 'These observations may suffice in reference to the means which the World-Spirit uses for realizing its Idea. Stated simply and abstractly, this mediation involves the activity of personal existences in whom Reason is present as their absolute, substantial being; but a basis, in the first instance, still obscure and unknown to them.' (Paperback edition [1956], p. 37.)

great book reads like a Wagnerian saga in which the forces of evil (portrayed by a mysterious spirit called 'the Academy') are assailed by heroes who, instructed only by nature,[1] and animated only by altruistic zeal, perform superhuman feats of obstetrics to enable the *Zeitgeist* to give birth to the true architecture of the age. But the trouble with such sagas is that they are, by their nature, interminable; just as 'Tarzan' was inevitably followed by 'Son of Tarzan', so the fifth edition of *Space, Time and Architecture* has inevitably introduced the 'third generation' of heroes, represented by Jørn Utzon; and the reader may well wonder whether the *Zeitgeist*'s perpetual spiritual pregnancy does not effectively preclude any possibility of reliable architectural judgement, in the way that constant political revolution would similarly preclude reliable legal judgement.

In the 1958 reprint of *Vers une Architecture*, Le Corbusier concluded his new preface with the remark: 'Perhaps it is a good thing to be still criticized abusively (*engueulé*) at the age of 70!!!' But why should a Pioneer of the Modern Movement still derive so much satisfaction from being abusively criticized, after having been awarded gold medals and honorary degrees by the leading academies and universities in the Western World? Few leaders of any profession, however suffused with reformatory zeal, can have made such a boast at the very height of their fame. But then few professions have been consistently led for half a century by pioneers who based their whole philosophy on a scorn for the professional 'Establishment' and the official dignities it bestowed. It is an attitude we associate less with the idea of a profession than with the mystique of the '*Salons des Refusés*', of '*Le grand artiste méconnu de son vivant*',[2] of political or religious minorities which derive spiritual strength from being in a constant state of rebellion and dissent.

If, as I believe, the architectural principles traced in *Space, Time and Architecture* constitute the basis of today's orthodoxy, then the uniqueness of the creations of contemporary 'Form-Givers' may be less significant than the values they share in common. But whatever

[1] Compare S. Giedion, *Space, Time and Architecture* (1941), p. 407: 'Le Corbusier's spirit was never ground to a smooth specialization at a university.' This also was omitted from the 5th edition (1967).
[2] G. Rivière, *Cézanne* (1936), p. 166.

the contribution of such 'Form-Givers', there is little doubt that if unorthodoxy—however popular and lucrative—is to be regarded as the essence of architectural creativity, then the search for criteria must be abandoned, leaving T. G. Jackson's rhetorical question 'Why is it thought to be possible to protect the world from bad architecture while we are to be left to take our chance of escaping unfortunate investments in worthless canvas and dishonoured marble?'[1] to triumph without any effective response. We all know that the architectural profession must constantly adapt itself to the needs of the day, just as the activities of the legal profession and the medical profession need to be continually re-appraised by its members if the latter are to do their duty toward society. But the fact that they *are* professions, achieving their improvements by accumulated experience freely shared by the dissemination of knowledge, placed at the disposal of individual clients or litigants or patients, means that the technique of self-improvement must be fundamentally different from improvements in painting and sculpture. Indeed, it is widely held by specialists in such matters that 'the Fine Arts' do not 'improve' in the way professions improve. 'Fine Art' of high quality is to be found in every age and at every intellectual level, because it does not depend on advances in technology and in the social sciences to keep abreast of the needs of mankind. Whatever may be the lessons which painters and sculptors can give to architects, their technique of staying 'contemporary' is not one of them; and whilst architects can continue to learn much from the visual sensibility of our leading painters and sculptors, it is time practitioners and teachers of architecture began to concentrate more seriously on understanding what a profession *is*, so as to realize more effectively the totality of society's environmental needs.

[1] *Architecture, a Profession or an Art?* (1892), p. viii.

CHAPTER TWELVE

The ideals of judgement

In an article entitled 'Adhocism', published in the July 1968 issue of the *Architectural Review*, Charles Jencks commented on the importance of the Archigram Group's rejection of the term 'ideals' in favour of the word 'preoccupations'. 'Instead of universals', he wrote, 'we now have fashions. Architecture, embedded in the market place, in the opinion and the cultural situation of the moment, has marched out of Plato's Ideal Realm right back into his Cave. But this, according to Adhocism, is much more realistic and honest; for that is exactly where it has always been. And this can be seen by the process of design. For one thing, the form of a building is always shaped by the climate of opinion'.[1]

Mr. Jencks's essay (which deals primarily with the South Bank Arts Centre discussed in the first chapter) raises a number of fascinating issues relative to the problems of architectural judgement, not the least of them being the concept of a 'non-building', (which seems to bear close analogy with the anarchist concept of non-law). But there is one point of particular relevance, namely the view that 'architectural ideals' are an old-fashioned concept of the 1920s, and should now be discarded. Mr. Jencks instances, as an example of this outmoded concept, the Lincoln Centre in New York, which, he claims, is 'a wonderful specimen of a closed and moribund aesthetic'.[2] In contrast to this, he asserts: 'The adhocist designer is as much opposed to the radical invention which results in a space capsule as he is to the tenets of "good design" or "modern

[1] *Architectural Review*, vol. cxliii (July 1968), p. 30.
[2] *Ibid.*, p. 28.

architecture". What he proposes is a lively and fumigated eclecticism.'[1]

The reaction of the younger generation of architects against the traditional concept of 'architectural ideals' is understandable and, by their definition, to some extent justifiable. During the last two decades, there has been a tendency to pass off as 'architectural ideals' too many ideals which are not really architectural at all. Moreover, since idealism is essentially a type of nympholepsy (in that its very nature is to be unattainable), pragmatists are understandably frustrated by the apparent idiocy of trying to achieve something which, by definition, is incapable of fulfilment. Little wonder, therefore, that Archigram has abandoned 'ideals' in favour of 'preoccupations', thereby making do with what is ready to hand, instead of dreaming up schemes for approximating to perfection.

Nevertheless, despite the attractions of 'fumigated eclecticism', its main defect as a philosophy of either law or architecture is that it relies too heavily for its justification on nebulous terms like 'climate of opinion'. The danger of confusing 'justice' with 'public opinion' has already been discussed. Similar confusions exist in architecture with respect to 'climates of opinion', whereby 'what the public thinks' can easily be confused with 'what the public ought to think'.

For example, as far as the 'climate of opinion' of the South Bank Arts Centre is concerned, we know at least three major *facts*. The first is that, acoustically, the concert hall seems satisfactory both to audiences and (to judge from Yehudi Menuhin's comments)[2] performers. The second is that, structurally, the building has so far shown no major defects. The third is that, as a result of a statistical survey conducted by a popular newspaper, 46 per cent of five hundred engineers voted it to be 'Britain's ugliest building'.[3] Now leaving aside for the moment any consideration as to what Mr. Jencks's reaction would have been if the engineers had voted it 'Britain's most shoddily constructed building' or 'Britain's most cacophonous auditorium', it is surely fair to assert that he is rather naïve in saying that 'whether this judgement "ugliest" will be taken as a compliment or insult depends on the philosophy of the indi-

[1] *Ibid.*, p. 29.　[2] *R.I.B.A. Journal*, June 1968, p. 256.
[3] *Architectural Review*, vol. cxliii (July 1968), p. 27.

vidual'.[1] He has every right to consider ugliness an architectural merit, and may even be right when he asserts that the architects themselves 'probably intended the building to be conventionally ugly';[2] but there can surely be no doubt that the two hundred and thirty engineers who considered it the ugliest building in Britain were signifying that it was uncongenial to their 'climate of opinion'.

Mr. Jencks's statement is particularly confusing because it would seem perfectly reasonable to argue that since some kind of compromise was (as in all such buildings) inevitable, the appearance of the building mattered less than its functional efficiency and the economic efficiency of its structural components. This may well be what 'fumigated eclecticism' is really all about. But the confusion is due to a verbal ambiguity, whereby 'Platonic Ideals' are identified with the newer concept of ideals which developed round about 1800. It is generally accepted among lexicographers that, for Plato, an idea (or ideal) was an eternally existing pattern of any class of things, of which all individual things were imperfect copies. But this is rather different from the nineteenth-century notion of an ideal (a neologism which, in English, has not been traced earlier than the 1790s)[3] as meaning simply a standard of excellence. No High Court judge believes that all his judicial opinions are but an imperfect copy of some immutable pattern of divine justice. No architect believes that every building he designs is but an imperfect copy of the Perfect Building existing in the mind of God. Judges and architects who have ideals believe simply that the possession of certain standards of excellence creates a greater probability that they will bring justice or good architecture into the world than if they did not possess any standards at all.

The problem is thus essentially that in all professions, the factors which must be taken into account when making a judgement are so numerous, and so difficult to evaluate, one against another, by a common measure, that unless those responsible for judging have some standard of excellence, no rational compromise is possible.

---

[1] *Ibid.*   [2] *Ibid.*

[3] The *O.E.D.* traces it no further back than a reference to C. M. Wieland's 'exquisite dissertation on the Ideals of Greek artists' in a book review published in 1798 in *The Monthly Review*, vol. xxvi, p. 481. The author was apparently William Taylor who, according to the *D.N.B.*, had a mania for neologisms.

By taking refuge in such terms as '*bricolage*',[1] the Archigram theorists seem to be implying that their techniques of compromise are either irrational (in the traditional Rationalist sense of the word) or amateurish. I suggest that they are neither, and that the clue to the significance of their doctrine is to be found in Mr. Jencks's criticism of the Lincoln Centre as 'a specimen of a moribund aesthetic'. Environmentally, the South Bank Arts Centre is essentially nothing more than a specimen of a different 'aesthetic'. This 'aesthetic' may be the result of a technique of evaluation comparable to that of nineteenth-century eclecticism, whose devotees contended, very sensibly, that functional and structural values should (in the then current crisis of the 'Battle of the Styles') take precedence over archaeological values.[2] But such a contention is as much an *ideal* as the ideal which prompted the architects of the Lincoln Centre to adopt a scale of values based on the precedent of Italian *piazze*. Whether or not the Archigram 'aesthetic' is based on the techniques of Action Painting (i.e. spaces and forms which just happen, and are thereby considered as constituting a stimulating environment by virtue of their spontaneity) or on the technique of Pseudo-Action Painting (i.e. spaces and forms which give the impression of spontaneity, but are as artfully and carefully contrived as any mock-ruin in an eighteenth-century landscape), is something which only its exponents can decide.

I would contend that the real problem of professional ideals has nothing to do with rival aesthetic theories of the plastic arts, but is the result of a dilemma which confronts all those who practise a profession with full awareness of their human frailty. That dilemma is the extent to which any professional expert can really trust his own judgement. The whole essence of a profession (as this essay has sought to demonstrate) is that it does involve judgement, and cannot be based on rule of thumb. An intelligent bricklayer, an intelligent conveyancer, an intelligent butcher, after serving a full apprenticeship, clearly has to use some primitive kind of judgement occasionally; but for the architect, the lawyer and the surgeon, judgements of a highly complex kind are the very essence of his

---

[1] i.e. amateurish fixing-together. Mr. Jencks explains this fundamental proposition of 'Adhocism' on p. 28 of his article.

[2] Cf. *Revue Générale de l'Architecture*, vol. xi, col. 446 (1853).

skill, for which book-learning provides merely the raw materials of intellectual creativity.

The dilemma is, of course, as apparent in the realm which Mr. Jencks himself labels 'aesthetics' as in any other aspect of architectural creativity; but this merely illustrates the extent to which the 'aesthetics' of any profession are inseparably bound up with the nature of the profession itself. Much of the criticism of architects' architecture and lawyers' law is justified; but much of it is due to the layman's reluctance to face the inescapable fact that only a trained lawyer can really appreciate *elegantia juris*, and only a trained architect is really sensitive to the essential elegance of a well-constructed and properly functioning building. Laymen inevitably judge professional expertise superficially, and become impatient with technicalities they cannot be expected to understand. Indeed, in this respect, it is interesting to note that one of the most significant miscalculations in the programme of the Royal Courts of Justice Competition concerned the excessive provision of space for lay spectators.

In the 1860s, when the organization of the police force was in its infancy, the judiciary's main concern, when deliberating upon the size and means of access to public galleries, was to ensure that the administration of justice would not be interrupted by demonstrations or riots.[1] But anyone who now visits those galleries will find them almost totally empty, and the reason for this is, in retrospect, perfectly obvious. The type of crowd which, before the age of electronic home entertainment, would have queued for hours to hear some great forensic orator, like F. E. Smith or Marshall Hall, addressing a jury in a lurid criminal trial, never had any interest in listening to legal niceties expounded in a Court of Appeal. However appreciative the Lord Chief Justice might be as he listens to an unusually felicitously phrased exposition of some ambiguity in the Road Safety Act (1967), such eloquence is unlikely to arouse similar emotions of appreciation in a lay audience. Similarly, the

---

[1] Para. 25(e) of the *Book of Instructions for the competing architects*: 'That the accesses to the Courts for mere public spectators should be entirely distinct from all other accesses, and as far as possible from each other, and should enter directly from the street.' 25(f): '. . . No standing room should be allowed. In short, that the utmost precautions be taken and means provided by which the quiet of the Courts may be secured.'

elegance with which the architects of the South Bank Arts Centre resolved certain dilemmas imposed, for example, by the fire regulations, is unlikely to be savoured by anyone who has not been faced with the same type of problem himself.

The credibility gap between professional comprehension and public comprehension, as regards the elegance of the solution of legal and architectural problems, may be a modern phenomenon due to the increased technicality of each profession. Perhaps in the days of Cicero or Vitruvius, thundering rhetoric and flashy façades delighted professional colleagues as much as they delighted the mob. But the situation today was probably best expressed—as far as the law is concerned—by Judge Frank when he remarked in *Ricketts v. Pennsylvania Railroad* (1946)[1] that 'fortunately most judges are too common-sensible to allow, for long, a passion for aesthetic elegance, or for the appearance of an abstract consistency, to bring about obviously unjust results'. Perhaps the members of Archigram were trying to express the same sentiment about *venustas* (or what Alberti more accurately defined as *amoenitas*) at the South Bank Arts Centre.

The main cause of the current professional reaction against architectural prettiness is undoubtedly a result of the art-historical tradition of asserting that 'it is especially in elevations that the genius of architecture manifests itself',[2] or of defining architecture as a term which 'applies only to buildings designed with a view to aesthetic appeal'.[3] Despite the fundamental difference between the ideals of harmony in architecture and the ideals of harmony in law, the latter demonstrates that whereas *elegantia juris* is as much a legal virtue as oratorical skill, neither have ever been allowed, by legal theorists, to take a prominent part in definitions of judicial ideals. Yet 'aesthetics' have long enjoyed undeserved prominence in definitions of architectural ideals; and although it can be argued that there is a good and obvious reason for this difference, in that *amoenitas* is a fundamental part of the final result of architecture, whereas rhetoric is only incidental to the process of legal decision-making, the difference is in fact less real than might at first appear. Rhetoric is indeed only

[1] 153 F. 2d. 757 (U.S. Second Circuit, 1946).
[2] Charles Blanc, *Grammaire des Arts du Dessin* (1867), p. 76.
[3] N. Pevsner, *Outline of European Architecture*, Introduction.

a small part of the juridical process as finally recorded; but it nevertheless exerts a powerful influence on the process of reaching final
decisions. And those final decisions are not only things that the
plaintiff and the defendant have to live with for the rest of their
lives; they are facts of life which (especially if it is a case of first
impression) a vast number of other people will have to adjust to.
The problem of the place of 'aesthetics' in law or architecture is thus
not simply one of exclusion or inclusion, but of the establishment of
priorities; and the success of the total end-product, whether we like
it or not, is only determinable by those with the professional skill to
understand the nature of these priorities, and the professional
wisdom to take them into account when judging their influence on
the final result.

Insofar as a building like the South Bank Arts Centre is important, it is not because it is a manifesto proclaiming that visual
amoenitas should be ignored, but because it seems to be an assertion
that there are occasions when, in the opinion of the architects
responsible for the design, the sacrifice of certain traditional concepts of visual elegance is as essential to a realization of the true
ideals of architecture as the sacrifice of oratorical elegance is to the
true ideals of law. When a Mr. MacPherson[1] achieved legal immortality by being injured because his brand-new automobile
collapsed as a result of a defective wheel, he had probably never
heard of *elegantia juris*, and must have been dumbfounded when
this concept rendered his claim for damages so debatable that the
case was taken to the New York Court of Appeals. He must have
been even more dumbfounded when Chief Justice Willard Bartlett
argued (in his dissenting opinion, on the basis of *elegantia juris*) in
favour of the defendants (i.e. the Buick Motor Co.), by basing his
argument on the English decision in *Winterbottom v. Wright*[2] (when
a mail-coach collapsed in similar circumstances in 1840). In
Winterbottom v. Wright (which was a case of first impression), the
plaintiff, who was lamed for life when the wheel collapsed, was told
by Baron Rolfe that this was unfortunately a case of *damnum absque
injuria*.[3] Art-historians might profitably recite this legal maxim

---

[1] *MacPherson v. Buick* (1916) 217 N.Y. 382.   [2] 10 M. & W. 109.
[3] 'loss without a wrongful act', i.e. a loss which does not give rise to an action
for damages against the person causing it.

whenever the ceiling of a Rococo church collapses on them; and it may even console them, as they are driven to hospital, to reflect on Burchard and Bush-Brown's dictum: 'A building of high artistic merit, measured solely in visual terms, is architecture even if it is badly built'.[1]

But the problem of establishing architectural ideals today is not so much due to the difficulty of weighing the relative importance of *firmitas, utilitas* and *venustas* as to the difficulty of creating a realistic understanding in the lay mind of the difference between price and value. In the days of Louis XIV, this sort of distinction presumably had little importance (though J. F. Blondel almost ruined his career by charging fees which Louis XV's Superintendent of Buildings considered exorbitant). Today, the lack of comprehension of the distinction is sapping the roots of all professional idealism, and nowhere more clearly than in architecture.

Sometimes, of course, this dilemma can have unexpectedly beneficial results. There can be no doubt that Auguste Perret's abilities were very effectively stimulated by inadequate financial resources, and that his finest building was the church at Le Raincy, where his extraordinary ingenuity in turning the need to economize into a source of architectural inspiration was well demonstrated by the shell vaulting, which was based on existing form-work designed and used previously for a factory. Similarly, the 'New Brutalism' emerged as a direct result of financial limitations (though whether the philosophy it propagated was as profound as its protagonists have claimed, is debatable). It is generally acknowledged that the 'New Brutalist' philosophy emerged as a result of the completion of a school at Hunstanton in 1953. The commission was won in open competition in 1950 by Peter Smithson (who had graduated two years earlier), and his wife (who graduated in 1949). The design was clearly inspired by the work of Mies van der Rohe (whose work neither had seen except on photographs), and the extremely precise structural detailing, characteristic of Mies van der Rohe's buildings, was the work of R. S. Jenkins, a partner of Ove Arup (probably the leading firm of structural engineers in England). The 'Brutalism' seems to have been due to the fact that whereas the maximum price stipulated by the clients (i.e. the School Board) was £131,000, the

[1] J. Burchard and A. Bush-Brown, *The Architecture of America* (1961), p. 3.

building had already cost £147,900 by 1953. Thus this figure was presumably only maintainable by leaving the doors unpainted, the pipes uncovered, and the walling rough. Whether or not the idea of deliberately dispensing with conventional 'finishes' was a stroke of genius, or a subterfuge for disguising their youthful inexperience in dealing with the financial practicalities of the building trade, is immaterial.[1] What matters is that whereas the client was concerned essentially with *costs*, the architects were naturally concerned essentially with *values*, as the careful detailing of their subsequent work demonstrates.

The current inability of laymen to distinguish between price and value embitters every aspect of professional activities, and has done so for centuries. Lawyers' obsessions with fees have been a standard witticism among dramatists since the time of Shakespeare; and if doctors and architects have been spared such gibes, it is only because the medical profession has, since the time of Molière, been easier to deride for ignorance and malpractice, whilst resentment against architectural remuneration is difficult to express in literary satire because the fees are percentages of the building costs. Few laymen are prepared to acknowledge that intellectual creativity is of high monetary value. Indeed, cynics brought up on Parkinson's law might justifiably define the layman's idea of a profession as 'a learned skill for which the remuneration demanded is always ludicrously in excess of the value of services performed'.

If (as in the medical and legal professions) the relationship between price and value were confined only to the assessment of fees, architectural ideals would not be subject to any special dilemma. The trouble is that, in architecture, the price-value credibility gap also affects the quality of the building produced. The reason for the layman's inability to appreciate the nature of the architect's dilemma is of course only too obvious. In the ordinary circumstances of life, a layman normally only purchases finished articles, which he has inspected before any decision is made as to the price he is willing to pay. Show him a second-hand automobile, and he has little difficulty

---

[1] Perret also left the concrete surfaces *brut de coffrage*, so it might be claimed that he invented *béton brut* in 1922–23. In this context, however, it is of more significance that in 1922 he was nearly fifty, and had spent half his life-time as a building contractor specializing in reinforced concrete construction.

—however ignorant he may be of mechanical engineering—in deciding whether or not the quoted price is reasonable. Show him an old house which is being offered for auction, and he will bid for it with full confidence that he knows a good bargain when he sees one. But show him the sketches and working drawings of a building he has commissioned, and he will find it inconceivable either that so few drawings are worth 5 per cent of the estimated cost of the building, or that the architect cannot make immediate alterations so as to halve the contractor's price without sacrificing any of the amenities.

In the Common Law, the problem of distinguishing price from value received its classic expression in 1602 in *Pinnel's Case*,[1] where the Court of Common Pleas, being asked to give judgement with respect to a claim by the defendant that he had paid Pinnel £5 2s 2d in full settlement of a debt of £8 10s 0d, logically decided that no sum of money can ever equal a larger sum of money, even though the value of a chattel can be assumed to be whatever price the purchaser is willing to pay for it. This latter doctrine is the basis of the idea of a 'peppercorn rent', whereby it is a rule of English law that a debt for any sum of money may be perfectly well discharged by the creditor's acceptance of 'a beaver hat or a peppercorn',[2] or in fact any other object. However, the real dilemma of distinguishing between 'price' and 'value' only began to appear when courts were asked to settle disputes over executory contracts—i.e. contracts concerning future acts for which the *quid pro quo* was to be determined on completion. As an illustration of the problem it may useful to compare *Leaf v. International Galleries* (1950)[3] (which has already been discussed in the first chapter), and *Hoadley v. McLaine* (1834)[4] where Sir Archibald McLaine commissioned a new, fashionable and luxuriously appointed coach in accordance with precise specifications, and then refused to pay for it.

In *Leaf v. International Galleries*, Mr. Leaf had not only inspected the painting of Salisbury Cathedral before paying the purchase price, but had enjoyed contemplating it for five years before discovering that it was not painted by Constable, but by some person or persons unknown. On what reasonable grounds, one may there-

[1] 5 Co. Rep. 117a. [2] See *Harvard Law Review*, vol. xii, p. 521.
[3] 1950 2 K.B. 86. See note (3) on p. 19. [4] 10 Bing. 482.

fore ask, could he assert that the price paid did not correspond to the value received? As the Master of the Rolls pointed out: 'What he contracted to buy and what he bought was a specific chattel, namely, an oil painting of Salisbury Cathedral . . . the attribution of works of art to particular artists is often a matter of great controversy and increasing difficulty as time goes on . . . there may turn out to be divergent views on the part of artists and critics of great eminence, and the prevailing view at one date might be quite different from that which prevails at a later date'.[1] Now although this litigation concerned a painting, the issue is nevertheless of fundamental importance to architectural theory. For example, it was a basic tenet of the nineteenth-century Rationalists that anonymity was the secret of progress in all forms of building. Writers like James Fergusson and Viollet-le-Duc never tired of comparing the constant improvements in ship-building with the lack of progress in architecture, the backwardness of the latter being the result (according to them) of the decline of mediaeval Masonic traditions. There may be some good reason why a genuine painting of Salisbury Cathedral by Constable should fetch a higher price than a copy of one of his numerous depictions of this splendid building; but there is no logical reason why a terra-cotta panel from a building by Louis Sullivan should be more highly prized or more highly priced than an identical panel newly cast from the same mould. Both are equally 'genuine', although one may well have a higher mercantile value than the other because of its historical association.

In *Hoadly v. McLaine*, the problem in dispute would have appealed to the Pioneers of the Modern Movement, because they liked analogies with vehicles, and indeed often designed them.[2] The essential facts of the case have already been stated. Sir Archibald McLaine knew what he wanted, specified in writing what he wanted, got what he wanted, and received delivery on the stipulated date. But he disputed the coachmaker's claim that it was worth £480.

[1] 1950 2 K.B. at 93–4.

[2] In some ways it is regrettable that Nikolaus Pevsner changed the title of *Pioneers of the Modern Movement* to *Pioneers of Modern Design* in later editions, because it is one of the more significant minor characteristics of the era that after 1750 architects began designing vehicles. Robert Adam designed a sedan chair; Sir William Chambers designed the British state coach; Viollet-le-Duc designed the Imperial railway carriage for Napoleon III.

The coachmaker sued for breach of contract, and brought a number of other coachmakers to testify that the coach 'was of such exquisite workmanship, and so highly ornamented as to be cheap at the price'. As a result, the jury gave a verdict for the plaintiff, with £200 damages, which was upheld in the Court of Appeal.

The case's special relevance to the point under discussion lies on its reliance on a change in the law produced by a modification of the Statute of Frauds.[1] The original Statute of 1676 had regulated the validity of contracts for the sale of goods 'for the price of ten pounds sterling or upwards'. But by an act passed in 1828 (usually referred to as Lord Tenterden's Act) this stipulation was modified to extend its provisions to executory contracts, whereby the phrase: 'for the *price* of ten pounds sterling' was changed to: 'for the *value* of ten pounds sterling'.

The importance of the rewording was commented upon by Chief Justice Tindal in his opinion in *Hoadly v. McLaine*. 'The extreme accuracy of mind of the framer of the Act', he said, 'is shown in this that while the Statute of Frauds, in its enactments touching contracts for the sale of goods, employs the word price, the framer of the latter act has substituted the word value, so that, where the parties have omitted to fix a price, it may be open to a jury to ascertain the value in dispute'.

When Lord Tenderden's Act was replaced by the Sale of Goods Act of 1893, the latter retained the term 'value of £10', rather than 'price of £10'; but those who drafted the United States Uniform Commercial Code preferred the wording of the seventeenth-century Statute of Frauds (as re-enacted in the New York Revised Statutes of 1836) except that the phrase 'the price of $50 or more' was changed to 'the price of $500 or more'.[2] In view of the fact that the Uniform Commerical Code cost half a million dollars to draft, the monetary change seems reasonable. What is surprising is that

---

[1] 29 Car. II c. 3: 'An Act for the prevention of frauds and perjuries' (effective from 24 June 1677). Para. 17 stipulated that for a contract to be valid, the buyer must accept and receive part of the goods so sold, *or* give something in earnest to bind the bargain, *or* in part payment, *or* that some note or memorandum in writing of the said bargain be made and signed by the parties to be charged by such contract.

[2] Art. 2–201.

American jurists seem to have deliberately chosen to exemplify, in legal form, Oscar Wilde's definition of a cynic, whom he described as a person who knows the price of everything and the value of nothing.[1]

The architectural importance of the distinction was dramatically brought to public attention in 1963, when Mies van der Rohe's Seagram Building was the subject of litigation caused by the New York Tax Commission's decision to evaluate it twenty per cent above the value claimed by the owners.[2] Architectural journalists, especially in New York, were quick to publicize the dispute, and the *Architectural Forum*, in an editorial entitled 'How to Ban Architecture', characterized the unanimous decision of the Appellate Division of the New York Supreme Court (which had supported the Tax Commissioners) as 'culturally illiterate'. 'Who are these judges', the editor asked, 'to set the New York architectural standard at the lowest going?' And he concluded his diatribe by stating: 'Make no mistake; if this outrageous decision is permitted to stand, its effects on our three-dimensional cities will not be superficial, but disastrous. The power to tax architecture on its quality is the power to prevent it'.[3]

Encouraged by such wide professional support, Messrs. Seagram took the case to the Court of Appeals where, in addition to the usual battery of legal arguments arrayed by the appellants and respondents respectively, a number of briefs were submitted by *amici curiae*. In this, the ultimate appeal, the Bench was divided, in that four of the judges upheld the earlier unanimous decision of the Appellate Division, whilst three judges dissented on a point of law. The point of law was to the effect that it was erroneous to consider the cost of construction as prima facie evidence of the value of a newly-erected structure, when that structure was built especially for prestige and advertising value as well as for the headquarters of its owner.[4]

It will be perceived that this point of law was rather different

---

[1] *Lady Windermere's Fan*, Act III.

[2] See Appendix A. It was taxed at the rate of $34.00 per square foot of rentable office space, as compared with the Lever Building opposite (Skidmore, Owings & Merrill, 1952), then being taxed at $25.50 per square foot of rentable office space.

[3] *Architectural Forum*, May, 1963, p. 97.

[4] 251 N.Y.S. 2d. at 463 (reprinted in Appendix A, *infra*).

from the issue for which the editor of the *Architectural Forum* fought so strenuously. The editor, by claiming that the municipality was taxing the building's *quality*, argued as if the cost of construction had been, *mutatis mutandis*, the same as that of the less admired but much cheaper Colgate-Palmolive Building. Yet none of the judges ever asserted that it was unreasonable to assess a building which cost $36m. at considerably more than a building of the same floor area which cost only $18m. (the 'value' claimed by Messrs. Seagram). The only difference of opinion concerned the extent to which an element of a building which was unique to the owner (such as the advertising value of the building's name) could be regarded as a real property value inherent in the building itself.

This distinction can perhaps be expressed more clearly by using hypothetical cases. Let us consider, for example, what would have been the reaction of the architectural profession if Mies van der Rohe had charged only $2\frac{1}{2}$ per cent fees on the grounds that, in terms of rentable office space provided, this was equivalent to the minimum fee of 5 per cent with respect to a building of the same size constructed with cheaper materials and fewer amenities. Can we doubt that the American Institute of Architects would have insisted that the fee must be calculated on the actual cost of the building, rather than on the rateable value in terms of capitalization of the residual rent? Similarly, what would have been the reaction of the *Architectural Forum* if the Tax Commission had assessed it at double the construction cost, on the grounds that its artistic value was certainly equal to—and hence additional to—the market value of the materials and workmanship? The untenability of such hypotheses must surely make us question the fairness of criticizing the Appellate Division for having 'ended up by making a value judgement'.[1] The plaintiff had specifically asked the Court to determine the building's value, so what else could the Courts do but give a value judgement? We all know that the artistic value of an artifact is often greater than the market value of its component materials. It is also indisputable that if municipalities were to tax expensive architecture at the same rate as cheap architecture, clients would have one less incentive to build cheaply. But the artistic value of the Seagram Building, in terms of its environmental *quality*,

[1] *Architectural Forum*, July 1964, p. 7.

or the extent to which it enhanced the value of adjoining property, was never at issue. The only point at issue was whether the property should be taxed at its nominal rental value (i.e. on the basis of rents which were clearly unprofitable in relationship to the cost of the building) or at its replacement value; and the most telling argument in favour of the Tax Commissioners' assessment was unwittingly provided by one of Seagram's own expert witnesses, who, ignorant of the fact that the building had cost $36m., asserted on oath that the cost of reproducing it would only be $19m.![1] Little wonder, therefore, that the judges in the Appellate Division should have considered the additional $17m. as a form of 'advertising by means of Conspicuous Waste'.[2]

Thus the New York City Tax Commission, by demonstrating the most irksome aspect of Mies van der Rohe's doctrine that 'Less is More', performed a useful service in inviting architects to reconsider the validity of the arguments in Ruskin's 'Lamp of Sacrifice': arguments which distinguish between 'architecture' and 'building' in a manner understandably distasteful to architectural theorists of the present century, yet surely pertinent to such buildings as this. Could Mies van der Rohe have produced such a noble building if he had been limited to a budget equivalent to the capitalization value claimed by Messrs. Seagram (i.e. $18m.)? Could Jørn Utzon have won the Sidney Opera House Commission with a design constructable at the price indicated in the Competition? If not, we should recognize candidly that so-called skill in 'design' is nowadays largely dependent upon the use of costly materials, costly techniques, or both.

Another vexatious problem which tends to militate against the establishment of consistent and universally acceptable architectural ideals is the difficulty of establishing the nature of rules or norms. The way in which the legal profession dealt with this delicate problem has already been discussed at some length; and it was then pointed out that the very nature of Law, as a social institution, requires that rules of some kind must exist, and must therefore be formulated as unequivocally as possible. But in architecture there is no such social imperative. The inhabitants of an attractive city may well ask the civic authorities to determine the principles which

[1] 238 N.Y.S. 2d. at 234.   [2] 238 N.Y.S. 2d. at 230.

are the apparent source of its harmony, and even oblige them to establish 'rules' which seem to correspond to those principles. But even the most enthusiastic supporters of zoning regulations would find it difficult to demonstrate that these regulations derived either from the nature of architecture or from the nature of man, whether they regard the latter as an individual or as a member of a group. In fact, such rules are more comparable to the idea of 'customary law' as conceived by Blackstone in his *Commentaries*, where 'customary' does not mean 'what is usually done for obvious reasons' but 'what has been done since time immemorial for reasons which no living person can recollect'.

Nevertheless, despite the difficulty of justifying rules which cannot be based on indisputable scientific analysis, it is a curious fact that the most influential architect of the present century, namely Le Corbusier, was obsessed throughout his long career by the belief that objective rules of proportion must exist. This obsession is all the more remarkable in view of his hostility towards 'academic' theories. Though he derided those who used the Petit Trianon as an architectural prototype, he went to considerable trouble to demonstrate that his own buildings could be 'proved' to be just as beautiful by the same geometric techniques which 'demonstrated' the perfection of the Petit Trianon's proportions.[1] Indeed, his enthusiasm for such demonstrations, however implausible, occasionally led him to curious errors, as for example when he exemplified the technique by reference to a photograph of the Porte S. Denis,[2] a structure which (as J. F. Blondel proved by measurements taken two centuries ago) does not in fact correspond to the proportions claimed for it by its designer.

Le Corbusier's early insistence on *'tracés régulateurs'* can perhaps be explained by the essentially historical character of *Vers une Architecture* (where so many arguments are based on Greek and Roman precedents), and by his evident determination to beat, as it were, the enemy on his own ground. But his elaborate researches on proportions undertaken during World War II, culminating in his invention of the Modulor, cannot be explained away so easily; and one is forced to conclude that his belief in the existence of some ideal rule of proportion stemmed from deeper roots.

[1] *Vers une Architecture* (1923), p. 61.　　[2] *Ibid.*, p. 49.

The ideals of judgement

Few architects have ever used the Modulor, despite the publicity it has received, and the authority of its progenitor. But there are three aspects of the Modulor which suggest that it should not be dismissed out of hand. The first is that Le Corbusier had enough faith in it to use it on such important buildings as the Unité d'Habitation at Marseilles, which is widely acclaimed for its harmonious proportions.[1] The second is that it is unique among rules of proportion in that it combines both a rule of progressive proportion and a rule of human scale. The third is that the solution to the problem, as envisaged by Le Corbusier, was only made possible by abandoning the metric system in the initial experimental stage, and calculating the ratios in feet and inches.

This last aspect seems of particular interest, now that English architects are obliged to abandon their traditional measures in favour of the Continental System. Whether or not feet and inches are more 'human' or more 'natural' than metres and millimetres is hard to say on the historical evidence available. Perhaps French buildings designed according to the metric system are less attractive than French buildings designed before the Revolution; but even if they are not, it is a curious fact that, despite the wide variations in standard measures which existed in Europe before the Napoleonic era,[2] the old European units of measurement were always based, ostensibly at least, on the scale of the human body. And Le Corbusier may well be right in claiming that harmonious environments can only be achieved by relating buildings to the height of an ideal Anglo-Saxon, whether this be expressed as six English feet or 1,829 millimetres.[3]

[1] P. H. Scholfield, *The Theory of Proportion in Architecture* (1958), pp. 122–3, points out that 'the "Modulor" provided the dimensions of the individual apartments . . . but not, apparently, the larger dimensions of the building'.

[2] The *Encyclopédie* lists about sixty measures in use in Europe in 1750. Taking the English foot as 1,000 units the relative length of the French foot was 1,068, Amsterdam 942, Antwerp 946, Leiden 1,033, Mechlin 919, Strasbourg 920, Cologne 954, Mantua 1,569, Venice 1162, etc., etc.

[3] The official legal measure in the Province of Quebec is still the pre-revolutionary French foot, despite the fact that no such rules have been obtainable in Canada for two centuries. For arithmetic convenience, French architects regard the height of a man as 1m75; but Le Corbusier's six-foot man would, according to the metric system, be 1m95 (the old *pied-du-roi* being equivalent to 324.8 mm.).

However, despite Le Corbusier's efforts, it seems more than likely that whatever industrial module is accepted in the future, research into the ideals of architecture will concentrate more on social relationships than dimensional relationships, and this, as has already been pointed out, involves two basic juridical concepts, namely the obligations imposed by the voluntary act of individuals, and the obligations imposed by the nature of society.

The architect's contractual obligations are too well known to merit comment here, but they are worth contrasting with those of law and medicine. In English law, barristers have no contractual obligation whatsoever to their clients. From the client's point of view, this is occasionally an advantage, since the barrister is legally incapable of suing for his fees; but it is particularly advantageous to barristers, who, for the same reason, cannot be sued for negligence. Medical practitioners, on the other hand, are so vulnerable to actions for negligence (often involving vast sums of money in damages) that American Medical Associations are under strong pressure from insurance companies to expel members who testify on behalf of a plaintiff. Indeed, there was one celebrated occasion, namely *Agnew v. Parks* (1959),[1] where a plaintiff sued a group of Californian doctors for 'conspiracy to obstruct the ends of justice' because they refused to testify as expert witnesses in a medical malpractice case. Yet despite the wide discrepancies in the relative legal obligations of doctors, architects and lawyers towards their clients, the enforcement of ethical obligations by the respective disciplinary bodies of *all* professions is extraordinarily lax. The reluctance of members of a profession to inflict exemplary punishment on their colleagues is understandable; but it makes nonsense of the sociological concept of the main function of a professional association as being 'to guarantee competence and integrity' in their members.[2] In many countries, such disciplinary powers as exist are not vested in the professional association, but in a State Registration Board. But wherever disciplinary power may reside, the only real remedy against professional incompetence is by taking legal

[1] 172 Cal. App. 2d. 756.
[2] Barrington Kaye, *The Development of the Architectural Profession in Britain* (1960), p. 16.

proceedings,[1] since neither architectural associations nor medical associations are inclined to strike members off their registers for anything less than convictions of fraud. Even then, such incompetence must be both indisputably flagrant and indisputably gross if legal proceedings are to succeed.

Professional controls over an architect's obligations to society in general are even harder to impose. It is doubtful whether the elected officers of any architectural association would ever reach unanimous agreement that any such obligations had been contravened. Even if they did, they would still be faced with the dilemma that, despite all the fine phrases about 'men united in the pursuit of a learned art as a public service',[2] the architect is still legally his client's agent, and there is not much the architect can do about a misanthropic client except resign the commission to a less scrupulous colleague. Indeed, it is now a well-known technique in the United States for land-developers who wish to construct blots on the landscape to engage Emeritus Form-Givers as their consultants. The Emeritus Form-Giver may be violently criticized in the professional press; but he can always retort that if he does not accept the commission, some less reputable architect will accept it in his place, and thereby fail to make the best of the bad job which is, in any event, inevitable.

However, one of the most striking distinctions between architecture and other professions is that whenever a reputable architect does accept a commission which, in the opinion of his confrères, will spoil the landscape, he is often criticized publicly, despite specific prohibitions of such criticism in Ethical Codes. Why the architectural profession should be more prone to indulge publicly in this kind of moral indignation than lawyers and doctors is unclear. Perhaps it is just another proof of the endemic psychological syndromes surviving from Renaissance art-theory, with its emphasis on competition between rival geniuses. Perhaps it is a survival of youthful dedication to social reform. But whatever the cause, and however altruistic the motives of those who thus take it upon themselves to fight the good fight against urban blight, it seems doubtful

[1] Though, as indicated in Chapter eight, this is *not* a possible remedy in England when the professional adequacy of a barrister is challenged.
[2] Roscoe Pound, 'The Professions in the society of today', in *New England Journal of Medicine* (8 September 1949), vol. 241, p. 351.

whether acrimonious exchanges in the public press help architects to fulfil their responsibilities to the general public. The highest ideals of the most competent and conscientious architects can only be achieved if the whole architectural profession is held in public esteem; and there must surely be better ways of increasing the general competence of the whole profession than by conducting derisive controversies in circumstances where the medium is too easily confused with the message.

This is not to deprecate architectural criticism. On the contrary, it has already been emphasized more than once that serious criticism, based on questions of principle, is the indispensable condition of professional progress. But it is a curious fact that whereas every other profession produces authoritative criticism by means of learned periodicals, the standards of architectural journalism have deteriorated so rapidly in the last twenty years that there scarcely remains a single professional journal worthy of respect. This is so, not merely with regard to commercial architectural periodicals, but also with regard to those which are ostensibly the official organs of professional associations. The temptation, as advertising rates increase, and as techniques of 'sales promotion' develop, for architectural periodicals to become less concerned with the dissemination of knowledge, and more concerned with the accumulation of wealth, has proved irresistible; and the point is now being reached where the 'Journal of the Institute'—whichever architectural institute it may happen to be—is virtually indistinguishable from any of the other trade brochures thrust under the door.

A detailed comparison between nineteenth-century and twentieth-century architectural magazines shows just how far the profession has degenerated in this respect, though such a comparison would serve little purpose in the present context, since it would simply invite some retaliatory platitude to the effect that *tempora mutantur et nos mutamur in illis*.[1] It is therefore far more useful to compare current architectural periodicals with current law journals, since the latter (unlike medical journals, which have the support of pharmaceutical companies) cannot count on revenue from advertisements. Law journals are produced by all the leading Law Schools and Law

[1] 'Times change, and we change with them' (Harrison, *Description of Britain* [1577] part 3, ch. iii, p. 99).

Societies; and even a casual inspection of one of the six hundred major journals in circulation will demonstrate to an architect what the term 'learned periodical' really means. It would be no exaggeration to say that these periodicals constitute the essential mechanism by which the ideals of the legal profession are progressively elaborated and improved. When any new and important point of law emerges, it will sooner or later be scrutinized and criticized by an authoritative scholar. If any judicial decision has some potentially undesirable implication, it will not be long before an expert on this aspect of law demonstrates its dangers. If changes in social, commercial or industrial relationships make new legislation desirable, some authoritative writer will indicate the basic principles on which new laws might best be framed.

Such journals are naturally concerned only with general legal problems, and not with individual behaviour. However numerous or scholarly, they will never reduce the number of shabby lawyers who 'prey alike on the victims of accidents and those responsible for accidents',[1] or any of the other riff-raff of the profession who have scourged it for centuries. Similarly, whatever improvements are made to architectural periodicals, they will never rid the profession of hacks. But they must inevitably raise the profession's standards as to how its products and its practices should be judged.

When Dean Roscoe Pound lectured on 'The Professions in the Society of Today',[2] he was addressing a medical society, and limited himself to four professions: medicine, law, the ministry and teaching. But his concept of a profession was, by analogy, equally applicable to architecture. 'The professional ideal', he stated, 'promotes effective individual treatment, individual counsel and forensic exertion, individual ministry and individual teaching, to the best of the powers of the individual practitioner . . . Each profession is an art in which the individual approach of a skilled practitioner to the task immediately in hand is of first importance. He cannot be made to a model so that everyone can have the benefit of a professional man exactly as good for every purpose as everyone else has. The required combination of training, native skill and experience makes each practitioner in some measure and in varying degrees unique'. It would of course be highly gratifying if every school of

[1] Roscoe Pound, *op. cit.*, p. 352.   [2] *Ibid.*, pp. 351–7.

architecture could so devise its curriculum that every graduate was guaranteed to have such perfect taste, such complete technical competence, such encyclopaedic mastery of all relevant data, and so strict an ethical code that he would be certain of fulfilling his obligations to society with complete integrity whatever situations he might encounter throughout life. But the attainability of such an ideal has little importance, as compared with the fact that it *is* an ideal; and although the ideal of universal perfection within a profession must always be that of a star whose worth is unknown, although its height be taken, it is the lodestar we must identify if the architectural profession is to charter its future progress so as to provide the maximum benefits for the good of mankind.

Joseph E. Seagram & Sons, Inc.
v.
New York Tax Commission
Court of Appeals of New York
June 10, 1964
(251 N.Y.S. 2d 460)

DESMOND, Chief Judge.

In this proceeding to review tax assessments the contest is as to the values ($20,500,000 in two of the years, $21,000,000 in the third year) assigned by the Tax Commission to the building which was completed just before the first of these tax years at a cost of $36,000,000. Summarized, the position of appellant is that capitalization of rental income, including estimated rent for the offices occupied by appellant itself, would not justify a building value of more than about $17,000,000.

(1) Unlike many of the real property tax proceeding orders reviewed in this court, this order comes to us from an Appellate Division affirmance of Special Term so that questions of fact and of weight of evidence are not before us. We cannot reverse or modify in such a situation unless the record is without any substantial evidence to support the conclusion below or there has been error of law in the use of an erroneous theory of valuation, or otherwise. We find no such errors here.

(2) Although we do not concur in everything said in the two Appellate Division opinions, we agree that for an office building like this, well suited to its site, the actual building construction cost of $36,000,000 is some evidence of value, at least as to the tax years

soon after construction (Matter of 5 East 71st St., Inc. v. Boyland, 7 N.Y.2d 859, 196 N.Y.S.2d 994, 164 N.E.2d 866; Matter of 860 Fifth Ave. Corp. v. Tax Comm. of City of New York, 8 N.Y.2d 29, 32, 200 N.Y.S.2d 817, 819, 167 N.E.2d 455, 456). Petitioner urges, however, that for a building built to rent and rentable, capitalization of net income is the only basis for valuation and that the building assessment here can be justified only by assigning an inflated value to the office space occupied by petitioner itself. This, says petitioner, really means that petitioner, having for its own reasons constructed an unusually costly and beautiful building, is being taxed ostensibly for building value but really for the prestige and advertising value accruing to petitioner because the 'Seagram Building' has become world-renowned for its striking and imposing beauty. We do not agree with this interpretation of the opinions and order of the Appellate Division.

(3) Usually, the assumed rent for the space occupied by a building owner would for purposes of capitalization of net rent income be computed at about the same rate as the rents actually paid by other tenants. But there can be many reasons why, as both of the Appellate Division opinions state, 'the building as a whole bearing the name of its owner includes a real property value not reflected in commercial rental income' since 'the owner did not build for commercial rental-income purposes alone, and, as a consequence, capitalization of such income without adjustments produces a false result' and, therefore, 'one must not confuse investment for commercial rental income with investment for some other form of rental value unrelated to the receipt of commercial rental income'. In other words, the hypothetical rental for owner-occupied space need not be fixed at the same rate as paid by tenants. This does not mean that advertising or prestige or publicity value is erroneously taxed as realty value. It certainly does not mean that a corporate sponsor of esthetics is being penalized for contributing to the metropolis a monumental and magnificent structure.

The order should be affirmed with costs.

BURKE, Judge (dissenting).

We do not suggest that cost of construction is not relevant, that it may not be taken into consideration as bearing on value. That it

may be so considered is an old rule recognized in many cases prior
to Matter of 5 East 71st St., Inc. v. Boyland, 7 N.Y.2d 859, 196
N.Y.S.2d 994, 164 N.E.2d 866, and Matter of 860 Fifth Ave. Corp.
v. Tax Commission of City of New York, 8 N.Y.2d 29, 200 N.Y.S.2d
817, 167 N.E.2d 455. (See, e.g., People ex rel. Amalgamated Props.
v. Sutton, 274 N.Y. 309, 8 N.E.2d 871; Ettlinger v. Weil, 184 N.Y.
179, 183, 77 N.E. 31, 32; People ex rel. Four Park Ave. Corp. v.
Lilly, 265 App. Div. 68, 37 N.Y.S.2d 733; Matter of Melcroft
Corp. v. Weise, 256 App. Div. 291, 10 N.Y.S.2d 27; Great Northern
Ry. Co. v. Weeks, 297 U.S. 135, 56 S. Ct. 426, 80 L.Ed. 332; cf.
People ex rel. Rome, W. & O.R.R. Co. v. Hicks, 105 N.Y. 198, 11
N.E. 653 [a railroad property tax case].) In fact, in the 5 East 71st
St. and 860 Fifth Ave. cases, the over-all return under ordinary
commercial operations supported the cost of construction; whereas
here, the rent return under ordinary commercial operation con-
cededly fails to support the cost of construction. We do criticize as
erroneous in law the holding of the Appellate Division—and also the
holding of this court insofar as it refuses to meet the issue—that cost
of construction is prima facie evidence of value in the case of 'a
newly-erected structure built especially for prestige and advertising
value as well as for the headquarters use of its owner.' (Matter of
Pepsi-Cola Co. v. Tax Comm. of City of New York, 19 A.D.2d 56,
59, 240 N.Y.S.2d 770, 774-775.)

While the well-settled rule is that capitalized net income is the
best measure of the value of commerical rental property[1] (People ex
rel. Parklin Operating Corp. v. Miller, 287 N.Y. 126, 38 N.E.2d
465; Matter of City of New York [Madison Houses], 17 A.D.2d 317,
234 N.Y.S.2d 799), it has now been decided that this measure must
be displaced as 'false' where the building is of such renown that the
court feels that its owner must benefit economically thereby, over
and above the rental commanded by the building. In such a case, it
is said, the rental value of the space occupied by the owner-tenant,
Seagram, must be valued not in proportion to the value of space
occupied by the other tenants but at some higher value that reflects
the business advantage accruing to one whose name is associated
with such an outstanding and well-known building. Since the

[1] The city offered no testimony as to economic value, i.e., capitalization of
net income.

petitioner failed to so value its space it is held to have failed to carry the burden of showing excessive assessment.

Although this court has no general power to review the fairness and accuracy of real property assessments (Matter of City of New York [Fourth Ave.], 255 N.Y. 25, 173 N.E. 910), yet where the Appellate Division has made explicit its method and the elements of value considered, any errors of law therein are presented to us for review. (People ex rel. Kings County Lighting Co. v. Willcox, 210 N.Y. 479, 492, 104 N.E. 911, 914, 51 L.R.A., N.S., 1; People ex rel. Jamaica Water Supply Co. v. State Bd. of Tax Comrs., 196 N.Y. 39, 53, 89 N.E. 581, 585; People ex rel. Rome, W. & O.R.R. Co. v. Hicks, 105 N.Y. 198, 202, 11 N.E. 653, 654, supra; Matter of City of New York [Exterior St.], 285 N.Y. 455, 458, 35 N.E.2d 39, 40; cf. People ex rel. Hotel Paramount Corp. v. Chambers, 298 N.Y. 372, 83 N.E.2d 839.) The Appellate Division could have granted leave to appeal in this case for no other reason than to bring its legal theory of value up for review.

The narrow and highly technical character of the rule applied by the Appellate Division may be highlighted by comparison with Matter of Pepsi-Cola Co. v. Tax Comm. of City of New York, 19 A.D.2d 56, 240 N.Y.S.2d 770, supra, decided by the same court three months after the instant case. There, the court was confronted with a brand new structure quite similar in novelty to the Seagram Building in that it 'is unusually distinctive and individualistic in appearance, [and] is set back approximately 14 feet on Park Avenue and 34 feet on 59th Street to provide on said sides a promenade and plaza ornamented with plants and shrubbery.' (19 A.D.2d p. 57, 240 N.Y.S.2d p. 773.) Yet the court held that it is not 'in the same category as the Seagram Building, that is, a newly-erected structure built especially for prestige and advertising value as well as for the headquarters use of its owner.' (19 A.D.2d p. 59, 240 N.Y.S.2d p. 774). Since both are new, held for business rental, and used as headquarters for the owner, the only difference is the presumed benefit accruing to the Seagram Company from having its name associated with an architecturally superior and well-known building.

'Value' under section 306 of the Real Property Tax Law, Consol. Laws, c. 50-a, is market value given willing sellers and buyers (Administrative Code of City of New York, § 158-1.0; People ex rel. Parklin Operating Corp. v. Miller, 287 N.Y. 126, 129, 38 N.E.2d 465, 466; People ex rel. Gale v. Tax Comm. of City of New York, 17 A.D.2d 225, 233 N.Y.S.2d 501). In our view, this approach to value necessarily excludes any element that is unique to the present owner of a building. Any increment in Seagram's outside business enterprises deriving from public appreciation of the Seagram Building will not pass to a buyer of the building in a sale. Such an element would disappear if the building were sold to another investor, engaged in another business or in no business at all, other than real estate investment. The good will follows Seagram and cannot be regarded as real property value inherent in the building itself.

Of course, the prestige of the Seagram Building undoubtedly enhances the value of the building in any hands. This is undoubtedly real estate value—value which is transferable in a sale, and for which a buyer will pay. Such value also affects the rental commanded by the building. But, if tenants are willing to pay more for space in the Seagram Building than for similar space elsewhere, that is fully reflected in the capitalization of earnings. In turn, it would seem to follow that such capitalization adequately comprehends any increase in value that the building would bring in a sale—without resorting to concepts foreign to real estate value.

By the consideration of a so-called value element without regard to its place in light of the ultimate statutory norm of market value, and thereby displacing income capitalization as an acceptable measure of value and giving undue prima facie effect to cost, the Appellate Division has committed legal error for which the order appealed from should be reversed and the case remitted for reconsideration without regard to any supposed theory that the building is a specially built structure representing more of a real estate investment in its owner-occupant's business than a commercial office building.

DYE, FULD and BERGAN, JJ., concur with DESMOND, C. J.

BURKE, J., dissents in a separate opinion in which VAN VOORHIS and SCILEPPI, JJ., concur.

Order affirmed.

INDEX

215

Index

Index

217

Index

Index